THAT THEY MIGHT LIVE

THAT THEY MIGHT LIVE

Power, Empowerment, and Leadership in the Church

Edited by Michael Downey

CROSSROAD • NEW YORK

1991

The Crossroad Publishing Company
370 Lexington Avenue, New York, NY 10017

Copyright © 1991 by Michael Downey

Printed in the United States of America
Typesetting output: T_EXSource, Houston

Library of Congress Cataloging-in-Publication Data

That they might live : power, empowerment, and leadership in the
   church / edited by Michael Downey.
      p. cm.
   ISBN 0-8245-1072-0
   1. Laity—Catholic Church. 2. Christian leadership—Catholic
Church. 3. Power (Christian theology) 4. Catholic Church—
Government. 5. Catholic Church—Membership. I. Downey, Michael.
BX1920.T46 1991
262'.15—dc20   90-44036
                                                                  CIP

CONTENTS

INTRODUCTION

Michael Downey

"All power tends to corrupt, and absolute power corrupts absolutely."
This aphorism of Lord Acton, the nineteenth-century Catholic historian, has become a commonplace in discourse about power and its exercise in the church. But Acton's point of view is only one view of a point. And there is much more to be said about power.

Several factors in our own day call for further discussion of power, empowerment, and leadership in the church. Among them the most frequently noted is the decline in the number of ordained ministers and vowed religious, particularly in the United States and Western Europe. Then there is the increase in the number of nonordained persons assuming various responsibilities and leadership roles once reserved for the ordained and for vowed religious. A third factor is the apparent tension between local churches and the Vatican brought on, at least in part, by what is often called Roman centralization. These are just a few of the factors that necessitate a reexamination of the nature and function of power in light of Christian sources, as well as a reconsideration of how power is appropriately exercised.

This volume offers a variety of perspectives on power, empowerment, and leadership. The contributors include theologians and church leaders, ordained and nonordained. Each presents a view of power considerably more nuanced than what is expressed in Acton's axiom. Power may tend to corrupt, but it may also enhance life. It may be hoarded or it may be shared. It may be understood as something held in the hands of a few, or it may be viewed as the life and breath of God loose in the world, the Spirit at the heart of all creation.

Credit for the initial idea for this volume goes to Fernando Moreno, presently director of the Office of Campus Ministry at Loyola Marymount University in Los Angeles. Upon return from a meeting of the Campaign for Human Development in Las Cruces, New Mexico, in 1988, he expressed his concern that ordained church leaders seemed at a loss for a solid theology of empowerment, which, as he correctly suggested, continues to be a pressing need in the church. He asked if I would be willing to invite, coordinate, and edit a col-

1

lection of essays on the theme of empowerment for leadership in the church. At the outset, he hoped that the essays would address ordained ministers in terms of their responsibility to empower lay persons for leadership in the church.

At the early stages of planning, it became clear that the essays should not be addressed exclusively to clergy, but to a much wider readership. More importantly, it seemed to me that much more needed to be done in a volume on power and empowerment than simply spell out the responsibilities of the ordained to empower the nonordained for leadership in the church. What was needed was a thoroughgoing theology of empowerment. And that need has only increased since the time of the project's inception.

It is my contention that most discussion about lay ministry and leadership in the church is undertaken because of very pragmatic considerations. The "bottom line" in such discourse goes as follows: There are just not enough priests and nuns any longer to do the work of the church. But there are good, committed lay persons who are willing to devote themselves to service in the church. Let's count our blessings. Maybe the "vocation shortage" is a work of the Spirit calling lay people to ministry.

The problem with this view is the implication that if there were enough priests and religious, then the services of the laity would not be necessary. Underlying this view is the assumption that laypersons are "pinch hitters" in a crisis. They form a "second string" of church ministers. They are, in the last analysis, not essential to what most judge to be the essential ministry of the church — the ministry of the ordained.

I reject this view. Even if we did not find ourselves in the midst of the "vocations crisis," there are theological, not simply pragmatic, reasons to recognize and call forth the gifts of all the baptized. It is the very nature of the church to be and to build the Body of Christ, and this requires the flourishing of the gifts given each one by incorporation into the Body through baptism.

The essays that follow address the issue of empowerment in very different ways. No one contribution presents a tightly-knit theology of empowerment. But taken as a whole, the essays constitute a reliable theological and pastoral resource for theologians, students, and ministers, ordained and nonordained, who seek a fuller understanding of power, empowerment, and leadership in the church past and present.

The volume opens with a New Testament study from a feminist perspective. Tina Pippin's "The Politics of Meeting: Women and Power in the New Testament" provides an understanding of power based on an interpretation of the meeting of Elizabeth and Mary, traditionally known as the "Visitation," and the Magnificat that follows

(Luke 1:39–56). Using this text as a paradigm, Professor Pippin argues that the gospel narratives have potential for transforming the material world through a "radically different" reading of the text that is both textual and contextual: political, revolutionary, feminist, and hermeneutically constructed. Pippin's own hermeneutical vantage "is part of cultural politics that draws from Western and non-Western sources" and presupposes the "view from below" that gives room to the marginalized, space for their speech, and privilege to their point of view. She maintains that in the Gospels the meeting of women with one another and the encounter of women with Jesus creates a different kind of power. Jesus enters into relationship with those who are furthest from power — slaves, women and children, the sick, the physically handicapped, the racially unacceptable. These are the "revealers of the heart" (Rita Brock) who break through the structures of power and oppression and manifest a type of power that is "non-hierarchical, relational, and experiential," allowing for difference and multiplicity of expression.

"Power and Authority in Early Christian Centuries" by David Power offers an understanding of power based upon an examination of key New Testament texts reflective of the authority of Jesus, of Paul, and of the reality of authority within the churches of the New Testament period. David Power shows that, in the generations that followed the New Testament era, the task that faced the churches was that of interpreting the Scripture, formulating the apostolic tradition, and celebrating Christ's mystery in liturgy. The evolution of the episcopacy is traced in relation to the service of this task. In charting the development of episcopal authority, attentive to other kinds of authority that existed alongside it, Fr. Power takes up the issue of how the life of the church and the empowerment of the faithful were affected by a sharply marked distinction between clergy and laity, noting that "the office of bishop became the sole holder of authority in the church rather than the servant of its manifold presence." He maintains that clerical, particularly episcopal, authority was emphasized to the gradual neglect of charismatic authority held by other believers. This regrettable cleavage cannot be properly understood as the result of benign, divine guidance. The author suggests that the most vital factor in a renewed understanding of power and authority in today's church is the cultivation of a deeper awareness of the presence and work of the Spirit among the faithful "so that it may serve as an ecclesial, rather than an individual, criterion of true faith and apostolic community." He concludes with an invitation to recognize that the greatest challenge given by the Spirit today is to include the socially, politically, and ecclesiastically marginalized within the communion of faith and worship as testimony to the power of God.

The essay by Wayne Hellmann, "Rebirth of the Word: Empowerment in the Middle Ages," provides an explanation of the various ways in which persons were empowered by the Word in the Middle Ages. Beginning with the Cluniac retrieval of an appreciation for the humanity of Christ as discerned in gospel text, Fr. Hellmann demonstrates that there were very different understandings of the function of the Word. The Cistercian reform fostered an approach to mystical union based on deep desire and intimate love, which leads to contemplation of and participation in the humanity of the Incarnate Word mediated through the gospel text. The Victorines focused on sharing the Word in concrete community experience, which edifies and, thereby, empowers. Alan of Lille emphasized public preaching for love of others as that which expresses the full power of the Word. According to Francis of Assisi, the gospel empowers concrete choices in the manner of imitation of Christ. The gospel "empowers choices that allow the Christian to participate in Christ's choice of obedience to his Father and in Christ's choice of poverty for a life with the lepers of this world." For Dominic, the gospel was experienced as empowering the apostolate of preaching. The needs of others conditioned his approach to the Word. Dominic was "empowered by the Word in his realization of the need of others for the Word."

For Hellmann, these various approaches are all expressions of the power and empowerment of the Word. He maintains that a common thread running through this multifaceted impulse of the gospel is the attentiveness given to the humanity of Christ mediated through the Word and encountered in human experience. This gives rise not only to the surge of evangelical life characteristic of the Middle Ages, but also to the evangelical theology by which "the whole church, clerical and lay," was empowered.

"Religious Life as a Space of Empowerment" begins by focusing on religious life as a gift of the Spirit for the holiness of the church, as expressed in the documents of the Second Vatican Council. This, Mary Milligan maintains, is the context for speaking of religious consecration as a source of empowerment. She describes religious life as a specific way of concretizing the basic orientations in the life and ministry of Jesus. This entails the choice to eschew external power in favor of the power of the Spirit through which one "authors" one's life and choices according to the mind and heart of Christ. This choice is the basis for a theology of the vows as empowering. "The vows invite the Christian into identification with the powerlessness/ empowerment of Jesus," and to find therein that one is "a fragile human being who ... receive[s] all from God." Far from distancing religious from others, the vows empower them to touch a common humanity shared by all human beings.

Sr. Milligan then draws attention to a form of religious life rooted in the monastic tradition stressing its eschatological dimension. Such an approach considers religious life as an alternative community wherein one is empowered to transcend the human condition. This she contrasts with the apostolic congregations of women religious, most of which began in the sixteenth and seventeenth centuries in contexts fraught with obstacles. She avers to the social and ecclesiastical restrictions that were unsupportive of the apostolic desires of these women, but that did not thwart their approach to religious life as a means of empowerment for service and mission. In spite of the obstacles, these congregations continued to provide a context for women to develop talents in those areas that the larger society did not encourage. The author finishes with a description of the impact of the Sister Formation Movement, which empowered "a whole generation of women religious for intelligent, competent service in the American church, a service springing from a renewed theological vision and spiritual depth."

"John Paul II's Vision of Collaboration and Empowerment" presents a brief overview of the life of Karol Wojtyla, attentive to his longstanding appreciation for collaboration in mission. Leonard Doohan observes that some suggest that the papacy has hindered Wojtyla's previous collaborative approach. But Professor Doohan insists that in his writings, he emphasizes "a prophetic service, calling the universal church to communion, mutual appreciation, coresponsibility, and shared mission." He argues that John Paul II does not see collaboration and mutual empowerment simply as means of being more efficient. Rather they are ways of more fully realizing the nature of the church as communion. According to Doohan, John Paul II underscores interdependence as part of his vision of church as communion, recognizing the dignity and rights of the laity, and stressing the roles and responsibilities proper to them deriving from their distinctive condition, i.e., the secular condition of lay life. Some of the responsibilities and roles in the church being assumed by lay persons arise from the sacraments of initiation while others, according to John Paul II, require ecclesiastical missioning for the sake of order. When lay persons participate in areas of church life that relate to the function of the ordained, John Paul II "sees the need for empowering, for permission, and for control." But, Doohan insists, "nowhere does Pope John Paul present the hierarchy as a source for empowering the laity in their distinctive, baptismal mission, as if the hierarchy's permission were necessary for this." John Paul II presumes the laity know what the world needs, take responsibility in addressing such needs, and have a mandate to do so by virtue of baptism. The essay draws to a close with a helpful analysis of John Paul II's *Christifideles*

Laici, the apostolic exhortation that resulted from the 1987 Synod on the Laity. Here again we find a theology of collaboration and an understanding of mutual empowerment in service of the church as communion, which calls for a "hierarchical ordering of communion rather than the clerical hierarchy's ordering of the faithful."

In "Charism, Power, and Community," Bernard Cooke begins by noting the power shifts occurring among various segments of the church. Such shifts are indicative of a more deeply rooted revolutionary appraisal of the notions of power and authority as they apply to the Christian community. This reappraisal is due, in part, to feminist thought as well as to current studies of Christian origins. Professor Cooke's analysis of power and authority in the New Testament provides a basis for questioning "the unquestioned acceptance of the patriarchal/hierarchical view of power that has reigned relatively unchallenged for centuries." He maintains that the later emphasis on the jurisdiction proper to those who occupy official positions in the church is out of step with understandings of power that derive from a careful reading of the New Testament. These later views of power are based upon a "political" or "organizational" model for thinking about Christian community. Power and authority in the New Testament are not based upon this model, but rather on a "life model," a model of a living social reality. This latter model is rooted in "the divine creative power that we have come to call 'the Holy Spirit,'" which empowers a community to live a life of discipleship motivated by faith, hope, and love. Empowerment comes through participation in the life of this community of grace and Spirit.

Cooke maintains that what is happening in the church today is a simultaneous revision of our ecclesiology, pneumatology, and christology. Taking this renewal to heart, he offers an explanation of the power exercised by the ordained celebrant of the Eucharist, which casts the notion of *in persona Christi* in a new light. Those in positions of power who lead the community at prayer and worship are not *above*, but *of* and *for* the community whose members they are.

In "Empowering Lay Leadership: Challenges and Responsibilities," Robert Morneau maintains that ordained ministers have both a responsibility and an opportunity to assist lay persons in exercising appropriate leadership within the ecclesial community. In light of John Paul II's affirmation in *Christifideles Laici* that, in case of need, laity can be entrusted to fulfill certain tasks ordinarily reserved for the ordained, Bishop Morneau makes ten assertions about empowerment for lay leadership. He insists that "empowerment is not an option. It resides at the center of responsible leadership." The author holds that theological education and the development of professional skills are necessary components in the empowerment of lay persons. But

Morneau notes that there is often a lack of attention to the theological and intellectual formation of lay persons. He raises this question as a gentle reminder: "Has pragmatism... become so dominant as to downplay if not negate the value of the intellectual life? Put more boldly: Is there an unconscious anti-intellectualism afoot that makes theological formation a mere option if not a waste of time?"

At the heart of Morneau's understanding of empowerment for lay leadership is a critique of the notion that "the world" is the sole locus for lay ministry. He maintains that though the tradition has affirmed that the primary ministry of the laity is in the world, not in the formation of the ecclesial community, our contemporary situation calls for an appreciation of the latter responsibility. "The important distinction between ministry *ad intra*, that is, nurturing the development of our own ecclesial life, and ministry *ad extra*, that is, reaching out to the needs of the broader world, must not be used to subvert the empowerment question." He holds that, given the present circumstances in the church, it is too narrow and unrealistic to insist that the ordained and religious will do the *ad intra* ministry while the laity will attend to *ad extra* concerns. Thus, empowerment of the laity takes place at two levels: "in being missioned to permeate the world with gospel values and in the building up of the ecclesial community itself."

In "Priests and Laity: Mutual Empowerment," Roger Mahony treats the ministerial relationship between clergy and laity, focusing not only on the responsibilities of clergy to empower laity, but also on the responsibilities of the laity to enable ordained priests to exercise their ministry. He notes that, as we come to the end of the twentieth century, theological and cultural developments converge to call for new patterns of relationship between clergy and lay persons. Gaps between clergy and laity have narrowed to some extent, causing some concern about "overlaicizing the clergy and overclericalizing the laity." He reminds both clergy and laity that "we are all first and foremost baptized Christians."

Archbishop Mahony then provides a fuller explanation of his position on the nature of "lay ministry," expressed in his intervention at the 1987 Synod on the Laity. He explains that sometimes non-ordained ministers "are subject to the vicissitudes of changing pastors and administrators." Dioceses could " 'use' these ministers as long as it is convenient without affording them protections appropriate to one who is committed to church ministry." His intention is to recognize and "protect" these ministers by granting them "formal status to act in the name of the church." His concern "is not to strip lay ministers of their lay status." It is rather "to respect what it means to the church and to the individual to give one's life as a minister of the church."

Mahony maintains that full participation in the communion and mission of the church on the part of all the baptized will be enhanced by acknowledging the distinctive roles and responsibilities of clergy and laity. This, in turn, requires "that we are clear about the full incorporation of new ministries into the structures of church ministry." Finally, mutual empowerment for ministry demands a deeper appreciation of all ministry as service to the Body of Christ and the needs of the human community.

James Jennings's "From Paternalism to Empowerment" traces the evolution of the Campaign for Human Development during its nineteen years as an "experiment in empowerment," one of the longest temporary arrangements of the United States Catholic Conference. Jennings describes the CHD as a program aimed at empowering poor and low-income communities to share in the decision-making processes that affect their lives and thereby take a greater part in the political and economic life of the nation. He maintains that the lengthy temporary status of the CHD resulted from uncertainty regarding the appropriateness of direct involvement on the part of the church as institution in the empowerment of the poor. Jennings explores some of the historical factors that presented obstacles in resolving this issue, as well as those factors that led to its definitive resolution. Here he offers a quick survey of the church's social teaching beginning with Leo XIII, followed by a review of some of the events of the 1960s that led to the church's nuanced worldview. Jennings demonstrates that the "church's efforts to address human concerns have evolved along a twisting trail from paternalism to the poor to the empowerment of the poor." He is quick to point out that the CHD's part in this evolution has sometimes been threatened by the persistent "nagging right-wing criticism" that the CHD supports "leftist political activists." This criticism notwithstanding, the experimental, tentative status of the CHD ended in 1988, when the United States bishops voted overwhelmingly to grant the campaign the status of a standing committee of the United States Catholic Conference. This recognition marks a new chapter in the story of the church's struggle to empower the poor, and a new stage in its evolution.

"Liturgy and Empowerment: The Restoration of the Liturgical Assembly" takes up the issue of power and empowerment within the context of the reform of the liturgical life of the church initiated by the Second Vatican Council. Bob Hurd treats the liturgy as a political phenomenon and a site of empowerment. He maintains that while the particulars of the conciliar liturgical reform have been implemented fairly quickly, its political meaning and implications are far from being realized. This, Dr. Hurd suggests, is because the conciliar reforms presume a political unit, the assembly, that has not existed for centuries. A quite differentiated pair, priest/congregation, has predominated in liturgical life since the Middle Ages. The author charts the development of an "assembly model" of liturgy from early Christian centuries to the point when it was eclipsed by the "priest/congregation model" in the Middle Ages. Both models display a different "politics of liturgy," i.e., different expressions of power relations. Hurd maintains that the *General Instruction of the Roman Missal* is a document of empowerment because it restores the assembly-centered model of the liturgy as the norm. The document reiterates throughout that the primary agent of the liturgy is the assembly. The *GIRM*'s "political substance is basically democratic in the sense that it envisions every human person as a co-responsible agent of salvation history.... Persons are not to be reduced to mere objects, patients, or consumers in their own religious histories." And this reduction, or dis-empowerment, Hurd suggests, is the effect of the "priest/congregation model," which still holds sway in much liturgical practice. In conclusion, he offers practical suggestions for empowering the church through the implementation of the introductory rites and the presentation of the gifts in ways more in keeping with the primacy of the assembly that he is working to restore.

In "He Has Pulled Down the Mighty from Their Thrones, and Has Exalted the Lowly," Susan Ross offers a feminist reflection on empowerment. Rather than basing her discussion on one of the major Christian sources, e.g., Scripture or early Christian tradition, she draws from feminist theory and theology those aspects that suggest different ways of looking at the issue of power and empowerment. Professor Ross argues that the situation of women at the margins of power "enables us to imagine new and more creative forms of empowerment." Drawing on theological, philosophical, and social-scientific works in feminist theory, this essay attempts to describe forms and uses of power in ways that enhance the dignity of all human beings and promote the transformation of the self and the social body. Women's understandings of power and empowerment, for Ross, revolve around five principles basic to feminist thought: solidarity, marginality, embodiment, knowledge, and transformation. Taking as her inspiration "the example of the most powerful one, whose power did not coerce and manipulate but was shared," together with the five feminist principles, Ross describes some of the ways in which women, working in relationship to and on the margins of the structures of the church, are forging new patterns of empowerment and leadership in the church.

"The Church and Hispanics in the United States: From Empowerment to Solidarity" by Roberto Goizueta offers an examination of "the preferential option for the poor" and its implications for a theology of empowerment. The author understands the option for the poor not as an ethical imperative but as a precondition of faith. This leads beyond a theology of empowerment to a theology of solidarity with the poor, which gives rise to new understandings of faith and discipleship. He argues that liberation theologians have taken the preferential option for the poor to its logical conclusion. What is revolutionary in liberation theology, according to Dr. Goizueta, is not the struggle for justice, but the epistemological priority afforded that struggle. That is to say that those persons whose own vantage point is outside the power structure of the dominant ideology stand "as the guarantee of God's transcendence." The preferential option for the poor tells us nothing about the moral quality of the poor themselves. "Rather, it tells us something about God."

Goizueta argues that the very notion of empowerment is to be questioned because it conveys the notion of redistribution of power from the powerful to the powerless. True empowerment, he suggests, is based in solidarity with the struggling poor and marginalized. The most basic expression of empowerment is found when the powerful keep silence so that the powerless can speak and be heard. Perhaps the poor and marginalized do not want more power or a greater slice of the political and economic pie. Perhaps they will speak of a way of living that is altogether different from that of the dominant social group.

Goizueta reminds that the ever-growing Hispanic-American community is issuing a call to solidarity and conversion. They are a *mestizo* people born from a history of racial, ethnic, cultural, political, economic, and religious conflicts. They are a marginalized people, who mediate a transcendent, marginalized, outcast God. To empower the Hispanic-American people is to recognize that Anglo society has something to learn from them, something about the very nature of God, calling all "to strive for a genuine pluralism whose very definition is forged in the struggle for justice, not imposed by the dominant social groups."

In "Looking to the Last and the Least: A Spirituality of Empowerment," I offer an explanation of power and empowerment from the perspective of the marginalized, those at the periphery of social and religious institutions. Using a hermeneutics of marginality, the essay examines the Spirit at work in remembrance of the Kenotic Christ and in the parabolic power of the Word that orients, disorients, and reorients to a new vision of God's future. The understanding of power that results from this remembrance and from hearing the Word in this way confronts understandings of power that undergird the socio-symbolic order of "the center" with its dominant ideology. Exercises of power at the center stand in opposition to a "relational" view of power that is unified and interdependent because of its origin in the unity and interdependence of divine and human power, which is the Holy Spirit. From this perspective, power rests at the heart of all creation, even and especially in the most vulnerable. Empowerment, I suggest, is not a matter of giving those at the margins a share in the power of those at the center of church and society. It is a matter of recognizing new ways of perceiving and being more in keeping with the word and the work of the Crucified and Risen One whose power was disclosed in his refusal to lay claim to the power of lords, kings, priests, and patriarchs.

This collection represents the work of many. It is likely that each contributor would offer a word of thanks to a colleague or friend for encouragement and support received. But, as editor, it falls to me to express gratitude to those who have assisted the project as a whole. Mike Leach of the Crossroad Publishing Company welcomed the idea for the volume with great enthusiasm and has been of good cheer all along the way. Frank Oveis, editor at Crossroad, has once again been masterful in his craft and steadfast in his support, both professional and personal. Finally, a word of thanks is extended to Fernando Moreno for suggesting that the project be undertaken, and to Mary Milligan who, as on so many other occasions, offered such sound advice.

The title of this volume derives from the Gospel of John 10:10 — "I have come so that they may have life and have it to the full." I have judged the title appropriate because of the shared conviction that power, empowerment, and leadership in the church are to be exercised in such a way that others might live.

1

THE POLITICS OF MEETING: WOMEN AND POWER IN THE NEW TESTAMENT

Tina Pippin

> I think you can only refuse something morally if there is a space which is radically different. And I'm not sure those of us in the first world have a space like that, although we maybe at least can gain strength from identifying those spaces in other parts of the world without being able to make them ours exactly.[1]

> Right now and for the imaginable future we have no intellectual, professional, or political base for alliances between radical theorists and dispossessed people.... North American intellectuals need to move beyond theory, tactics, and great dignified moral sentiments to support, in the most concrete ways possible, people harmed or endangered by the guiltless counterrevolutionary violence of state power.[2]

The space of the Third World, in which we hear the voices of the oppressed, is a space that relatively few First World theologians and biblical scholars physically enter. The gospel of liberation theology is "overheard" through the writings of Third World theologians and the news of political struggles from the point of view of the marginalized. Listening is an art that concerned First World Christians develop in order to hear and then converse with the Third World. The stories of suffering and violence, hope and liberation are constantly encountering the "psychic numbing" of the oppressors. This psychic numbing is overcome only if the oppressor enters the space of the oppressed — either by being physically present or by participating as a reader or hearer of the texts of liberation. I propose that the gospel narratives (with the Gospel of Luke as a paradigm for this study) serve as such spaces that are "radically different," spaces that are always present to the First World reader of these texts and always hold the potential (at least in the deep structures) of transforming the material world. This potential requires a rereading (revision, reconstruction) of the text that is textual and also contextual: political, revolutionary, feminist, and hermeneutically constructed. This new hermeneutic is part of cultural politics that draws from Western and non-Western sources. Presupposed in this hermeneutic is the "view from below" — allowing the marginalized to speak and their point of view to be dominant.

ON THE CONCEPT OF DIFFERENCE

Feminist biblical studies have called attention to the need for a dialogical method. The "view from below" has several dimensions (class, race, gender, sexuality, culture) and can be fully heard only through open dialogue and experience (the practical struggle of living the biblical message in daily life in a particular context). Reading from the point of view of the oppressed means a radical transformation from the traditional, post-Enlightenment methodology of a rational search for the "true meaning" of the text. There is a switch in the dominant ideology when other voices and other ways of knowing are included. Rosemary Radford Ruether shows how this inclusion works:

> Feminist theology makes explicit what was overlooked in male advocacy of the poor and oppressed: that liberation must start with the oppressed of the oppressed, namely, *women* of the oppressed. This means that the critique of hierarchy must become explicitly a critique of patriarchy. All the liberating prophetic visions must be deepened and transformed to include what was not included: women.[3]

This shift in emphasis is the future shift in biblical scholarship. The workings of the biblical text in the lives of marginalized and oppressed people are beginning to be seen in places like South Africa, Latin America, South Korea, and Eastern Europe. The Christian community in these oppressed regions has been flourishing in ways that are not being told.

Rather than seek a unified reading of the New Testament understanding of power and authority, feminists are beginning to suggest that *difference* is necessary.[4] This difference is culturally and socially determined. Difference counts. Difference implies possibilities — for dialogue and for change. White feminists no longer assume they speak for women of color. The gospel texts do not transcend issues of gender and class but rather raise the issues of empowerment of the oppressed. Feminists have answered Ruether's question "Can a male savior save women"[5] with both yes and no; those who answer yes find in Jesus a paradigm for the powerless — one who accepted people and affirmed difference.

There is still resistance to using a dialogical method when reading biblical texts. Literary criticism and hermeneutical studies are eclectic and often esoteric. In a graduate seminar in New Testament at a prominent institution an objection was raised recently by a male doctoral student to the inclusion of feminist criticism and theory in the syllabus: "But that's not bread and butter exegesis!" This statement points to the very ideology that feminist criticism challenges: that the central reading is white, male, and Western.

But there is another critique of a pluralistic model that comes from feminists. Elizabeth Meese points to the use of pluralism as cooptation (by males to weaken the power of feminist observation and by females to slip into the dominant system). Also, pluralism is a First World privilege, and the marginal tend to remain marginal.[6] First World interpreters and exegetes have the power to produce texts that are inclusive or not of different alternatives. Feminist and materialist readings of biblical texts are reminders of the richness of biblical interpretation — the richness that comes with shared power and the decentering of the male subject.

NOT AN IDLE TALE: READING AS A WOMAN

Now it was Mary Magdalene and Joanna and Mary the mother of James and the other women with them who told this to the apostles: but these words seemed to them an idle tale, and they did not believe them. (Luke 24:10–11)

Translating into contemporary literary theory means that the reader has the power in interpreting a text (reader-response criticism). Traditional biblical education has taught men and women to read as men (to think rationally and scientifically — seeking to be an "objective" reader), but feminist criticism explores the difference in reading the text *as a woman*. Jonathan Culler relates, "When we posit a woman reader, the result is an analogous appeal to experience: not to the experience of girl-watching but to the experience of being watched, seen as a 'girl,' restricted, marginalized."[7] The dominant interpretation of the New Testament has left woman as other, marginalized, and alienated from the sharing of power in the church. Women tell "idle tales," but men preach and have the voice of authority.

Women reading biblical texts as women have brought slow but deep change to the power structures of the church. But even the powerful readings of Elisabeth Schüssler Fiorenza and Rosemary Radford Ruether have not brought down the centrality of patriarchal readings. Reconstructing women's history — the stories of biblical women to be remembered and retold and the history of women's interpretation of the Bible that is global — requires a conscious choice on the part of the reader. Literary critic Patrocinio Schweickart rightly points to the "commitment to emancipatory *praxis*," which leads to

> the necessity of *choosing* between two modes of reading. The reader can submit to the power of the text, or she can take control of the reading experience. The recognition of the existence of a choice suddenly makes visible the normative dimension of the feminist story: She *should* choose the second alternative.[8]

Reading for the gender codes in the text (or subtext) gives the reader responsibility, and with this responsibility comes the openness to be changed by the text. This issue of difference raises the idea of deconstructive theory.

THE DECONSTRUCTION OF POWER

Studies of power in the New Testament and in the stories of Jesus have traditionally dealt only with male power. Woman is other, outside, and is identified with power only through the male. In traditional studies women are given a kind of "secondary power" that emanates from Jesus or is apportioned out by the disciples (or the male scholars!). But women in Luke's Gospel have power when they meet on their own terms, and also when they actively seek the healing of Jesus, actively challenge Jesus, or actively follow Jesus. Reading the text as a woman is essentially deconstructive; the power relations in the text and outside the text break down. The dominant ideology is questioned and decentered. The woman reader takes control of the reading process. Gender becomes a significant rather than an insignificant category of concern.

In more traditional studies power is seen in terms of its religious and political implications and, in particular, the relation of Jesus to the religious and political powers of his time. The history of religions approach to the problem of power generally begins with the adult Jesus and is imbued with an apocalyptic focus on the future world of God. The Roman Caesar is not the focus of Jesus' message. Martin Hengel provides an easy example of this type of traditional study. For Hengel the philosophical definition of Max Weber is central: " 'Power' is the probability that one actor within a social relationship will be in a position to carry out his own will despite resistance, regardless of the basis on which this probability rests."[9] Hengel summarizes: "the power of Christ is able to 'carry out [its] own without resistance,' but that this in no case can happen through external coercion, but only through genuine persuasion of the person addressed, *sine vi humana sed verbo* — 'without human power, simply by the word.' "[10] The tension between this reading of Jesus and the force of Mary's reading of God's power in the Magnificat is strong.

An alternative way of philosophically defining power comes through Jürgen Habermas's reading of Hannah Arendt's understanding of power. Habermas suggests that Arendt's view of power is grounded in her reading of the Greek city and relates to "the communicatively produced power of common convictions." He summarizes this definition of power as follows:

> Hannah Arendt regards the development of power as an end in itself. Power serves to maintain the praxis from which it springs. It becomes consolidated and embodied in political institutions which secure those very forms of life that are centered in reciprocal speech. Power therefore manifests itself (a) in orders that protect liberty, (b) in resistance against forces that threaten political liberty, and (c) in those revolutionary actions that found new institutions of liberty.[11]

Power as a goal and an external end is redefined by Arendt. Habermas relates finally that "legitimate power *arises* only among those who form common convictions in unconstrained communication."[12] In the Lukan story of the meeting of Elizabeth and Mary we have a scene in which two women are engaged as equals in "unconstrained communication" away from the "constraining" presence of the dominant male. Men are present in outline only — the outline of the womb and the outline of the political, religious, and social hierarchies. The women express the creative use of power — power that at once reproduces and also creates an entirely new social and political order.

Perhaps this image of power emerges in the mother image. This mother image represents a kind of "politics of motherhood" and a "poetics of motherhood" through the poem of Mary. Janice Capel Anderson notes that the birth narratives "associate female gender with the realm of birth and nurture" and thereby "reflect a male cultural view that this realm is a source of female power and difference controlled by patriarchal...arrangements";[13] this is certainly true on one level. Anderson observes the instability of the narrative in the middle of patriarchal ideology, since Mary and God have a direct relationship.[14] But the birth narratives operate on many levels, and reading for the gender codes of the narrative in Luke reveals a rare glimpse of female reproductive power as nurturing *and* politically revolutionary.

The image of mother is central to the meeting of Elizabeth and Mary. According to Barbara Johnson, "The figure of mother should be analyzed as the subject of discourse rather than as the source of life or the object of desire and anger."[15] The women in this story are more than the traditional reproductive vessels and objects of desire. Elizabeth and Mary image — they imagine — power. This imaging/imagining is possible through their mutual discourse and aggressive pronouncements.

Centuries of the male reading of power relations have created a politics of violence against women. The powerful women of the Bible have been coopted or silenced by the institution — made into submissive role models for women and for the laity in general. Barbara Johnson clearly understands the oppressive role of institutions:

> It is as though institutions existed precisely to create boundaries between the unreal and the real, to assure docility, paradoxically, through the assumption of unreality. Yet institutions are nothing if not *real* articulations of power. They are strategies of containment (to use Jameson's phrase) designed to mobilize some impulses and to deactivate others. Always ideological, they are also heuristically, if not existentially, inescapable.[16]

Biblical women work and meet outside the male institutions. They know directly the power of the institutions of the Roman government and the Sanhedrin. The power of institutional law maintains the marginalized existence of women in the church and world. The poetry of women's lives and voices is drained out of the text. Women reading women meeting brings the poetry back into the reading process and is inherently deconstructive. If poetry is "the repository of knowledge about the resistance of language to intentional dissolution" (Johnson),[17] then the presence of women in the biblical text creates new and "different" worlds. The reader enters into such worlds at her own risk, the risk of imagination and power. The following interpretation of a Lukan passage is an example of such a "different" world.

THE POLITICS OF MEETING: LUKE 1:39–56

Since the hardest stories to hear and critique are beginnings and endings (Genesis and Revelation), birth and death (virginal conception and the cross and resurrection), I have chosen to begin near the beginning of the story of Jesus in Luke's Gospel with the meeting of Elizabeth and Mary, traditionally known as the "Visitation," and the Magnificat that follows. In this section the role of women is unfamiliar; they take responsibility for subverting the existing order. Included in this "order" are economics, politics, gender roles, and class distinctions. What is said about each of these in this passage? Does what is said hold true throughout Luke-Acts? This section relates more than a meeting of motherhood but is a "politically charged" encounter with dangerous ethical implications for men and women in the first and the twentieth centuries.

The "politics" I am discussing are "sexual, textual politics"[18] with ramifications for the larger context of the Luke-Acts narrative. The meeting of Elizabeth and Mary in Luke 1:39–46 reveals (1) the power relationships and gender roles (1:42–45); (2) the decentering (and then recentering) of the male subject; (3) a critique of the ideology of class domination (the Magnificat).

The Gospel of Mark has traditionally been the focal point of political and materialist readings.[19] To move the political discussion to include the Gospel of Luke both social world studies (Richard Cassidy) and studies on narrative structure (Robert Tannehill) are necessary. The relationship between discourse and power is shown in the dialogue of the women. On one level the meeting of the two women to share the joy of their pregnancies is innocent enough; on a deeper level the force of their meeting represents political empowerment and the overthrow of the structures (and institutions) of oppression. "Dangerous memory" (J. B. Metz) and "prophetic hope" (Jürgen Moltmann) of the coming reign of God are proclaimed in this narrative — themes that recur throughout Luke.

Three varieties of critical theory will be applied to the text. First, materialist criticism (Marxist literary theory) provides a bridge between literary theory (narratology) and social world studies. Second, feminist criticism reconstructs women's roles in the text and enables the decentering of the male subject. Third, a liberation hermeneutic reads the text "from below," listening to the voices of the oppressed and taking their viewpoint. Third World responses to this text raise necessary issues for its contemporary relevance. These methods work together to produce a common goal: a political rereading of this section of the Lukan birth narrative and the political implications of the whole of Luke in light of this reading.

THE MEETING

The Gospels are subversive narratives; they are dangerous snares for those intent on maintaining the status quo. So is the meeting of Elizabeth and Mary a dangerous text; the women are empowered with the ability to *speak*. They are not silent; they speak to each other, and the reader overhears their conversation. According to Fernando Belo:

> *"Narrative" means a narrative of a subversive act, a subversive narrative....* By recounting the practice, the narrative subverts the ideological codes opposed to the subversiveness in question; being itself subversive, the narrative opens up within the text of the social

formation, the space for new practices. As the proclaimer of the subversive acts, the narrative makes it possible to read them, repeat them, enlarge upon them, and extend them. The narrative thus has an important and unappreciated role to play in a revolution.[20]

Belo is here revealing the basis of the materialist reading that lies in the production of texts[21] and how they function in social relations. The unspoken political meaning of the pregnancies suddenly becomes spoken: first by Elizabeth in proclaiming openly (after hiding herself for five months, 1:24) the joy of liberation and then outlined by Mary in the Magnificat. There are no passive heroines here; both speak powerfully and confidently.

The discourse of the women is embued with power, and there is a reversal of the dominant social relations of the time. Elizabeth and Mary are away from male protection in this scene, except in terms of the powerful male God who has entered their lives. Nonetheless, this discourse represents a political discourse. The women are talking about their roles in the overturning of the existing order (or oppressive Roman imperialism). Susan Wells makes an important distinction between private and public in feminist thought; private relates to intimacy and public to the broader social relations. She explains:

> For feminists, *private* is closely associated with *female* and invokes all those activities traditionally assigned to women; the creation of domestic life, care of children, even emotion and subjective life in general. *Public* refers to the themes traditional in masculine political discourse; parties and alliances, candidates and programs, economics and foreign affairs.... The great power of feminist critique has been to show the profound connection between these two seemingly independent spheres, enabling materials and themes that had been frozen into privacy to enter public discourse.[22]

Traditional readings of this narrative have focused on the private, domestic meaning of two pregnant women meeting to rejoice over being pregnant and fulfilling God's will and the will of the social order (retaining shame and honoring God and their men). In this narrative the spheres are dialectically merged, and the reader is given a rare glimpse of the feminine power. The women meet in private at "the house of Zechariah," but their discourse transforms the social order and is passionately public.

A certain social relationship is at once maintained (the reproductive function of the women) and overthrown (those of low degree are exalted). In this dialectic there is social unrest. Coward and Ellis relate that "struggle is then the only absolute principle of dialectical thought; its essence is to change the basis of reality."[23] The meeting is subversive because it reveals the power struggles of the first century C.E. The women take responsibility for their role in society and at the same time transform that place; i.e., make it public.

THE MAGNIFICAT

The ideology of the text is most strongly revealed in the discourse of Mary in 1:46–55. The statement by Conzelmann that "Mary disappears to a greater extent in Luke than in Mark and Matthew"[24] is just not true. Although her character is not fully developed to the end of the gospel, Mary is very much present at the beginning and is responsible not only for giving birth to Jesus but also in setting the radical theme of the birth.

A detailed analysis of the Magnificat has been done by Jane Schaberg in her book, *The Illegitimacy of Jesus*. Schaberg sees the song of Mary as a song of liberation from a woman who has been violated (raped, seduced). The surprise of the poem is "that she who was humiliated and degraded, and the child whose origin is in humiliation and degradation, were 'helped' by God (v. 54)."[25] Elizabeth in her barrenness and Mary in her "trouble" are both helped by God, but in Mary's case there is "God's overcoming of the deeper humiliation" or *tapeinosis*.[26] This parallelism between the stories of John and Jesus are continued throughout the gospel. Schaberg's analysis is important because the poem is reread from the point of view of the speaker, Mary, and not the Mary Virgin Mother that has traditionally been internalized by Christian women who use the Mary story as legitimation of their "humble" or submissive roles in religion and household. Schaberg salvages this narrative for women and men. The reification of the reader is overcome in the focus on the powerful reversal of the sexual humiliation of Mary.

As Tannehill relates,

> The reader must honor the unity of the text . . . sensing their mutual reinforcement or the tension between them. . . . the text enables us to see the mother and her baby as signs. . . . Its power as sign is dependent on the tensive unity of the text, which confronts us with the wonder of a particular event among humble people which has crucial significance for the ages.[27]

But in this part of the Lukan narrative there is as yet no baby born; he remains in the womb as a sign of hope and conflict with the existing social order. Julia Kristeva sees women as marginal in a patriarchal society because they stand at the line "between man and chaos; but because of their very marginality they will also always seem to recede into and merge with the chaos of the outside." Reproduction is especially mysterious, and "it is not *women* as such who is repressed in patriarchal society, but *motherhood*."[28] The humiliation of Mary is overcome, just as the humiliation of Israel will be reversed.

The poor in the Magnificat are not the "poor in spirit"[29] or the poor as "a traditional characterization of Israel understood in terms of its suffering and humiliation at the hands of the nations and as a result of its own disordered internal life."[30] Seccombe sees any liberation hermeneutic as misusing the "poor" as Luke intended and that no reversal theme is in the text.[31] Liberation theologians see Mary as a witness to God's liberating action on behalf of the oppressed. C. Hugo Zorrilla relates: "I see Mary as neither timid nor unwilling to risk all. Within the imperialistic regime and before the Roman oppression, she is a symbol of those who have no fear.... It is a relief and a challenge that we can look to Mary, who in a similar environment showed no fear because her confidence was in God her Savior."[32] In the context of the marginalized, poverty means real poverty, both physical and mental. Seccombe's rejection of a materialist reading leaves the concept of the poor too generalized and is contradictory to the real material poverty suffered by the Israelites under Roman rule. The Magnificat is directed against the state power. Mary is a subversive speaking a subversive text. The memory of the Exodus and the new Exodus is a dangerous memory, not some recapitulation of the traditional theme of the Deuteronomic history. Even Northrop Frye sees the Magnificat holding the "same theme of revolutionary upheaval" as the song of Hannah in 1 Samuel 2:7–8.[33]

Liberation readings of this text reveal its dangerous memory. Zorrilla states that if the Magnificat were sung publicly in almost any Latin American town, "I would not be at all surprised if one of those who is always on duty would not prevent the song from being finished, or at least see to it that it would be finished only in jail, assuming the Christian's health permitted."[34] The poem has a "revolutionary germ"[35] that is clear from the following dialogue at Solentiname:

I asked what they thought Herod would have said if he had known that a woman of the people had sung that God had pulled down the mighty and raised up the humble, filled the hungry with good things and left the rich with nothing.

NATALIA laughed and said: "He'd say she was crazy."

ROSITA: "That she was a communist."

LAUREANO: "The point isn't that they would just *say* the Virgin was a communist. She *was* a communist."[36]

The liberation talked about here is of course the violent overthrow of an oppressive military dictatorship. Could Mary be speaking of the same thing? Tannehill's conception of a triangular relationship of the tension of God, the oppressors, and the humble does not fit into a materialist reading where God takes sides and always takes the side of the oppressed. In the Magnificat there are binary oppositions rather than triangular tension. The narrative is extreme — extreme in its political orientation. The whole Lukan narrative gives order and stability to the story of Jesus and the early followers. But the meeting of the two women shows a deeper prophetic hope for the nation Israel and for the status of women.

CONCLUSION: POWER AS EROTIC POWER

In the Gospels the meeting of women with each other and the encounter of women with Jesus creates a different kind of power relationship. Rita Brock relates that the furthest from power (slaves, women and children, the sick, the physically handicapped, the racially unacceptable) are the "revealers of heart" — they break through the structures of power and oppression.[37] Brock states, "Actions to heal brokenheartedness shatter old orientations to self and power and open fissures that birth erotic power."[38] Brokenheartedness is a metaphor for oppression and sickness and destruction in culture. Brock notes that it "reveals our power to hurt each other and to heal each other."[39] In the gospel stories the victim is a catalyst in the process of healing and humanization. In the Lukan birth narrative Mary and Elizabeth stake a claim on justice. The racial and religious lines of injustice are erased, and the good news of Jesus Christ is heard in a new way.

This brokenheartedness is both male and female. Ruether and others are correct when they describe patriarchy as a system of brokenheartedness. Men and women alike suffer from patriarchy. Men are often threatened by the rage of women at the patriarchal system. How do men join in? First of all, it is important to understand rage/anger. Women are taught that the male system is the standard — the male way of knowing and thinking and reading and theologizing is standard. Feminist theologians reveal the importance of anger, for there is a new sensibility and a new way of knowing that comes out of this rage. Beverly Harrison explains, "Anger is a mode of connectedness to others and it is always a vivid form of caring."[40] The goal of anger is not to separate, but to reconcile, to join.

Power as defined in the Gospels is erotic power because it is nonhierarchical, relational, and experiential. Erotic power allows for anger and the telling of tales of violence and abuse. Erotic power allows for difference without alienation. Power becomes spiritual and is transformed, and the believer is thus transformed and empowered.

Men and women in the New Testament tales seek Jesus and confront Jesus and teach about Jesus and suffer because of their belief in Jesus. Schüssler Fiorenza says, "This history of women as the people of God must be exposed as a history of oppression as well as a history of conversion and liberation."[41] Her call for an "*ekklesia* of women" or women-church is a call to transform the misunderstanding of power as hierarchical and exclusive.

When contemporary women readers meet the biblical text as women, they begin to enter into those spaces that are "radically different." The choice to read as a woman is a choice of values. The dualism of the mind/body split that has haunted women throughout Christian history is overturned. As Jesus said to Mary of Bethany, "Mary has chosen the good portion, which shall not be taken away from her" (Luke 10:42). Discourse is power, and the involvement of women in the discourse of the church — as equal dialogue partners — is essential for the empowerment of Christian women but also for the empowerment of the church in the world. Feminist theologians point to a different choice for women and men and for the *ekklesia*, one "which shall not be taken away from her."

2

POWER AND AUTHORITY IN EARLY CHRISTIAN CENTURIES

David N. Power

As a contribution to the issue of empowerment and leadership in the church, I have been asked to explain the development of the notions and exercise of power and authority in early Christian centuries. The general title of the volume indicates the nature of the exercise involved. It specifies the question that is brought to a reading of the tradition and its texts. In a church that is looking for a correlation between its experience, its hopes, and its tradition, it is asked what light can be shed on current practice and aspirations from a reading of early Christian materials and from the attempts, however restricted in nature, to establish a reconstruction of the historical scene. The very presence in this volume of a New Testament study done from a feminist perspective is a reminder that we all bring specific ideas and interests to a study of tradition. Hence, at the beginning of this essay I want to carefully formulate my own perspective, as I think it fits the interests of the volume and its collaborative enterprise.

In order to relate to the concerns of the volume, I formulate the focus brought to the reading of the early tradition as follows: how is the grace of the Spirit communicated, and how is it conceived to be communicated, so that persons may participate fully in the life of the church, its mission, and its hopes? In an attempt to explain how and why they took place, I will further ask in what measure conceptual and institutional developments seemed to advance or hinder this reality.

At first one can look at the image of authority presented in some key New Testament texts as these reflect the authority of Jesus, the authority of Paul, and the reality of authority within churches of the New Testament era. Then it will be necessary to see how episcopal authority developed and what other kinds of authority existed along with it, and how diverse authorities interacted. After that, one cannot avoid the question of how the life of the church and the empowerment of the faithful was affected by the adoption of a sharply marked clergy/laity distinction. Finally one may ask how nonclerical forms of authority continued to be exercised despite this distinction, and whether there were ways in which episcopal authority was regulated so as to truly serve the body of the church.

AUTHORITY IN THE NEW TESTAMENT

This presentation is of necessity very limited, but it is pertinent to the issue to look first at how authority is associated with Jesus, then with Paul, and finally how it is located in communities.

The word describing Jesus' mission, which we roughly translate into English as "authority" or as "power," is *exousia* and is complemented by the word *dynamis*, which also has to be translated as "power."[1] The latter reflects what is received by the beneficiaries of Jesus' ministry, especially his healing ministry, and its perception is always the occasion of a wonder or amazement that sees God's hand in these works. Jesus associates this with the authority, or *exousia*, of his teaching, which has to do with the advent of God's reign. One might say that *exousia* combines the power to work wonders and to teach as one who knows personally whereof one is talking. It is this combination that evokes faith in others and inspires them to listen to the way in which Jesus interprets the law and the prophets, showing how they have come to realization and what they demand of believers. Ultimately the authority of Jesus comes from his personal consciousness of God's Spirit and his zeal for God's reign. This shows forth in his compassion, in his reprimands, in his works, and in his teaching. This naturally gives rise to the conviction that his is a personal authority, and whatever the varieties of christologies to be found in New Testament writings, this conviction is worked into them. The image and example of this authority is also ever present in the exercise of authority among the disciples, so that one commentator can cryptically say: "It was only as they shared in his mission that his disciples shared in his authority and charismatic power."[2]

Though the earthly exercise of authority by Jesus can be said to be an example for the exercise of authority in the church, it was of course the authority of the Risen Lord that was thought to hold command. The two are not unconnected, but what was represented in Jesus' earthly ministry was subsumed into the lordship given through his resurrection and exaltation. It was transmitted to the church by the pouring out of the Spirit and the gifts of the Spirit. Now of course the faith in God's reign and in Jesus as its messenger is confirmed and transformed by faith in the resurrection. The exemplar of how this authority flows over into discipleship and its exercise of mission is found in the figure of the apostle Paul.[3] Paul's authority is shown primarily in his preaching of the gospel of the death and resurrection of Christ in a way that commands faith, but it is not unassociated with his personal witness and even with some ability to work wonders, though in comparison with Jesus this is low-key.[4] In fact, Paul did more to point to the confirmation of the gospel in the deeds of others and in the charismatic gifts of the community than he appealed to his own charismatic powers.

Insofar as the Pauline writings elaborate a concept of authority, these points may be noted. First, Paul's authority has its origins in the personal commission given to him by the risen Christ. Second, it is one with his preaching of the gospel and with drawing people to faith in this gospel. Third, it is linked with the developing notion of *paradosis*, or apostolic tradition, and thus is verified in terms of fidelity to this tradition. Fourth, it is exercised in communion with the other apostles (both the twelve and others commissioned to preach). Fifth, the teaching is confirmed by the signs of the power of the Spirit, though not necessarily worked by Paul himself. Sixth, this has to imply the recognition by the apostle of the charisms and ministries generated in the believing community by the power of the Spirit. Seventh, though authority is chiefly couched in the preaching of the Word, it may be exercised in relation to specific judgments about conduct and practice in as much as these pertain to the living testimony to Jesus Christ expected of disciples and of the household of the faith.

In light of this last point, one has to ask how authority and the empowerment of the Spirit were shown in the lives of communities, and what sort of leadership was exercised in them. At the current stage of scholarship, it is prosaic to remark how complex this question is and how varied were the structures of different churches in different regions.[5] One may however be permitted three assertions. First, God's power is located primarily in the community of faith, worship, and service, and not in any particular person or manifestation of power. Second, discipleships were bound by fidelity to the apostolic word, in whatever forms it was given to them. By implication they owed obedience to the one received as an apostle, whether this person resided in the community or not. Third, discernment of spirits, of beliefs, and of conduct that duly testified to the Christ rested with the communities and in the communion that they formed. Some common activity, however diversified, is thus involved. Questions of structure and thus of office had to do with practical necessity, e.g., where to assemble, and most of all with appropriate ways to keep fidelity to God's Word and communion in God's love.

In the pastoral letters attributed to Paul, it already becomes apparent how much fidelity to the apostolic tradition and the question of church office were linked together. This invites treatment of the dilemma and the practical evolution of forms of authority in the postapostolic age.

MEDIATIONS OF POWER[6]

Unfortunately because of tensions in the church today, attitudes to this question tend to be polarized by suspicion of formal and ministerial structures on the one hand and by a heavy affirmation of their divinely given authority on the other. Only an effort at due differentiation can offer good insights from historical evidence. One way of formulating the question is to see the issue as that of appropriating the New Testament realities and images of authority within a time when the canon of the Word has to be set, beliefs more formally regulated, and the identity of the church forged through structures and through appropriate ritual expression. What in fact emerged as principal mediations of authority were the canon of the Scriptures, the rule of faith in creedal form, the liturgy celebrated according to its own recognized rules, and the episcopacy. Several risks were involved in this evolution. There was the temptation to identify these mediations with the authority and divine power that they served. There was a danger of giving one or other of the four undue governance over the others. There was the chance that the church might begin to suppress or ignore other, less regulated, exercises of the work of the Spirit. While some initial diversity existed in the ways in which different churches formulated these four principles of apostolic authority, it is necessary to note that over the centuries there was a drive toward a greater uniformity, in which the episcopacy and in particular patriarchal sees played a great role.

Since the church is brought into being through the Word of God and response to it, clearly the most basic issue was that of deciding on a fixed canon of the Scriptures. This could then become the concrete reference point for what was affirmed to be the apostolic word and the apostolic tradition. It was however always to be a living word, so that its transmission in worship and in teaching was actually constitutive of the canon. One of the primary concrete norms for deciding on what belonged to the canon was its use in liturgy, as dialectically deciding what could be used in worship was a way of expressing judgment about a book's canonicity. Since there were in early centuries competing canons, including the Jewish, the Marcionite, and the Ebionite, some collegial acceptance of what was the canon of catholic communion was important.[7] This ought not lead us to believe that strict uniformity on this point was reached in early centuries or even in the Middle Ages, as indeed the debates culminating in the decree of the Council of Trent testify. While the broad contours of the canon can be said to be determined from early church times, it may be true that its more rigorous boundaries remain a constant matter for diversity.

The Scriptures of their very nature require interpretation, as for the sake of inner cohesion the common life in Christ needs a more precise formulation of belief. Thus in the second century the churches evolved a common rule of faith that could be used as a test of orthodoxy and of catholic communion.[8] This was expressed in recitative creedal formulas, such as that which we name the Apostles' Creed, or in forms appropriate to liturgical usage. The interrogation on faith that went with pool immersion in the celebration of baptism is of the latter kind. The content of the Creed came to be more copiously spelled out and more precisely determined in face of unorthodoxy, giving us the Nicene Creed as well as the conciliar definitions on matters christological and trinitarian of the subsequent centuries. While the singing of the Nicene Creed at Eucharist is by no means a well established early church practice, it seems fair to say that there was always a doxological intent in early Christian creeds.[9] Right faith and right praise went necessarily hand in hand, and this helped to direct the notion and exercise of authority.

For the determination of both the canon of Scripture and the rule of faith, the congregation of the community for worship constituted the living context. This meant that these expressions of authority bore a living relationship to the mystery of Christ represented in the communion of faith. The real nature and purpose of authority is to bring God's grace and power into the living reality of the eschatological people. Doxology is the end of proclamation and of clearly formulated belief. The memorial and representation of Christ's mysteries, while it is begun in proclamation and in right faith, is culminated in the prayer of praise and thanksgiving. While on the one hand, and this was often the preoccupation, it can be said that right worship is that which follows right belief, it is also true that the power to bring to joyful and eschatological praise is a criterion whereby to assess the power of the word and the orthodoxy of the creed. This is but another way of formulating the dialectic between the *lex credendi* and the *lex orandi*, which can never be resolved solely in favor of one side of the interaction.[10]

EPISCOPACY AND AUTHORITY

The evolution of the episcopacy can be traced in relation to its service of the above three mediations of divine authority. It was both subordinate to them and their custodian. Its association in the church with apostolic authority is due to this. Such association meant first that it had to stand witness to the apostolic word, now expressed in Scriptures and in the rule of faith and brought to the celebration of

Christ's mystery in the liturgy. Second, it meant that bishops were conscious of the fact that like the apostles they needed to corroborate the witness of their teaching by the witness of the power of the Spirit in their own lives. Third, it meant that they needed to recognize the power of the Spirit even when it was exercised by persons not holding office and to give authority to these manifestations.

Since Ignatius of Antioch is usually taken as the first Christian writer in whose works we can find clear evidence of the episcopal form of church office, it is worth noting how much he felt it necessary to appeal to his own personal witness in support of his teaching of the faith.[11] In his case, the crowning witness was his martyrdom, something for which he longed and to which by anticipation he could make appeal when writing to other churches. Nowhere else in his life could the power of God be made more manifest or stand more obviously as corroboration of his teaching. The authority of his office and the authority of his witness could go together to confirm the case that he made against the false teachers who disturbed the communities, even to the point of denying the reality of Christ's fleshly appearance.

The second figure who looms large in the early evolution of episcopal authority is Irenaeus of Lyons.[12] This is because of his emphasis on the rule of faith and the criteria whereby to identify the genuine apostolic tradition as distinct from false creeds. While the role of bishops as authentic teachers is confirmed by his evidence, three aspects of this are important. First, he situates the teaching of the bishop in the context of the apostolic church. Second, Irenaeus does not identify the bishops with the apostles. In his episcopal lists, it is the first pastor after the founding apostle who is called a bishop. In this sense, episcopacy is an office and ministry that comes after the ministry of the apostles, the two not being identified with each other. Third, the teaching of the bishops deserves acceptance because of its link with apostolic tradition, as much as it is itself the guarantee of apostolic tradition. Irenaeus attributes the greatest authority to those churches that can trace their foundation back to one of the apostles or to one of their immediate disciples. The reason for this is that this temporal link is a kind of *de facto* guarantee of the authenticity of the tradition upheld in the church. There is something of a circular argument here in that the teaching of the bishop both upholds and is upheld by the tradition, but its circularity does not involve contradiction. What comes to the fore is that the tradition has primacy over the office and not the office over the tradition.

Unfortunately, the emergence of greater episcopal authority seems to have led to the gradual neglect of charismatic authority held by other believers. Charismatics are mentioned in church orders and get some recognition up until the fourth century,[13] but this is as much a remnant of former times as it is a full-blooded respect for their witness to divine power. The New Testament evidence would suggest that manifestations of divine power in the works of various members of the community ought to be a constant of church life. Its disappearance as an ecclesial phenomenon with importance for the church is as much evidence of neglect as it is an indication that people no longer possessed charisms. Nothing is fully a factor of communal life unless it is affirmed by leadership. Its neglect by leadership pushes it to the margins, and into legends. That charismatic power did continue for a long time appears from the legends of the saints, as it did also in the desire to promote charismatics to the ranks of the episcopacy. An outstanding example of this from the late fourth century is Martin of Tours, remarkable for the wondrous works that he performed both before and after his ordination. On the one hand, this kind of evidence shows that there was not an end to the gifts of the Spirit in the church. On the other, it shows how these very works were appropriated to build up the authority of the bishop.

The rather startling thing that the church has ever to face, and to face more pragmatically today than ever, is the early date at which a division is forged between the clergy and the laity.[14] This division cannot on any account be justified from New Testament evidence. It forces credibility to see it as a result of divine providence governing the church in developing its offices and structures. One can only say that along with the necessary emergence of a sacrament of order, there were too many other social forces and biases that brought the church to this cleavage. It is a development that in the light of cultural and social realities can perhaps be understood or explained, with whatever regrets, but it is not a development that can be equated with the results of a benign divine guidance. The difference between the images and configurations of authority in the New Testament and those in such works as *The Apostolic Tradition of Hippolytus* and the provisions of the Roman church of the fourth and fifth centuries, is too great not to be startled by it.[15] It is for that reason that there is some interest in seeing how various common qualities were in the course of time associated with the episcopacy, thus enforcing its authority. As common qualities in other persons they became less important, simple gifts that could be used for the sake of others but not supportive of any evidence of authority. In short, the office of bishop became the sole holder of authority in the church rather than the servant of its manifold presence. This is not to pretend that there were not bishops who served people well and showed great respect for others. It is rather to attend primarily to a social and official development in which individuals were caught up.

It is the wont of ritual to preserve the old even in the midst of the new. Hence, even before considering the evolution of an episcopal image, it is worth noting how elements of an earlier polity remained on in the practice and celebration of ordination, thus becoming an available tradition allowing for retrieval.[16] First, it continued to be affirmed as a principle that a bishop ought to be chosen or elected by the people of the church that he was to serve. Second, the people's approval needed to be expressed in the ordination service. Third, the proper circumstance for ordination was the gathering of the community for the celebration of the Eucharist, and it was the church rather than simply the presiding bishops that was accounted the ordaining body. Fourth, the celebration brought out in the laying-on of hands and the invocation of the Spirit, that no power exists other than that given by the Spirit, working where it will. There was in all of this some difference between the developments in East and West. The Western churches tended to accentuate appointment to office, whereas the Eastern kept alive the image of a divine taxonomy that was manifested in the holy mysteries or liturgy.

THEOLOGIES AND IMAGES OF THE EPISCOPACY

It may be important to note that I do not wish to question the existence and need for a sacrament of order in the church. Such a conclusion ought not to be drawn from a consideration of the various ways in which the episcopacy appropriated to its own benefit many things that belong to the body of the faithful in a more common way. That very exercise should only serve in the long run to bring out the necessary contours of the episcopacy, as distinct from its accretions. In pursuing this goal, first it will help to consider some typical theologies of episcopacy that amount to support of its unique power. Then we can consider an example of the development of an image of the bishop in the church.

Cyprian of Carthage was one who gave sharp impetus to the power of the bishop in the church.[17] He did this first in his way of exercising his authority in ruling the church in a time of persecution that needed strong leadership. Second, he did it by emphasizing that the bishop is the center of the life of the church and that no church communion can exist outside the community around the bishop. Third, he practically identified the office of bishop with that of apostle, referring to the twelve as the first bishops and finding the origin of the episcopacy in Christ's words to Peter (Matt. 16:18). Fourth, in depicting the role of the bishop in the Eucharist, Cyprian identified his actions with the actions of Christ. What he said was that in offering the great thanksgiving prayer and so sanctifying the gifts of bread and wine, the bishop repeats the action of Christ at the supper and so represents his presence in the church. In keeping with this idea,

Cyprian called bishops *sacerdotes* and presbyters *consacerdotes*, thus introducing priestly vocabulary into the designation of church office. However much this has been subsequently justified by theological argument, it still needs to be recognized that it was a remarkable shift from the fundamental New Testament image of the priestly people to the priestliness of office.

Augustine of Hippo is an interesting writer of whom to take note because of the many different factors that he held together in his depiction of church life.[18] As a bishop, he had a strong persuasion of the pastoral nature of his office among an at times wayward and often superstitious people, subject to the enthrallments of false teachers. He had much to say about evil and false shepherds, whose existence was all the more astounding for him because of what he considered the high nature of their calling. For Augustine, the clerical order was a calling to both service and greater sanctity. He could appeal to the New Testament images of authority to show that teaching needed to be confirmed by holiness of life, but he then appropriated this into a philosophical vision of cosmic order in which holiness of life and call to ministry belonged together and placed the clergy on a spiritual level higher than that of the faithful. It is well known how the ideal of order influenced clerical developments in the post-Constantinian age, but nowhere does it get so theological a conception as within Augustine's more boldly conceived notion of divine order.

Given this Augustinian position, it is of great interest to note how he wove more traditional concepts into his vision of authority in the church. To begin with, he believed in the accountability of bishop and clergy to the faithful. He was even ready to explain to the people some of the measures that he took in disciplining presbyters for infractions of the life that he expected the clergy of his diocese to live. This leads Yves Congar to remark:

> By giving all his flock an account of the way in which he wanted his priests and clerics to live with him, Augustine lifted the whole of the *ecclesia* onto so lucid a plane that he ensured for himself the enlightened and full consent of the faithful.[19]

The importance given by Augustine to the diffusion and explanation of the Scriptures is clear from his preaching and his theological treatises. Not only did he preach them, however, but he formally acknowledged their authority within God's plan and strove hard for the determination of the canonical Scriptures over against other writings. In the account of his own personal conversion that we find in the *Confessions*, he associates his turn to God with his discovery of the authority of the Scriptures, which he had previously tended to despise. In his treatise on Christian doctrine he formulates the principle of the canon as follows:

> Here is the rule [the believer] will follow in dealing with the canonical Scriptures. Those books accepted by all of the Catholic Church will be given preference over those which certain churches do not accept. Next, concerning those books not accepted by all, preference will be given to those books accepted by the more numerous and more important churches ahead of those admitted by the less numerous and those of lesser authority. Finally, if he should find some books accepted by the more numerous churches and others by the more important churches, although this is a tough one, I think that equal authority should be given them.[20]

In this quotation, we note not only the importance given to the canon but also the link between it and the faith of the church. Augustine is trying to combine a principle of universal consent with a respect for the more ancient or apostolic churches that is reminiscent of Irenaeus. The Scriptures, the faith of the church, and the authenticity of apostolic foundation merge together to constitute the authoritative word of God. With this there goes the rule of faith or Creed, something that Augustine carefully transmitted to the catechumens preparing for baptism.[21] All this, of course, though based in the church itself as a community of faith, was linked by Augustine with the responsibility of the episcopal office. Even in doing this, he placed a curtailment on the power of any individual bishop by the authority that he ascribed and in practice acknowledged to come from church councils. These were far better indicators of church faith and apostolic tradition than the teaching of any particular bishop.[22]

To pursue the development of the notion of authority to the end of what is often called the "patristic" era, one would have to attend to the power of the keys ascribed to bishops, since this combined sacramental, jurisdictional, and teaching authority in one reality. It came to the fore as a concept in the exercise of penitential discipline, where it belonged to the bishop to decide who was to be excluded and who was to be readmitted to the communion table.[23] At the end of this era, the giving of the keys to Peter is proffered as the origin of the New Testament priesthood by Isidore of Seville.[24] What Isidore places to the fore in this concept is the power to teach, since this is what he sees as distinctive of the New Testament priesthood in relation to the Old. With this power he associates sacramental celebration and the penitential discipline of binding and loosing. Together these constitute the episcopal or priestly ministry.

In a rather different way, Martin of Tours is an important figure in the development of the practice and image of the episcopacy. This is not attributable to any writing from his hand but to the writing of his life by Sulpicius Severus[25] and his assimilation into popular legend. So great was this latter, that centuries later Martin served as one of the models for the writing of the life of Francis of Assisi, thus serving ironically as support to an authority other than episcopal in the preaching of the Word of God.

The promotion of the figure of Martin as the ideal bishop is an excellent and influential example of how personal testimony and charismatic power were appropriated to the office of bishop, so that they could actually be used to win it respect. In the *Life of Martin of Tours*, holiness, the spread of the gospel through an itinerant ministry, the combat against demonic superstition, the founding of monasteries, the working of wonders, and suffering for the name of Christ all came together to conjure up the image of the ideal bishop and to confirm the importance of this ministry in the church. Even the assent to the election of Martin as bishop, which was still considered a necessary factor in ordination, was evoked by extraordinary divine intervention so that the people could not in good faith have refused it. For Sulpicius Severus, opposition to Martin's election was demonically inspired and in facing his accusers he was like Christ himself appearing before his accusers. As for Matthias, however, in the Acts of the Apostles, God intervened in the casting of lots and Martin stood out as a divine choice and no mere choice of the people. This moved subtly from the location of the choice of a bishop in the hands of the people to a divine vocation to which the people were expected to give their assent.

The theologies of Cyprian and Augustine and the practical example of Martin by no means exhaust all that deserves to be studied in the exercise of power and authority in early Christian centuries. They do however serve to typify an evolution. If one had to look more factually to "what happened" to the exercise of authority and power in the early church after Constantine, it would be necessary to give considerable attention to the place that bishops assumed in society as a whole. This means attention to their relation with the secular power, as well as their cultural and civilizing influence among the new Christians of the barbarian peoples. There is a factual reality here of great importance. In the first few centuries, bishops were foremost among the martyrs in testifying to the lordship of Jesus Christ against the claims of worldly powers. After Christianity's official recognition, they were the ones to keep the church on track and independent when secular authorities wanted to coerce it to other interests. They were often also the ones to hold diverse peoples together and to promote ancient ideals of civilization among the barbarian peoples. Could all of this have been done without assuming the vestiges of power and rank and

privilege? Could it have been done without placing the bishop so em-
inently above other faithful and without emphasizing the distinction
between clergy and laity? Could it have been done without associating with the faith some ideas and ideals that were not essential to it
and may have been indeed inimical to it? One would wish that all
this could have been possible, but one does not know.

RECLAIMING THE MARGINAL

Even while we see the development of the episcopal office and the
growing equation between it and the mediation of God's power in
the church, it is still important to note that it was meant to serve the
interpretation of Scripture, the formulation of the apostolic tradition,
and the celebration of Christ's mystery in the congregation's worship.
The empowerment of the people through the Spirit came not from the
bishop but from that which the office mediated.

It is equally important to keep the marginal in mind, in the recognition that it deserved and deserves to be more fully incorporated
into the church's mediation of power. During these centuries even
the most powerful of bishops recognized that in some measure he
had to exercise his office in the church in collaboration with others.
In other words, collegiality was a reality not only among bishops but
also on the level of the local church. Bishops constantly consulted and
sought the assent of their presbyterium.[26] At ordination, the assent of
the people was vital to the process. However much his policy was
that of taking initiatives rather than one of listening to the people,
Augustine thought that the church lived as church and passed on the
faith only in communion. One of the questions facing communities
today is whether this collegial aspect of church life does not need to
be given fuller canonical status.

Furthermore, as we have already remarked, charismatics never
disappeared. What happened rather was that their gifts and ministry
were looked on as extraordinary and were not given a place among
the criteria for the discernment of the operation of the Spirit in the
community, except when they belonged to a bishop. There seems to
have been some hesitation about this marginalization of the spiritual
power not associated with office. Martyrs through their death had the
power to confirm the church in its faith, their death being a confirmation by the Spirit of the faith that they professed. In the *Apostolic
Tradition* the confessor had an authority comparable to that of presbyters simply because of his witness.[27] The prodigies worked by holy
persons could always be taken as the Spirit's confirmation of the kind
of life that they led and so indirectly as an encouragement to the
church and an enlightenment of its faith. Except, however, when the
charismatic was ordained a bishop or a bishop operated as a wonder-

worker, this power was not directly associated with the criteria of a church's faith and fidelity.

Maybe the most noteworthy thing in the development of the notion and exercise of power in early centuries was this appropriation of charismatic power to the office of bishop. Once located there, its continuation in other quarters could be given less importance, relegated in legend to the edification of the people and effectually excluded from among the criteria of the authenticity of faith. Once located there, it could also be made a secondary factor in episcopal power, one whose eventual absence could not be seen as taking away from the authority of the office-holder, whether it be seen in terms of outstanding holiness of life or in terms of the power to work wonders. For a retrieval of tradition, it has to be admitted that it is a particularly hard reality to get a grip on, simply because we have no clear sense of what constitutes the wonders of the Spirit. Fundamentalist appeals to gospel miracles or to the legends of the saints do not help us much today. Could it be that the most vital factor for a reconceptualization of power and authority in today's church will be the development of a genuine sensitivity to the presence and work of the Spirit among all the faithful, so that it may serve as an ecclesial, rather than an individual, criterion of true faith and apostolic community? In the end, it is my suggestion, as I have written elsewhere,[28] this is something pointed to by today's liberation theologies. Sometimes they make direct appeal to the testimony of wonder-workers who are seen as evidence of the faith and of the Spirit among the poor people struggling to live or struggling for justice. More globally, they see the gift of freedom as the crucial point where practice and grace converge. For those oppressed to be able to find their own voice, to become the actors in their own lives, to pursue the thirst for justice in their own way, all in the name and memory of Christ, is perhaps today's outstanding charismatic gift and the one that points to the congregation of the true church.

CONCLUSION

Whatever judgments are made about the growth of office and about the growing association of authority with the episcopacy, for a retrieval of tradition it is rudimentary to note that the purpose of the office was and is to serve the congregation of the faithful in the one faith and the one worship and to bring the Word to life in the form of the Scriptures and the genuine apostolic tradition. It is however the Word of God, the gift of the Spirit, the preaching of the faith, and the celebration of worship that empower the faithful and the church community. None of these should be as tightly tied to the episcopacy as they became. Some pointers to the responsibility that all the faithful have for the transmission of the faith and for mutual empowerment are found in the documents of the Second Vatican Council. There is also an explicit warning therein that all charisms need to be properly discerned and recognized.[29] The practical acknowledgment of the various ways in which, and the various persons through whom, the power of the Spirit is mediated is more difficult to establish. In noting the criteria of discernment that serve in recognizing the authenticity of those churches in which the Spirit is working for the spread of the gospel, more attention has to be given to the works of the Spirit in the community. There are in fact many ways in which the Spirit gives witness to our witness. In New Testament times, it was through the many charisms that gave liveliness to the community. Later, it was through the witness of martyrs, the fidelity of confessors, and the work of healers, but these tended to be relegated to the background in favor of the claims of the episcopacy. In recent decades, some have thought to turn again to charismatic activities such as healing and tongues. These no doubt have their place, but are all too often found together with biblical fundamentalism. The Spirit seems to be speaking in new kinds of charismatic voices, voices that find their authentication in the fidelity and joy of a struggle for freedom from injustice and for a fuller participation in life of the socially, politically, and ecclesiastically marginalized. To include these within the communion of faith and worship as testimony to the power of God, the presence of Christ, and the truth of the faith, may be the great challenge and invitation that the Spirit is giving to the churches today.

3

REBIRTH OF THE WORD: EMPOWERMENT IN THE MIDDLE AGES

J. A. Wayne Hellmann

The Word of God empowers the life of the church. A magnificent flowering of this is seen in the late twelfth and early thirteenth centuries. Apostolic and evangelical movements among the laity gave new shape and form to the Word of God. The mendicant movements emerged. The early beginnings of all this are found in the yearning for reform characteristic of the eleventh century. It was the desire for monastic reform at Cluny within the Benedictine monastic tradition, even earlier in the tenth century, that initiated the journey toward a full flowering of the Word of God in the gospel life of St. Francis of Assisi and the gospel preaching of St. Dominic.

The Cluniac thrust for monastic reform gave birth to new directives or constitutions and facilitated new piety based on the liturgy and the Scriptures. With papal support, the Cluniac spirit reached Italy. When it eventually touched St. Romuald (d. 1027) and St. Peter Damian (d. 1072), another monk, Hildebrand, later known as Pope Gregory VII, was influenced. With full energy, he devoted the years of his pontificate (1073–85) to free the church from the abuses of lay investiture and to reestablish regular life among the monks as well as moral life among the clergy.

Institutional reform was the order of the day, and to this end canonists sought to clarify and organize law. The "Gregorian" canonists searched the libraries. Ivo of Chartres (d. 1116), Bernold of Constance (d. 1100), and Gratian (d. 1150?) with his *Decretum* offered direction for canonical development. Law and clear hierarchical authority were the key elements for church reform. The Lateran Councils (1123, 1139, 1179, and 1215) furthered and institutionalized the Gregorian reform.

Collateral to the papal and institutional attempts at monastic and clerical reform were other developments that sprung from Cluny and began to take hold in a different way and in a different forum. At

Cluny, an appreciation of the humanity of Christ and the maternity of the Virgin found humble beginnings. In the Italian peninsula, in the writings of St. Romuald (d. 1027) and St. Peter Damian (d. 1072), these devotional forms were developed further.[1] Here, the voluntary and penitential pilgrimages, as practiced by the lay penitential groups, found a new spiritual and affective foundation. This growing appreciation for the humanity of Christ and the cause of his human connection, Mary, his mother, was furthered also by the Cistercians of the twelfth century. Out of this emerging piety, a new approach to the gospel was born.

CISTERCIAN APPROACH TO THE WORD OF GOD

While the attempts at reform of the clergy fostered the development of canon law, in monastic reform the Cistercians led the way. In the renewal of the monastic vocation, a spirituality of the humanity of Christ came into full play, and this, of necessity, brought the monks to the gospel text in a new way. As he contemplates and participates in the humanity of Christ mediated through the gospel text, the monk is renewed. There, in touch with the human Christ, the monk experiences deep desire and intimate love.[2] The soul of the monk desires Christ the bridegroom. As St. Bernard (d. 1153) writes in his *Song of Songs*, "The mouth that kisses signifies the Word who assumes human nature."[3] The Incarnation provides the greatest intimacy possible.

Thus, for the monk, the gospel text fosters involvement in the human life of Jesus. Each gospel follower of Jesus teaches how to love him. The Word of God is the source of every spiritual delight:

> For his living, active word is to me a kiss, not indeed an adhering of the lips that can sometimes belie a union of hearts, but an unreserved infusion of joys, a revealing of mysteries, a marvelous and indistinguishable mingling of the divine light with the enlightened mind, which, joined in truth to God, is one spirit with him.[4]

The Word of God, tied to the humanity of Christ, empowers the monk's lips to taste the sacred kiss of the Incarnation. The Word offers delight and leads to the sweetness of a mystical love. Aelred of Rievaulx (d. 1167) in his *On Reclusion* offers an example of the use of the gospel for guidance in the life of contemplation. The gospel invites the monk to enter into and live within the very life and experience of Jesus, empowering him toward the goal of the monastic experience: contemplation in the passionate love of the "kiss" of God.[5]

VICTORINE APPROACH TO THE WORD OF GOD

The genuine yearning for more authentic Christian life in the humanity of Christ characteristic of the twelfth century found root in the regular canonical life, another development flowing from the Gregorian reform. Of the many canonical groups, the Victorines in Paris were the most famous. While St. Bernard and the Cistercians were no strangers to the canons, the Victorines' approach to the gospel and their understanding of the Word of God in Christian life took a different twist.

The Victorines do not approach the Word in the ecstatic and contemplative manner of the Cistercians. For the Victorine canons, the Word must be shared if it is to empower, and this sharing is done through edification. The Word empowers when good example is given.[6] "For a holy life is not sufficient to us unless there is also good reputation," writes Hugh of St. Victor (d. 1142).[7] In the context of the shared experience of canonical community life and worship, one is empowered by the Word to the extent that one empowers the community with the Word through good example and reputation. The Word is thus experienced historically and it empowers history itself. It is in this way that the Victorines discovered the literal and historical power of the Word. The Word is not to be allegorically tasted as much as it is to be historically exemplified in concrete life and experience. Therein lies the truest contemplative wisdom.[8]

The Word of God, then, empowers to the extent that one brings the hermeneutic of one's historical and lived experience to the Word: "Do you wish to see Christ transfigured? Ascend this mountain; learn to know yourself."[9] Only in connection with an understanding of the historical self in community, and all that this implies, can the Word of God take power in human life. Thus, the Word reveals its power in the concrete historical and personal example of Christian life. Good example in Christian community life enfleshes the Word and manifests the redemptive and restorative power of the Word. Good example, given to another, is the way the Word of God is shared with others. Good example conditions the historical experience of one's neighbors, and it enables them to bring that experience to their hearing of the Word. In a community that practices mutual edification and good example, one empowers others with the Word and one is empowered by the Word.

ALAN OF LILLE

A contemporary of this twelfth-century Cistercian and Victorine spiritual renaissance is Alan of Lille (d. 1202). His *Art of Preaching* demonstrates that the Word of God achieves full power when it is communicated to others because of love for them. This moves the Word beyond personal contemplative experience and even beyond the good example of shared community experience. In the active and conscious engagement of preaching the Word to others, one experiences the Word and finds its power. The Word is received as preached, and its power is felt in the preaching.

In the preface to his work, Alan refers to Jacob's ladder, the model of ascent that represents the progress of the Christian to full spiritual and human development. Repentance characterizes the first rung of the ladder. Alan writes further: "The sixth rung is reached when the reader himself expounds Holy Scripture to others. He climbs the seventh rung when he preaches in public what he has learned from the Scripture."[10]

One therefore profits most from the Word when one can "show how profitable it is to hear the Word of God"[11] in preaching. In commenting on Alan of Lille, M. D. Chenu states that "we have come far from the monastic program, not only by the steady introduction of *quaestiones* but by the treatment of a divine word which now appeared as a word directed to men."[12] There is a movement from the monastic mystical kiss, to the Victorine immediacy of concrete historical community experience, and, finally, to Alan of Lille's emphasis on public preaching. All are expressions of the power and the empowerment of the Word of God.

FRANCIS OF ASSISI

Francis of Assisi (d. 1226) focuses on the power of the Word in the ecclesial and sacramental experience of the church. The Word provides a concrete pattern for practical Christian living. It is not so much tasted, exemplified, or preached as it is to be experienced as a power effecting both tangible worship and concrete daily living. In his *Letter to the Custodians*, Francis urges that the written words of the gospel be venerated because of their sacramental power. He urges the custodians of the friars to "beg the clergy to revere above everything else the most holy Body and Blood of our Lord Jesus Christ and His holy written words which consecrate His Body."[13] The holy words of the Scripture, like the sacrament, are to be venerated. "Likewise, wherever the written words of the Lord may be found in unbecoming places, they are to be collected and kept in a place that is becoming."[14]

In the gospel Francis discovers his Lord Jesus Christ as one who made choices and one who acted. The gospel is to empower that same praxis in the life of the Christian. In encouraging the friars to a discipline of life and obedience, Francis holds out for all to see the model of Jesus, who "gave his life that He might not lose the obedience of the most holy Father."[15] Francis never ceases to marvel at what the Christ of the gospel has done: "Oh, how holy and how loving, pleasing, humble, peaceful, sweet, lovable, and desirable above all things to have such a Brother and such a Son: our Lord Jesus Christ, Who gave up his life for His sheep and who prayed to the Father saying: 'O Holy Father, protect those in your name.' "[16]

Jesus in the gospel is not simply the Bridegroom to be embraced in a contemplative kiss. It is what the Bridegroom has done in relationship to the Father and to the Christian people, his sheep, that is the great marvel. The salvific action of God is to be contemplated so that salvific action is effective, and realized to be effective, in the life of Christians. The Word effects both sacrament and salvation.

This power effects salvific choices. Mary, the first disciple, made Jesus' choice her choice: "Though he was rich beyond all things, in this world He, together with the most blessed Virgin, His mother, willed to choose poverty."[17]

Within the heart of the Christian, the gospel empowers the ability to make choices according to the pattern of Jesus' life. The gospel presents and makes possible a specific life to be lived, and it is the gospel itself that Francis enjoins on his brothers. The *First Rule* begins: "The rule and life of these brothers is this: ... to follow the teaching and footprints of Our Lord Jesus Christ,"[18] and, again, in the *Later Rule*, the life of the brothers is "to observe the Gospel of Our Lord Jesus Christ."[19]

According to Francis, the gospel empowers concrete choices in the manner of imitation. Intimacy with Christ is experienced in the active imitation of Christ, and it is the action and effective power of Christ that is marvelled at and contemplated. The gospel empowers choices that allow the Christian to participate in Christ's choice of obedience to his Father and in Christ's choice of poverty for a life with the lepers of this world. Therein is the "kiss" of ecstatic love.

St. Bonaventure (d. 1274), who borrowed heavily from the twelfth-century Cistercian and Victorine traditions, integrates Francis's approach to the gospel within this tradition. In his influential work *The Tree of Life*, a series of meditations on the life of Christ for those who desire "to conform perfectly to the Savior," Bonaventure "endeavored to gather this bundle of my rrh from the forest of the holy Gospel."[20]

"A bundle of myrrh is my beloved to me; he will linger between my breasts," a text taken from the Song of Songs,[21] characterizes the spousal language of the Cistercians.[22] In Bonaventure's approach to the Christ of the gospel, he develops mystical union in the affective "kiss" of delight, but this is a mysticism that moves toward imitation and conformity of choice and will. The intimacy of the bundle of myrrh becomes the conscious and willed identification with Christ

Crucified.[23] Only when one shares in the choice of obedience to the Father with Christ Crucified is one fully alive and empowered by the Word of the gospel.

Francis and the Franciscan tradition turn to the gospel to find a pattern for imitation. Franciscan preaching exhorts all to follow the "footprints" of the Christ of the gospel. The gospel empowers the believer to make choices, and so the Word offers the practical moral direction necessary if one is to taste of the love of God and neighbor. It puts one into proper relationship with God and with one's brothers and sisters. The Word empowers relationships, and thus it has an ecclesial and universal dimension. The obedience of following the Christ of the gospel is not separate from obedience to all creatures,[24] nor from obedience to the Lord Pope.[25] For Francis, the gospel empowers in a way that is sacramental, because it effects the Eucharist and it fosters living in the full range of human and divine relationships.

DOMINICAN EXPERIENCE OF THE WORD

As much as Francis of Assisi was moved to embrace the gospel life of imitation, Dominic (d. 1221) and his followers approached and understood the gospel as a commission or mission. The gospel was experienced as empowering the apostolate of preaching. Indeed, for Dominic, this preaching apostolate, conditioned by the catechetical, doctrinal, and moral needs of the people, is primary to the gospel life.

This focus differs from that of Alan of Lille. For Alan preaching is on the seventh rung of Jacob's ladder and it empowers union with God. The gospel as preached effects union with God. For the Dominicans it is in preaching, as explicitly conditioned by the needs of others, that the Word effects union with God. For Dominic, the point of departure is the need of others. It is their need, particularly the heretics' need, to be empowered by the truth of the Word that urges him to embrace the gospel. His whole life with the Word of God is defined and determined by the need of others for the preaching apostolate. He is empowered by the Word in his realization of the need of others for the Word.

Dominic himself wrote very little. The articulated vision of the Dominican spirituality of the gospel was left to the fifth Master of the Order, Humbert of Romans (d. 1277). In his work *On the Formation of Preachers*, he helps his brothers understand and appreciate their vocation as gospel preachers. As Humbert comments, the gospel empowers the sending of preachers: "To see what a noble job preaching is, we must notice that it is an apostolic job: it was for this job that the Lord chose the apostles. 'He appointed twelve to be with him and to be sent out to preach'" (Mark 3:14). Or, again, in the same first chapter, he continues: "Further, it is a divine job. God became man precisely to do this job. 'Let us go into the neighbouring villages and towns so that I may preach there too, because it was for this purpose that I came'" (Mark 1:38).[26]

Experience of the divine "kiss," or intimacy with God, is found in the Dominican response to ignorance, error, and hunger of the market place. For this purpose the Dominican is called to pray, to study, and to live a life above reproach. In short, the Dominican is to serve the Word of God and allow the Word to make fertile the earth: "Again, without preaching, which sows the word of God, the whole world would be barren and without fruit."[27]

In the subsequent century, the fourteenth, there arose the need for a new kind of Dominican preaching. It was the apostolic need of German nuns and of the Beguines for nurturance in the mystical life that gave rise to the preaching of Meister Eckhart (d. 1327), Henry Suso (d. 1366), and John Tauler (d. 1361). This new need drew them to the gospel texts in a way different from the earlier Dominicans. Through the preaching of these Dominicans, the Word empowered the whole German mystical movement.

Just as the Word frees from ignorance and speaks the truth in the market place, so also the Word is the source of the deepest mystical experience within the heart. In his "German Sermon IV," Meister Eckhart addresses the birth of the Word in the soul. His preaching empowers the mystical experience:

> The Father gives birth to his Son in the eternal knowledge, and the Father gives birth to the Son in the soul just as he does in his own nature. He gives birth in the soul as its own, and his being depends on his giving birth to the Son in the soul whether he likes it or not. I was once asked what the Father does in heaven. I answered: He gives birth to his Son and this activity pleases him so much and is such a delight to him that he never does anything else but give birth to his Son, and the two of them cause the Holy Spirit to blossom forth. Where the Father gives birth to his Son in me, there I am the same Son and not a different one. We are, of course, different with respect to our humanity, but there I am the same Son and not a different one.[28]

This is one of Meister Eckhart's more difficult passages. He penetrates into the deepest empowerment of the Word within the intimacy of "sonship." This participation goes much further than the affective kiss of the Bridegroom experienced by the Cistercians. He moves beyond intimacy and imitation to actual metaphysical identification.

However, even in his mystical and metaphysical preaching, Eckhart remains true to the Dominican approach that places even this empowerment of identification with the Word within the active apostolate of service. In his "German Sermon LXXXVI," Eckhart reverses the interpretation of the story of Martha and Mary, a passage so dear to the monks:

> But Martha was very steadfast in her being and hence she said, "Lord tell her to get up," as if to say, "Lord, I would wish that she were not sitting there just for the pleasure of it. I would like her to learn life so that she might possess it in being. Tell her to get up, so that she might become perfect."[29]

Perfection is not in resting at the feet of Christ but in meeting the needs of Christ. Therein is the power and perfection of the Word.

GOSPEL VS. INSTITUTION

In the development of spirituality from the Cistercians to the Dominicans, the Word empowers in different ways. A common thread weaving through this multidimensional impulse of the gospel is the humanity of Christ encountered in human experience. Cluniac piety, which rediscovered the humanity of Christ, opened the door to the gospel text. This opening, in turn, allowed the gospel text to inspire and empower the human experience. The humanity of Christ and personal concrete human experience came together in a new and dynamic way.

This development is often called the evangelical awakening of the earlier Middle Ages. Although the examples and texts used to illustrate this evangelical development are taken from movements that later became institutionalized, their origin and inspiration arose out of the lay impulse for reform. Francis of Assisi and his early brothers, for example, are numbered among the laity. None of what has been considered in this essay can be understood apart from the lay penitential groups, the pilgrims, the Poor Men of Lyons, the Waldensians, and even the Cathari. All these had one thing in common: Desire for the gospel life according to the model of Jesus Christ.

The lay and evangelical renewal of Christian life focussed on the pattern of Christ in the Gospels. The Word was preached and copied. All this developed concomitantly with institutional reform. The Gregorianists rediscovered canonical texts to clarify and give force to institutional structure and authority. In the work of the *Decretum* of Gratian, sacraments were further delineated, and the clerical status was defined. The Lateran Councils were called. Two different experiences and dynamics of Christian life developed. M. D. Chenu comments:

Since the evangelical awakening took place not by a revision of existing institutions but by a return to the gospel that by-passed these institutions, one could predict what its dynamics had to be: witness to the faith, fraternal love, poverty, the beatitudes — all these were to operate more spontaneously and sooner among laymen than among clerics, who were bound within an institutional framework.[30]

Christian life expanded beyond the inherited institutions just as these institutions were in the process of new organizational and moral reform. Even as monasticism reformed itself under Cistercian impulse, the traditional monastic rules were gradually eclipsed in favor of direct reliance on the gospel. The "apostolic life" expanded to embrace all walks of life inspired by the gospel. A new question arose: From where does authority flow, the gospel or the canons espoused by the hierarchy?

It is not within the scope of this essay to answer that question. Suffice it to mention that the eventual crisis of the question was headed off for a while by the wisdom of Pope Innocent III. He integrated gospel movements into the structural reform of the hierarchical church. Francis's way of life is a key example of this. His gospel life was lived in acceptance of the sacraments and in obedience to the pope.

EMPOWERMENT OF THE CHURCH

Monastic piety, which gave rise to a new discovery of the humanity of Christ, and the monastic thrust for structural reform, which influenced Pope Gregory VII, opened the door for a new way of empowerment for the whole church, clerical and lay. The key to this broad empowerment was a theology that bridged what threatened to become an ever-widening gap. It brought about both the institutionalization of groups originally lay in character and the eventual evangelization of the hierarchy. In this theology, which developed from gospel empowerment, the whole church, clerical and lay, found a rebirth.

The Word of God was not only to be lived in a human way, but it was also to be explained and understood in a human way. The message and truth of the gospel was to be incarnated in the human mind. No longer was the transcendence of revelation to be shelved beyond human modes of thought. Reason could penetrate and be penetrated by the Word of God.[31]

As the gospel Word of God empowered a more human pattern of life according to the pattern of the Word Incarnate, a more human theology, in the embrace of reason, was inspired in the minds of those who followed and obeyed the Word of God. The gospel, as it inspired a life and choice according to the human "footprints" of Our Lord Jesus Christ, also empowered a new theology and the choice of reason according to that same human pattern.

The Word empowered evangelical life and evangelical theology. Theology moved from the mystical kiss to the needs of the market-place. Dialectic and debate became the pattern. This theology, which moved forth from the lay gospel impulse, was accepted and promoted in many ways by the hierarchy and the papacy. Gospel life and insti-tutional structure could meet in the reason and dialectic of theology. The collection of the canons and the collection of the Scriptures were brought together. A Word-inspired theology, which was at home with human reason, provided the forum.

The Word of God empowers the human experience of the Chris-tian with the human experience of Christ. The gospel text is taken up, no longer in the mystery of transcendent allegory, but in a human, lit-eral, and historical way. The text is applied to human life, and human life in turn, with the full capacity of reason, is applied to the text. Therein all that is human (i.e., personal, rational, and institutional) is empowered to speak and reveal Our Lord Jesus Christ. Thus the Word of God empowers, by the action of the Spirit, the real pres-ence of Christ in the vibrant flesh of a lay and clerical, mystical and dialectical, personal and institutional church.

4

RELIGIOUS LIFE AS A SPACE OF EMPOWERMENT

Mary Milligan

Any theology of empowerment in the Christian tradition is fundamentally a theology of the Holy Spirit and of the freedom that derives from the Spirit of God. To be free is to be led by God's Spirit; to be led by the Spirit is to be empowered to act.

In reflecting on religious life as a place of empowerment, then, a necessary starting point is pneumatology. This essay will initially lay theological foundations from the teaching of Vatican II on the charismatic nature of religious life. It will then look at religious consecration as an age-old attempt to live in the freedom of the Spirit. Finally, it will consider religious congregations as prophetic spaces of apostolic empowerment. Some concluding remarks on the apostolic experience of women religious in the United States since the nineteenth century will indicate how congregations in a pioneer situation drew on a theological understanding of religious life to exercise a role in the world that society denied them.

THE CHARISMATIC AND PROPHETIC NATURE OF RELIGIOUS LIFE ACCORDING TO VATICAN II

The action of God's Spirit within the church is a theme of the Vatican II documents. *Lumen Gentium* clearly states that in the various types and duties of life, one holiness is cultivated by all those who are moved by the Spirit. Within the one holiness to which all Christians are called, various modalities are specified. Religious life as a specific modality is situated within this gift of one holiness to the church.

Lumen Gentium initiates its chapter on religious by referring to the "life according to the counsels" as a gift of the Spirit given by Christ to the church.[1] Through this gift as through all gifts of the Spirit, the holiness of the church is made manifest. Vatican II states that it is the action of the Holy Spirit that inspires certain Christians to follow Jesus in a particular way of life that concretizes in a stable way the basic options evident in his life.

49

Among the benefits that "religious families" give their members is "liberty strengthened by obedience."[2] Though the nature and expression of this liberty are not specified in the document, freedom is indicated as integral to life within a religious family.

Not only the birth of religious congregations but their evolution as well are attributed to the work of God's Spirit.[3] It is the Spirit who raises up the founders and foundresses of religious congregations and who inspires certain members of the church, both lay and cleric, to an intimate following of Jesus through a life structured on the fundamental dispositions evident in his life: virginity, poverty, and total dedication and obedience to the will and mission of God in the world.

Lumen Gentium likewise sees the Spirit at work in the approval of congregations and their constitutions. This approbation is not seen as an attempt to control or uniformize congregations but rather as empowering them to exercise ecclesial ministry in an official and public way.

The work of the Spirit is one of diversity in unity. Each founding person lived in a particular historical situation, had a unique personality, and responded to the gospel in a personal way. Various apostolic congregations came into existence because the founding person(s) saw needs that were not being met and responded to those needs in a creative and courageous way. The diversity of religious congregations is underlined in *Perfectae Caritatis*, which attributes the "wonderful variety of religious communities" to the influence of the Holy Spirit. Indeed, "it serves the best interests of the church for communities to have their own special character and purpose."[4]

Finally, Vatican II underlines the particular grace each congregation has to contribute to the life of the church; indeed, "they have contributions to make which are as various as the graces given to them."[5] This diversity is not located only in their origins but in their life and ongoing renewal as well: "A necessary diversity will have to distinguish [each congregation's] path to a suitable renewal."[6]

Throughout the conciliar statements, it is clear that religious life is seen as a gift of the Spirit for the life and holiness of the church. The particular gift or "charism" of each congregation is in fact an empowering by the Spirit of the original founding person(s) in such a way that his or her gift attracts others and becomes "communalized." Those called to a particular congregation experience a certain affinity with this charism and are themselves empowered by the Spirit to respond. This conciliar understanding of religious life as a gift of the Spirit provides the context for reflecting on religious consecration itself as a means of empowerment.

RELIGIOUS CONSECRATION AS EMPOWERMENT

The fundamental intuition that gave rise to a life of celibate chastity, communal poverty, and obedience in the church was that the Christian was to be like Jesus in all things, that the mystery of the life and death of Jesus was to be relived in the individual and in the community. The diverse forms and expressions of what has since the Middle Ages been a *vowed* life are attempts to incarnate this fundamental insight at various times and in diverse circumstances, according to the particular graced insight of a group. The forms are affected by many factors, one of which is the group's understanding of Jesus and his mission.

In seeing religious consecration and the vows in particular as empowering, one enters the world of paradox so fundamental to the gospel: one must die to live, give one's life to gain it, leave all to experience the hundredfold. Here one must let go of external and illusory power in order to tap the source of true *authoritative* power, that is, the power whereby one *authors* one's life and choices.

Throughout the Gospels, and most expressly in the Fourth Gospel, Jesus is presented as the Servant of Yahweh, as one who has nothing except what he has received. He speaks and does only what he receives from God; his disciples and his glory are not his own but God's. His every step is led by the Spirit of God, and even his death is the accomplishment of God's hour. Jesus holds on to nothing, not even to "being equal with God." Paradoxically, this radical emptying and poverty are the source of his true power. Others, recognizing his authority, question him on the source of his power: "They were astonished at his teaching, for he taught them as one who had authority, and not as the Scribes" (Mark 1:22); "Where does this man get this wisdom and these mighty works?" (Matt. 13:54).

Jesus consistently refused to do anything that would alienate him from or elevate him above the human condition. As Johannes Metz points out in *Poverty of Spirit,*[7] the synoptic accounts of the temptations in the desert underline this radical acceptance. Turning stones into bread, jumping safely from the pinnacle of the Temple by relying on the intervention of angels, coming down from the cross: all these temptations, expressed symbolically or not, are basic appeals to be above and outside the ordinary condition of mortals. Jesus invariably refused any kind of power used for his own glory or recognition: "I do not seek my own glory, but the glory of the One who sent me" (John 8:50). It is this choice not to rely on external power but rather on the integrity of one's own humanity that founds a theology of the vows as empowering.

Jesus' refusal of external power and his acceptance of the human

condition enabled him to enter the life of others at their most vulnerable point. He recognized human hunger and thirst as points of
vulnerability apt for God's action. Sickness, sorrow, and mourning —
experiences common to all persons — are *par excellence* occasions of
empowerment for him. The need for forgiveness, the desperation of
failure are realities that he recognized and used for entering into the
life of another. And his entrance was always empowering. Those Jesus
encountered experienced God's power within their own limitation.
The story of the woman who was bent over for eighteen years is a
strong symbol of this empowerment of persons. She was "bent over
and could not fully straighten herself." But through her encounter
with Jesus, she was "immediately made straight and she praised God"
(see Luke 13:10–17). Through the encounter with Jesus triggered by
her infirmity, she found within herself resources of dignity and praise.

The vows invite the Christian into identification with the power-
lessness/empowerment of Jesus. To be one with Jesus in the poverty
of humanity is to renounce all that could give one the illusion of being
other than one is — a fragile human being who does, in fact, receive
all from God, a person created in God's image with intrinsic dignity.
For religious, as for Jesus, the temptation is to want to find power
in extensions of themselves rather than in their own hearts, in the
spectacular or the dominative rather than in their own truth.

Luke's Gospel preserves the story of a person who sought to find
eternity — not part of the human condition — in possessions. "I will
pull down my barns and build bigger ones... and say to my soul: 'My
soul, you have plenty of good things laid by for many years to come.'
But God said to that person: 'Thou fool'" (Luke 12:18ff.). In reiter-
ating the danger of material goods for the disciple, Luke touches on
a key human illusion: that we are what we have, or that we are more
because of what we have. Possessions can be considered an extension
of oneself. How often the rich and wealthy are admired as if they were
intrinsically better or more important because of their wealth! Possessions can lead people to believe that they are efficient, important,
powerful, or even, as in the passage from Luke's Gospel, immortal.
Only with great difficulty can a life of convenience or affluence, a life
encumbered by material goods, witness to the radical dependence on
God that is part of the human condition.

One might also hope to "be somebody" because of the people with
whom one associates, because of friends or family. One might vicar-
iously gain power by associating with prominent or powerful people.
Or it might be one's own accomplishments or profession that give
an illusion of intrinsic greatness. Success in work can give a sense
of personal indispensability just as failure can cloud one's sense of
worth. Social position or position within a community can likewise

give one the illusion of being better than others. The apostles' discussion about who would be first in the reign of God is surely a reminder that the Christian community is far from immune from this search for the first places.

The life of the vows can help the religious to assume the human condition without adornment. They can empower those who profess them, like Jesus, to say "no" to extensions of themselves through possessions, posterity, profession; to say "no" to anything that could give the illusion of being other than fully human. By their profession, religious declare in the church their desire to stand with unveiled faces and with empty hands before God, before others, and before themselves. They promise to identify with Jesus in his own humanity, with Jesus who did not hold on even to his "rank," as the Letter to the Philippians reminds the Christian community. In a world where it is common to seek to be "Number 1," this is unquestionably a prophetic stance.

Our humanity is the source of our greatest dignity. To be human is to be like God, an image of God. The vows are meant to help religious to be truly human, to confront the solitude and emptiness that are part of the fabric of all human life. They invite one to live in gratitude, to receive all as a gratuitous gift from God. Lived at their deepest level, the vows bring religious into communion with all humankind by calling them to let go of masks and illusions. In inviting religious to become like Jesus in the radical poverty of his humanity, the vows mark a solidarity with those who are poor and defenseless throughout the world. Far from alienating religious from others, they help them to touch what is shared by every woman, man, and child — a common humanity.

The vows of chastity, poverty, and obedience are meant to form and purify one's heart. They form one to love, to choose, and to serve with open hands and in freedom. They are meant to be opportunities not only for personal freedom but are intended as well to structure the lives of religious in a way that stands against so many of the destructive trends of our world. To hold all goods in common is a word of denunciation in a society where the unequal distribution of goods forces some to live in subhuman conditions while for others the most excessive luxury is taken for granted. Religious are not personally enriched by salaries or gifts but put those benefits at the service of their sisters or brothers and of the disadvantaged of the world.

A celibate lifestyle for the sake of the Absolute contradicts the image of male-female relationships presented so commonly in the media. How often the female (or male!) body is used to sell cars, cigarettes, or liquor. Shallow, dominative, temporary, or manipulative relationships can seem to be the norm for human relations. For a community to love without possessiveness and exclusiveness is a prophetic witness in our times.

A life of obedience lived in a community of equal disciples of Jesus can likewise be a powerful witness. A community where authority is exercised as service rather than as power, where one makes no significant decisions without incorporating a community into those decisions, has an eloquent word to say in a world of hierarchical and dominative power. The graceful, joyful, and chosen transition of authority such as occurs within religious congregations today is not a typical phenomenon in society. Communal discernment, a sincere and shared search for God's will in the circumstances of one's life, provide religious with an ongoing context of empowerment.

To present the vowed lifestyle as a space of empowerment is not to say that all those who make religious profession are so empowered. The mystery of grace and sin, of human failing and freedom, is as operative within this space as within any other. In religious congregations there are those whose lives are shriveled and closed, as there are elsewhere. But an authentic life of trying always to be more like Jesus, poor, chaste, and obedient in his humanity, hones the heart to freedom, a prerequisite for discerning and responding to the presence and action of the empowering Spirit.

ALTERNATIVE COMMUNITIES OF EMPOWERMENT

This view of the vows as means to enter fully into the human condition by a receptive authoring of one's life in freedom stands both in contrast to and in continuity with another view that sees religious life as a way to create an alternative community where one is able to transcend the human condition. In this eschatological understanding of religious life, the vows are understood primarily as empowering one to live "untouched" by this world, already sharing in the world to come. In this view, religious who now eat at a common table and are nourished by a common bread and a common word witness already in this life to the messianic banquet where all God's people will sit at the one table.

The long monastic tradition of religious life can be seen as a history of empowerment in this regard. This tradition did in fact create what were meant to be alternative communities reflective of the life to come. The tradition traces its roots to the ascetics of the early Christian centuries. Among the basic traits of their asceticism as described by Origen is "constant meditation on the other world, aiming at a mystical vision of God; renunciation of the world by abstaining from sexual intercourse and from the exercise of a worldly calling and possession of goods."[8] The creation of a visibly eschatological space was indeed a fundamental impulse of monastic life and "the external characteristic of the monk was...withdrawal from human society."[9]

The alternative community of monks and nuns was a society parallel to that prevailing "in the world." It was founded on values different from those current in civil society. Individuals could withdraw into these spaces and, as monasteries became self-sufficient economic units producing their own food, clothing, and books, the group as a whole was also able to "withdraw" from dependence on external society for the provision of goods.

The ideal of virginity especially was seen as creating an alternative space of freedom. Peter Brown claims that marriage and sexual intercourse in early societies were ways in which a person, especially a woman, was "conscripted as a fully productive member by her society."[10] By the fourth century, "the body, indeed had become a tangible *locus* on which the freedom of the will could be exercised, in choices that intimately affected the conventional fabric of society."[11] In monastic religious life, the virgin withheld his or her body from society, thus witnessing again to a different vision of human solidarity and community.

> To have withdrawn the body as a whole from society was to make a particularly concrete and intimate statement about the nature of one form of human solidarity — the common bonds of society, expressed at their lowest common denominator in terms of sexual needs, of sexual joining, and of the natural forms of union that sprang from such joining: family, offspring, kin. It was to assert, instead, the right of the individual to seek for himself or herself different forms of solidarity, more consonant with the high destiny of free persons, able to enter into a freely chosen harmony of wills, which, so Christians of late antiquity believed, was the particular joy of the undivided life of the "angels in heaven."[12]

Chastity as the "angelic virtue," then, was far from a denial of human bodiliness; it was rather a call to enter into community, to create a solidarity like that the angels were understood to enjoy.

The tradition of obedience to a common father or mother was likewise intended to express here on earth the order of the age to come. In a world where all realities were ordered hierarchically — angels, human beings, nature — the ordering of the monastic community was seen as reflecting the heavenly order itself.

The history of monasticism certainly has its darker moments when abbeys were populated by those who were unwillingly put there. The various monastic reforms throughout the centuries witness not only to the constant conversion intrinsic to all Christian life, but they also point up the distance from the ideal that in fact existed within certain monastic groups. Be that as it may, the monastery did in fact provide a physical space and a real community support for those who chose religious life as a way of union with God. The reality of the vows was lived by many who did in fact become models of freedom in the Spirit and authentic holiness.

APOSTOLIC EMPOWERMENT OF WOMEN

Post-Reformation Europe saw the first attempts to incarnate an apostolic vision in a complex world with needs unknown to previous generations. Europe was at the heart of the discovery of new lands and was being enriched culturally and economically by those discoveries. The church was not removed from the worlds discovered by the great explorers. Though in the message of the missioners Christianity was inextricably linked with European culture, the missionary achievements of the sixteenth and seventeenth centuries are truly awe-inspiring. In Europe itself, the population had expanded and moved to the cities, where disease and ignorance were common. It was most often in these cities that the Spirit called certain men and women to meet these new needs.

The earliest attempts to found religious communities of women devoted to apostolic work were fraught with difficulty. One might compare their origins with those marvelous unfinished statues of Michelangelo where the human figure is seen struggling to be released from marble. Indeed the society in which the apostolic insight struggled to take shape had many traits of marble. Following the Fourth Lateran Council in 1215, any new religious group had to adopt an already approved rule. While approved rules were not named, those of Augustine, Basil, and Benedict had long been recognized, and the Franciscan rule had been verbally approved several years earlier. The monastic and mendicant ways of life were the norm for new religious groups. As of the sixteenth century, however, certain founders and foundresses saw these rules as unsuited to their apostolic desires.

Women in particular faced serious difficulties. The social context was hardly favorable to the type of work outside a convent or monastery that the founding persons envisioned. The social customs and mores governing a woman's conduct at the time were restrictive and limiting, confining her sphere of action to the home. Women rarely participated in public life, were not to be seen alone on the streets, and were educated in quite specific fields.

Church legislation reflected and codified the social understanding of women. In 1566, Pius V's *Circa Pastoralis* decreed enclosure for all those solemnly professing chastity, poverty, and obedience. Cloister was considered an integral part of women's religious life, and only those with solemn vows and cloister were considered "religious."

Nevertheless, some Christians had a deep intuition regarding a life of the vows as empowering one for service. The history of some women's congregations gives evidence that certain groups were dedicated to a work or works before they formally adopted a vowed life of chastity, poverty, and obedience. Gathered together for *mission*, they formed themselves into "apostolic associations" or "pious unions" for the service of others. Some sensed, though, that a public commitment to those gospel realities would empower them in a special way for the service of the disadvantaged and the vulnerable. From the sixteenth through the nineteenth centuries, however, they knew too that public profession of the three vows would bring with it the inevitable cloister, often at odds with the apostolic project. Some of the more creative found various ways of avoiding the dilemma: formal promises rather than vows,[13] the profession of annual rather than perpetual vows,[14] establishment as local diocesan groups rather than as pontifical congregations.[15] While other motivations and historical factors may also be at the source of these creative solutions, a conviction of the vows as empowering for service and an understanding of the need for the free movement of the religious seem to be factors as well. Once again the vows were seen as creating empowering *inner* space where one's energies for mission were intensified and renewed.

To be sure, ecclesiastical legislation, especially that of enclosure, continued to hamper freedom of movement; indeed, one might legitimately write history from the point of view of restrictions imposed on religious, restrictions that were far from empowering. Such regulations consistently reflected the societal understanding of woman as needing both restraint and protection. But in spite of imposed restrictions, the apostolic congregations provided a context where women in particular could develop talents of scholarship, of organization, of leadership, of spiritual direction. Even where there was a degree of enclosure, schools and hospitals allowed sisters to meet the human needs of the ignorant and the sick, to serve their needy sisters and brothers without ever leaving the confines of the institution that in some sense was the extension of a monastery. And within those institutions, they became competent professionals — administrators, teachers, scientists, scholars, artists, leaders — in areas where society might not have welcomed their presence.

Apostolic religious congregations, especially those in the United States that had their own colleges and universities, formed women (and their own members) in fields from which they were traditionally excluded. They challenged the notion that a woman's education should be limited to the acquisition of certain "accomplishments" commonly understood to be suited to her sex. The education imparted by the members of these congregations stood in sharp contrast to the notion that a woman should acquire only "the knowledge essential to her sex, her condition, those things which are indispensable to fulfill in a holy way her duties as wife and mother and to keep order, cleanliness and economy in the house."[16]

The history of women religious in the United States has not yet been written. At present, the stories of the creative and courageous women who so greatly and generously contributed to the establishment of the faith on this continent is located primarily in the archives of individual congregations. A recent project, however, the History of Women Religious, is a hopeful sign that the many pieces of the mosaic may soon come together.[17] That mosaic will reveal that the vision of those pioneer sisters went far beyond the social and cultural barriers of their times. Those women found themselves in uncharted territory, sometimes confronting priests and bishops, working among the most neglected of society, travelling from continent to continent, creating solid works amid extraordinary material and moral difficulties. Their inner freedom to adapt to local circumstances, their clear intuition of the right thing to do in totally unforeseen circumstances, their single-minded devotion to the people they were called to serve — these were certainly "fruits of the Spirit" active in their own lives and congregations.

No reflection on religious congregations in the United States as places of empowerment would be complete without reference to the Sister Formation Movement. The movement had its beginnings in a providential confluence of factors. On December 8, 1950, Pope Pius XII convoked an International Congress of Religious, urging religious throughout the world to tap into the original inspiration of their congregations in order to meet the needs of the contemporary world. This assembly was followed a year later by the first International Congress of Teaching Sisters, also held in Rome. These two events were to be followed up at the national level. In 1953, Pius XII addressed the Major Superiors of Religious Congregations of Women specifically on the topic of formation.

In the United States, the soil was fertile for the reception of this message. At the turn of the twentieth century, the Catholic educational system was experiencing an extraordinary renaissance. In a generation, enrollment in Catholic elementary schools had more than doubled and had quadrupled in Catholic secondary schools. Catholic colleges and universities had increased their enrollment by more than 600 percent. Since women religious were the mainstay of this educational system, the call to a solid intellectual formation, to competency and professionalism ("equality with their colleagues"), had particular resonance among religious in the United States.

Most importantly, in this country the call to renewal was hailed by a prophetic group of women whose vision, creativity, networking, and persistence initiated an activity that would have far-reaching effects on the American church. That group founded the Sister Formation Conference, which established colleges for sisters, proposed a rigorous curriculum for their education, worked closely with universities and educational associations, and urged major superiors to spare nothing in the education of their sisters. As a result, institutions of higher learning across the country experienced an influx of sister students, most often during summer sessions.

From its inception, the initiators of the Sister Formation Movement saw it not only as an educational movement but as a response to new needs in a new age. The curriculum they advocated included a strong basis in the social sciences. What the Sister Formation Movement did was empower a whole generation of women religious for intelligent, competent service in the American church, a service springing from a renewed theological vision and spiritual depth.

CONCLUSION

Any truly Christian community is a "space of empowerment." As places where relationships are built on the love of God in human hearts, they are Spirit-inspired and empowered. History gives evidence of innumerable such groups; the phenomenon of religious life in the church provides a constant tradition of such communities.

Christians called to this life allow their hearts to be formed to the radical poverty of the human condition, a poverty that is the source of both dignity and freedom. Vows of chastity, poverty, and obedience are primary means of this formation to freedom. The support of a stable community of "God-seekers" likewise provides a locus where one is enabled to build permanent discernment into one's life.

Thousands of women have found apostolic religious congregations to be places of empowerment. Not only has religious consecration afforded its own source of power, but the call to respond to the needs of the church has likewise been a source of empowerment for them. The pioneer situation of many congregations in nineteenth-century America was an invitation to act in freedom and fidelity to meet those needs; the renewal of apostolic religious life in the twentieth century and the particular needs of American society today continue to be a challenge to act in fidelity and freedom.

5

POPE JOHN PAUL II'S VISION OF COLLABORATION AND EMPOWERMENT

Leonard Doohan

JOHN PAUL'S OWN LIFE AND EXAMPLE

On the day of his election as pope, John Paul II told the crowd gathered in the piazza of St. Peter's that with God's help and theirs he was ready to set out on a fresh stage of the history of the church. A creative dedication to further the history of the church in cooperation with others was a consistent feature of Karol Wojtyla's life. While his early childhood was filled with painful experiences, he soon learned to work well with others in planning religious and artistic events, in co-editing a student newspaper, in helping others with their studies, and in cooperating in students' self-governing organizations — eventually being chosen a vice-chairman. He emerged as a fine leader during the German occupation of Poland (1939–45), collaborating with fourteen others in the "living rosary" group and taking part in the underground university.

As a priest, Wojtyla evidenced both a vision of an intervocational church — stressing the vocation of lay life — and a willingness not only to work with others, but to study and socialize together too. His friends and associates refer to his ability to meet other people on equal terms. In fact, people who knew him then refer to an ease he had in gathering people and making friends, claiming this resulted from his openness, dialogic spirit, and involvement with others as friends or associates. After theological studies, he did postdoctoral work in ethics and became head of the Department of Ethics at Lublin Catholic University, where he was always a very popular teacher. Later, as bishop, he avoided distancing himself from his people and celebrated sacraments for them, sharing in their joys and pains. When appointed archbishop of Cracow on March 8, 1964, he said, "What I see most clearly is that my office of pastor is something we must build together. To be a pastor, it seems to me, one must know how to take what one's flock have to offer.... One must coordinate and integrate everyone's gifts into a single common good."[1]

As archbishop of Cracow he established creative and collaborative organizations for theological discussion, spiritual renewal, education, and family development. Close associates, including his own diocesan chancellors, spoke positively of his administration, emphasizing that he was a very good listener. The archbishop delegated a lot of responsibility, not because he could not cope with large amounts of work, but simply because he wanted others to do the work as part of their co-responsibility. He evidenced considerable skill in delegating to others, including laity, for whom he showed great trust.

Archbishop Wojtyla was made a cardinal on June 26, 1967, and although he did not exercise a leadership role in the Second Vatican Council, he was very supportive of Pope John's initiative, spoke enthusiastically of the council's broad representation, and told the seminarians of the Polish College in Rome that the council was a reinterpretation of the gospel. He spoke positively of administrative decentralization, including "a new relationship between the centre and the periphery" and "an upgrading of the role of laity in the Church" — including "a new conception of the people of God" that encourages laity "to be more mature, free and responsible."[2] When he returned to Cracow, he published *Foundations of Renewal: Studies concerning the Realization of Vatican II*, a collection of conciliar texts for study groups. Moreover, in 1972 he convoked an archdiocesan synod to initiate a diocesan-wide commitment to the community implementation of Vatican II.

Always a person of study, of responsibility, and of intense involvement with others, Karol Wojtyla was elected pope on October 16, 1978. His first address to the cardinals focused on the *Dogmatic Constitution on the Church* as the council's Magna Carta, and he drew out from its vision his first public commitment to collegiality, a position clearly in line with his previous ministry. The same theme emerged in Pope John Paul II's first spontaneous reaction to the enthusiasm of a general audience: "One Pope is not enough to embrace everybody...but luckily Christ had twelve apostles — we shall act in the same spirit of collegiality."[3] Thus, Pope John Paul II brought to Rome his vision of a postconciliar church dedicated to renewal through collaboration, and he proclaimed his commitment to this vision in his first encyclical, *Redemptor Hominis* (no. 5).

Pope John Paul II now seems very much at home in the papacy, and yet also seems personally hampered by his new life. Always a person of study, responsibility, and involvement, he no longer has the involvement he had in Poland, a shared involvement that previously energized him. He has had to sacrifice much that he valued in order to fulfill his present universal ministry. Some observers suggest he has drawn back from attitudes he demonstrated in his youth, as priest, and as bishop, and it now looks as if the papacy has stunted his previous collaborative approach.

Throughout his life he has been the embodiment of collaboration, but a climate of collaboration stimulates him to collaboration, and possibly he no longer finds it. He is a "listening person," but with all his responsibilities, when does he integrate what he has listened to? This question becomes greater with the passing of time in his papacy.

A wonderful leader in the many changing circumstances of his life, John Paul II now portrays himself as a leader who at times is inconsistent with attitudes shown in previous periods of his life. Perhaps he anticipated difficulties ahead when he confided to a friend, "For me the Curia's bureaucracy will be an insurmountable obstacle to directing the Church into progressive activity."[4] Some suggest communion, cooperation, co-responsibility, and mutual empowerment were so much a part of him that he really doesn't want to do what he's doing and needs to be helped to appreciate this. Pope John Paul II clearly has the potential of being a great collaborative leader. However, if the circumstances are personally oppressive for the pope and have possibly stunted his collaborative involvement, they have not dampened his vision, which we still consistently find in his writings — a prophetic service, calling the universal church to communion, mutual appreciation, co-responsibility, and shared mission.

A VISION OF A COLLABORATIVE CHURCH

In Pope John Paul II's first address to the world as bishop of Rome, he commented on the essential components of laity's "fidelity," stating it implied two dimensions, obedience to their pastors and collaboration in attaining one's mission.[5] Two days later, when addressing a group of lay faithful, the pope told them he was "thrilled to have your partnership in the gospel of Christ."[6] The pope sees the faithful's collaborative endeavors internal to the church's community life,[7] in its work of human cultural advancement,[8] in education and family development,[9] in the university environment,[10] among those who work for political stability and the causes of peace,[11] or who build up society[12] and create culture as an expression of humanity.[13]

When addressing members of Catholic Action, John Paul II confirms that they "are animated by the resolution to collaborate with ever-increasing responsibility in the hierarchical apostolate, in the task of evangelization that belongs to the whole Church."[14] While insisting that the task of evangelization belongs to the whole church, the pope is very convinced that the organization of the internal life of the church is entrusted to the clergy. Nevertheless, to the latter the pope says, "I... enthusiastically approve your concern to raise up collaborators, to form them to their responsibilities." But he adds, "It is necessary... to really know how to collaborate, without monopolizing all the tasks, all the initiatives, or all the decisions, when it concerns what is in the area of their competence and their responsibility."[15]

Speaking optimistically of the lay faithful's increasing desire "to take an active and responsible part in the apostolate, to help bishops and priests," the pope, considering this development a "consoling reality," affirms the lay faithful's willingness to collaborate with clergy and religious, but adds that it is necessary to "train priests to become conscious of it in their turn so that this enthusiasm, which is a real gift of the Holy Spirit for these times of ours, will not be suffocated and extinguished, or worse, deviated and led astray in mistaken and disappointing experiments."[16] Furthermore, John Paul II urges the lay faithful, individually and in organic lay groups, "to become aware of your complementarity" and thus to engage in "real collaboration" and "to establish links between the movements."[17] The pope is convinced that when groups of lay faithful live in union with the hierarchy they become signs of hope for the church and imitate the fidelity of the early Christian communities (Acts 2:42).

Lay faithful, "effective collaborators in the mission of establishing, developing, and fostering the life of the Christian community,"[18] also collaborate in the internal community ministries of the church, for example in the catechetical ministry. Some do this in their own families, and thus they "give evidence of the universal sharing by the whole people of God in the prophetic office of Christ himself."[19] Others are called to exercise a ministry of catechists and enjoy "a special sharing in the responsibility for the advancement of the gospel."[20] Elsewhere, the pope urges these dedicated lay ministers "to win over other collaborators," since "we all believe that one and the same Spirit, who guides the communities and the hearts of all people, has summoned your service in the Church into life."[21]

When dealing with the laity's ministry to transform the world, John Paul understands collaboration in the broadest terms. "Christians have the duty of collaborating with everyone for the building of a more human world."[22] This implies a unified effort to facilitate useful interventions of public authorities.[23] Pope John Paul II's teachings present a very positive appreciation of lay faithful.[24]

The pope sees that each person has a vocation and responsibility due to God's invitation and mandate. Lay faithful find their vocation in the major moments of each day, where the trends of modern life, frequently negative, become challenges to laity to minister with God's love and understanding. "You must create within you and around you wide spaces of humanity, spaces to accept and bring to maturity a wisdom about humanity."[25] In this mission the lay faithful have their own authority, but need to maintain a sense of love for the church and a dedication to strengthen their Christian and Catholic identity. This identity includes seeking spiritual nourishment from their pastors, obedience to the teachings of Vatican II, and respect for the nature of authentic freedom. It also means "being aware that our whole Christian being comes to us through the Church — faith, divine life, sacraments, life of prayer; that the centuries-old experience of the Church nourishes us and helps us to walk along ways that are partly new; that the magisterium is given to the Church to guarantee her authenticity, her unity, and her consistent and safe operation."[26] Above all, any ministry in the church involves communion. "The Church is essentially a mystery of communion: I would say that it is a call to communion, to life in communion." This requires that all Christians, whatever their vocation, try "to create unity in thoughts, in sentiments, in initiative"[27] to maintain the communion of the universal church. For the lay faithful the parish remains the fundamental place where they live out their community vocation in solidarity with other believers.[28]

The pope insists that each one is called by Jesus, endowed with a very personal vocation that includes evangelization, living as a good citizen, revealing to others the true meaning of life, welfare, and charitable actions, working for human rights, offering the world a new perspective on the dignity and humanness of work,[29] and building up family life.[30]

For John Paul, all the faithful participate in the church's mission to evangelize the world. Their authority to do this comes from the power of Christian unity presided over by the pastor. The authority of the ministerial priesthood is one of order, communion, faith development, and sacramental nourishment. The clergy must not impose themselves outside the specifics of their sacramental and nourishing roles but need to encourage laity in their own roles. In fact, clergy training needs to focus on real abilities to collaborate, empower, and foster awareness in laity of their own baptismal rights and obligations. This lay ministry of working to transform the world needs no permission, mandate, or authorization.

Some laity, partly in generous response to clergy shortage and resulting real needs, and partly in response to a new presence of the Holy Spirit's grace, engage in ministries that are more directly related to the offices of the hierarchy. Even here the first point to stress is that we are dealing with a mission of the church, and therefore all baptized have a natural association with it, even though it is a function reserved to the hierarchy. When laity participate in areas that relate to the functions of the hierarchy, the pope still rejoices and expresses his gratitude, but here he sees the need for empowering, for permission, and for control. Nevertheless, he shows no signs of insisting on greater control of laity by clergy, priests by bishops, or for that matter bishops by the Vatican. His vision is not a church divided into clerics and nonclerics, but a hierarchical church in which unity is preserved by respect and obedience, reciprocated by nourishment in faith, and guaranteed security in religion.

COMPONENTS OF POPE JOHN PAUL'S
THEOLOGY OF COLLABORATION

Recognition of the Dignity of Lay Life

Pope John Paul II sees lay life as a special vocation, solidly rooted in baptism and making the faithful salt of the earth and light of the world. It is a sign of hope that we all constitute one body in Christ and offer hope to the world, since we all share the same Spirit. "All Christians share in the only mission of the Church," and world transformation belongs to all vocations.[31] Baptism "is the root of the absolutely original and gratuitous new life which the Christian is called to develop and to give witness to." Through this sublime reality, "the Christian participates in the triple office of Christ: his priestly, prophetic and royal office,"[32] and this becomes the secret of maturing in Christ.

The lay faithful are active and responsible members of the church, who by their obedience to the Holy Spirit participate in the manifold renewal of the church.[33] In postconciliar years we have seen a rich and effective commitment by laity to participate in the church's vitality, aware more than ever regarding what it means to be church. The laity's dignity is directly related to their characteristic makeup as faithful dedicated to the local church and finding their life in the parish. Maturely accepting their responsibilities, laity give fruitful witness of their faith.

Insistence on the Proper Rights of Laity

The pope urges laity "to accept responsibility and prepare themselves for it by an adequate formation."[34] John Paul II speaks of all members of the church sharing experiences, concerns, initiatives, and hopes, "in the freedom and creativity of shared membership."[35]

Laity are an integral part of the people of God. In the church "there is no inequality," for all members "share a common dignity from their rebirth in Christ."[36] In fact, it is part of lay life "to help build up the church of tomorrow" through their renewal efforts and strivings for unity.[37] Lay faithful also have the right to be apostles in the church, individually and in organized groups. This is a "noble prerogative," "fundamentally a right and proper response, on the personal and community levels, to the Christian vocation."[38]

The Importance of the Lay Condition

Pope John Paul II stresses the secular condition of lay life. He challenges laity to have "a concrete and balanced knowledge of modern society," to develop "an attitude of involvement in current problems...of society," to be "sensitive and farsighted, seeking to understand particular situations,"[39] and to "live intensely, fully, and with total dedication...every situation in life, to give witness to Jesus Christ in your conditions as lay people, in your work place, in your profession, in your families."[40]

This secular calling does not exclude laity from roles of responsibility internal to the church community, including participation in church ministries, but it remains the defining characteristic of all lay response. Thus, he reaffirms, "It is within the everyday world that you the laity must bear witness to God's kingdom.... It is for you as lay people to direct all temporal affairs to the praise of the Creator and Redeemer."[41]

Christian lay faithful must first of all challenge the social dimensions of contemporary sin. Moreover, this "witness to the faith in truth and charity in all settings" is a moral and cultural contribution to society that produces "an ever deeper and more personalized Christian culture."[42]

Respect for the Interdependence and Mutuality of all Vocations

John Paul II sees the interdependence of the varied vocations as part of God's plan. Forming together the mystery of the people of God, the faithful have diverse tasks but should always manifest an essential equality in origin, grace, vocation, dignity, activity, and mission.[43] In the common mission entrusted to the church, "The role of the laity...has its own proper and irreplaceable originality, not reducible to that of the ordained ministry.... In carrying out this great mission of salvation, the clergy and the lay faithful assist and complement one another."[44] In this "reciprocal complementarity," pastors have the responsibility to recognize and promote the dignity and responsibility of laity, to help them fulfill those duties specific to lay life, and to discover and joyfully celebrate their charisms.[45] The best way to actualize this interdependence and mutuality is to have "a constant attitude of mutual availability and service."[46] This collaboration between clergy and laity is enriched also by the communion and ecclesial co-responsibility of religious communities. Religious life has its own fruitfulness to contribute to ecclesial communion.[47]

The vocational variety in ecclesial unity manifests the richness of the church and actualizes an ecclesiology of communion. "All the members of the Church, priests, religious and laity, assembled around their bishops, have thus been called to participate in the multiform richness of ministries and charisms in the unity of mission."[48]

Vision of Church as Communion

The pope points out that the goal of unity and communion is not only a vision, it is "a responsibility to be realized in its profundity and to be witnessed to in a visible and credible manner."[49] This implies educating oneself in the values of communion, combatting individualism, searching for solidarity, and identifying the specific services to which each member of the church has been called. All "must pay attention to their own role, to the service of which they have been called by their vocation. In this, they will have an appreciation and acceptance of the vocation of others, they will become receptive to mutual assistance and if necessary, to...correction in view of the one mission of the entire ecclesial community."[50]

This vision of universal ecclesial communion is lived out in the concrete conditions and structures of the local church. The Holy Father has frequently focused on the family as the basic foundational cell of church communion. Thus he proclaims, "The Christian family constitutes a specific revelation and realization of ecclesial communion," insisting that this is also a fundamental opportunity for building communion, "all members of the family, each according to his or her own gift, have the grace and responsibility of building day by day the communion of persons."[51]

Ecclesial Ministries Specific to Laity

Most of the duties of lay life arise from Christian initiation and commitment to the communion of the church. Laity, responsible for their own self-development and integral human growth, permeate this with the response to the vocation to holiness. For most, the family is the spiritual place, filled with love and joy, in which one's call to holiness is realized. Renewal, which is each one's personal responsibility, is a "continuous growing in the spirit," "reaffirming the value of the principles and of the criteria of the gospel" and emphasizing "the primacy of the grace of the Holy Spirit."[52] Lay faithful nourish this renewal with prayer in personal, family, and community forms. Such personal and mutual prayer builds up the family and parish communities, leads to ecumenical unity, and is a major apostolate of every baptized person.[53] Genuine renewal and conversion leads to a "growing and concrete solidarity with the disinherited," as Christian laity work to establish "the civilization of love."[54] With Christian courage and maturity the faithful dedicated to ecclesial communion acknowledge their lives will also include a solidarity in suffering, since "suffering, more than anything else, makes present in the history of humanity the powers of the redemption."[55]

Laity live out their vocation in the concrete conditions of their own lives. The family, a church in miniature, focuses the layperson's mission by stressing conjugal and family responsibilities and their resulting educational tasks. Called to reveal to the world "the new communion of love," laity build up and strengthen the church at this foundational level.[56]

A dimension of Christian foundational evangelization is the way laity work. Proclaiming a gospel of work implies reacting to sinful situations that may be met at work, working well, being good co-workers, broadening the horizon of solidarity, promoting creative forms of service, and contributing to modern progress.[57] Each one's professional vocation is an opportunity to shape society and to contribute to a better world.

As builders of society, laity are at the cutting edge of the integration of faith and culture, of the redirection of economic development to goals of justice and human dignity. This prophetic mission "is a tireless contribution to the building of... a civilization of solidarity,... a civilization of human love."[58] However, this common enterprise calls for the implementing of Christian moral and spiritual values into the basic fabric of daily life, struggling for justice and the legitimate interests of all, and proclaiming the demands of universal solidarity and the structural consequences it implies.[59]

Lay involvement in constructing world solidarity is rooted in baptismal responsibility. This is the vocation to strive for peace through reconciliation and international solidarity,[60] promoting a mentality of peace at every level of life. All people must resolutely commit themselves to establish a culture of peace,[61] abandoning domination and turning in service toward the spirit of Christianity.

These values are essential ecclesial ministries of laity and make up the major moments of their lives and vocations.

Ecclesiastical Mission and Responsibility
Baptism, confirmation, and Eucharist bind together church persons of different vocations. John Paul II emphasizes the duties and responsibilities of the pastors of the church to view their ministry from the perspective of service to the people of God. The Holy Spirit entrusts the local church to the bishop, and John Paul II, as a brother bishop, frequently addresses the nature of the ecclesiastical mission and responsibilities of the hierarchy. Succinctly he reminds the bishops, "Among the priorities of your mission as pastors is, without doubt, the Christian formation of the laity." If every effort is

made to improve pastoral care, the laity will become "a formidable force for...evangelization and humanization" of contemporary society.[62]

The hierarchy forms laity and challenges them to a greater awareness of their baptismal responsibilities. Pastors call the lay faithful to deeper holiness in the secular circumstances of their lives. The pope urges pastoral leaders to "vigorously involve the laity in the decisive dialogue of the Gospel with cultures."[63] This will mean conscience formation, new initiatives, deeper consultation, and the lived experience of ecclesial communion. Pastors not only call, challenge, and contribute to formation, but nourish and educate through the sacramental spirituality of the church.

John Paul considers that pastors' tasks include being stewards of the faithful, governing the people, and discerning authentic expressions of contemporary church life. In addition to pastoral rights and duties to oversee, the pope says bishops must know also when and what needs to be "loosed" to facilitate the growth of laity.

Thus, Pope John Paul II does not see collaboration merely as a way of being more efficient but rather as a way of more authentically being the communion of the church. He acknowledges the dignity and proper rights of laity, focusing especially on those roles that are exclusive to laity because of their distinctive condition. He highlights mutual interdependence as part of the vision of the church as communion. Some areas of lay responsibility arise from the sacraments of initiation while others require ecclesiastical missioning for good order.

JOHN PAUL'S UNDERSTANDING
OF MUTUAL EMPOWERMENT

Relationship between Laity and Hierarchy

All members of the church must remain in ecclesial union. "Charismatic gifts and hierarchical gifts are distinct but also mutually complementary."[64] Laity, as individuals or in groups, and hierarchical ministries "are coessential and share in fostering life, renewal and sanctification."[65]

Pastors nourish laity with the Word of God, confirm them in Christ's teaching, and respect their freedom in areas of ministry to the world.[66] The freedom to which laity have a right is a freedom with duties, since Christian freedom is not a "freedom from" but a "freedom for." It implies a dedication to the church's mission, and the pope, seeing this as authentically discerned by the hierarchy, complements freedom with obedience.[67] Laity who love the church maintain a Catholic identity, receive intact the deposit of faith, are nourished by the Word of God, and discover "that their own charisms are fully operative and fruitful."[68]

John Paul sees laity's specific mission to be their transformation of the world, a ministry that arises directly from baptism and makes each Christian a chosen partner with Christ in the evangelization of the world. This particular ecclesial role starts in the family and then includes social, professional, national, and international commitments. While there are no ready-made solutions to many of the complex problems affecting contemporary society, laity can receive from the hierarchy insights into their vocation to speak the truth in love, and renewed enthusiasm for a shared Christian vision of life.[69]

Lay movements and groups can contribute significantly to this evangelizing effectiveness, and it ought to be a concern of both laity and pastors to restore vitality to these apostolic groups.

All the baptized are called upon to be active in the church's life and mission, and pastors have an office to serve the common priesthood and facilitate the faithful's deeper participation in the church's communion and mission.

Collaboration and Empowerment
At the opening of the Synod on the Laity, Pope John Paul II declared that the interests of the lay faithful were his interests too, adding that he held a profound esteem for the laity and their gifts. The foundation of collaboration is the mutual sharing in the office and mission of Jesus, based on the relationship between the common priesthood and the hierarchical priesthood. From the first years of a child's life laity and clergy cooperate together in training for Christian life and service, in conscience formation, and in a sense of solidarity with the faith's transformation of the world. In the context of an ecclesiology of communion, the laity's contributions to the life and works of the church are necessary: "If the laity were not associated with it, their ecclesial identity would be obscured."[70] The pope, encouraged by the laity's increased awareness of "the prerogatives of the Christian vocation," urges discussion and collaboration in the local churches to help attain mature pastoral planning.

Well aware that collaborative approaches and mutual support are part of laity's daily family and professional situations, the pope praises the solidarity of workers, acknowledging that these experiences can be formative for the church. Collaboration and mutual empowerment within ecclesial communion are not only theologically, socially, and ministerially effective, they form the basis for peace in any community, civil or ecclesiastical. All must work for unity, building it solidly on recognition of equality, dialogue, common responsibility, solidarity, respect for the rights of others, and esteem for complementarity in a shared ecclesial mission.

The hierarchy empowers the laity by reminding them of their vocation, inspiring them through the Word, nourishing them with the sacraments, challenging them to persevere in the faith, and strengthening them in the unity of the ecclesial community.

Laity empower the clergy through their faithful response to their challenging proclamation, collaborative sharing in the local community, obedience to the common teachings of the faith, and participation in liturgical life. They also empower the hierarchy by extending the influence of their proclamation into all aspects of daily life, substituting for the clergy where they cannot go, offering their unique gifts to the local community, and contributing their proper ministries to the common mission of the whole church.

Sacramental Life as the Source of the Call to Ministry
The empowering of all Christians is to be found in the grace received in the sacraments of initiation, ever reenergized by the creative and prophetic Spirit of God. The faithful of all vocations need to recognize each other's dignity and welcome each other's gifts.

The lay apostolate is a response to the gift of baptism, where all discover that they are endowed with the common priesthood, Christ's threefold mission, a Catholic identity, and a sense of common mission. Baptism is the source of the faithful's life and hope; it is a new birth that incorporates us into the church, a confirmation of the common mission we share, and a sacramental bond of our unity. However, this initiation is only a beginning, for "we the baptized have work to do together as brothers and sisters in Christ."[71] Responding to the baptismal call to serve, laity find that the Eucharist becomes "a source of the Christian spirit" and "a challenge to our daily lives."[72] In fact, this sacramental life maintains intimacy with the Lord, which alone assures the efficacy of ecclesial ministry. This life gives rise to "a vast and consoling flowering of initiatives and works," especially when laity are without a local priest, and the pope rejoices in this consoling experience of collaboration and urges others to encourage its development.[73]

The Hierarchy's Ordering of the Lay Faithful
Pope John Paul calls all members of the church to a deepened awareness of their solidarity in communion. Laity recognize the hierarchy's ministerial and ordering charisms and the religious's charisms of specific dedication and witness, while other vocations recognize the laity's manifold gifts from the same Holy Spirit. The pope sees the church's pastoral ministers as encouraging, confirming, authenticat-

ing, discerning, and ordering the ministries, roles, charisms, and group organizations of the lay faithful. Even this presiding role is presented in the context of global ecclesial, mutual responsibility, by which communion is maintained and fostered. Nowhere does Pope John Paul present the hierarchy as a source for empowering the lay faithful in their distinctive, baptismal mission, as if the hierarchy's permission were necessary for this. Rather, he presumes the laity know best what is needed in the world, take initiative in accomplishing this task, and have baptismal responsibility to do so.

When the pope turns to consider those laity who contribute to ministries internal to the church community, he sees this dedication as "the universal sharing by the whole people of God in the prophetic office of Christ himself."[74] This special sharing in the responsibility for the advancement of the gospel is first given the theological context of God's will and Christ's mission before the pope focuses on needed authorization to maintain good order. Even this latter is a hierarchical ordering of communion rather than the clerical hierarchy's ordering of the faithful. "The Church is essentially a mystery of communion . . . a call to communion, to life in communion. In vertical communion, let us say, and in horizontal communion: in communion with God himself, with Christ, and in communion with others."[75] Thus, ecclesial ordering is the maintenance of this communion: Trinitarian communion is a model for collegiality, collegiality of bishops is a model for priests and religious, and all these are models for lay communion. Ordering includes obedience, not for reasons of power or control but for the purpose of maintaining communion.

JOHN PAUL II'S APOSTOLIC EXHORTATION ON THE LAITY

The apostolic exhortation *Christifideles Laici* resulted from the 1987 Synod on the Laity, and while synods are only advisory to a pope, John Paul II insists that this document "is not something in contradistinction to the synod, but is meant to be a faithful and coherent expression of it, a fruit of collegiality" (no. 2, p. 564).[76]

Synthesizing the sense and directions of synod representatives is no easy task. Out of 142 bishops' conferences 62 never contributed anything to the Synod Secretariat in the nearly three years of preparation. For others, however, this synod on the laity became a very important experience of a participatory and collaborative church. Thus, resulting synod documents generally strike a middle course between the enthusiasm of some parts of the world and the disinterest of others. The only synod that has produced a prophetic document is the second one, on peace and justice, in 1971. This present apostolic exhortation is hardly a prophetic document, especially for the roles of laity in the U.S. church, but it is a very fine document in both its spirit and doctrinal content. It gives an excellent synthesis of the road travelled by laity in the church since the council, and also offers some clarifications and fine tuning on debated topics, although it offers little direction for the future.

The introduction is an exciting challenge to laity to share in the evangelization of the world, since God the Father personally calls them, "from whom they receive a mission on behalf of the church and the world." Christ summons them "to associate themselves with him in his saving mission," and the Holy Spirit "has inspired new aspirations toward holiness and the participation of so many lay faithful" (no. 2, p. 563). The pope hopes that the result of the synod will be "the lay faithful's harkening to the call of Christ the Lord to work in his vineyard, to take an active, conscientious and responsible part in the mission of the church in this great moment in history" (no. 3, p. 564). Through faith and the sacraments, laity are incorporated in the church and receive an active part in its common mission. This call is intensified by an awareness of the problems, unrest, and defeats experienced by our modern world. Secularism, religious indifference, atheism, the phenomenon of de-Christianization, together with all the forms of manipulation or violation of human dignity and world conflict, all challenge the ecclesial vision and ministerial commitment of lay faithful.

Part 1 of the exhortation deals with the dignity and identity of lay faithful, since "only within the context of this dignity can their vocation and mission in the church and in the world be defined" (no. 8, p. 565). This section is very positive and respectful of the lay faithful's belonging to the church through faith and baptism that regenerates, unites, and anoints us all (nos. 10–13), making all sharers in Jesus' priestly, prophetic, and kingly mission (no. 14). Pope John Paul summarizes the common dignity of all Christians: "Because of the one dignity flowing from baptism, each member of the lay faithful, together with ordained ministers and men and women religious, shares a responsibility for the church's mission" (no. 15, p. 567). There follows an excellent section on the lay faithful's way of realizing this mission and their specific function within this common mission. "But among the lay faithful this one baptismal dignity takes on a manner of life which sets a person apart, without however bringing about a separation from the ministerial priesthood or from men and women religious" (no. 15, p. 567). This specific secular character of lay life is theologically and ecclesiologically significant, insofar as it is the place of the lay faithful's personal call. Thus, as salt, light, and leaven, "The lay faithful's position in the church, then, comes to be fundamentally defined by their newness in Christian life and distinguished by their secular character" (no. 15, p. 568). This secular function determines their mission, way of holiness, and responsibility in the church.

The sense of equality, common mission, and mutuality that permeate part 1 continue in part 2, which speaks of the participation of the lay faithful in the life of the church as communion. Modeled on the Trinity, Christians experience union with Christ and with one another — a union that is the mystery of the church. This organic communion implies diversity and complementarity and is lived out through mutual appreciation of varied ministries, charisms, and roles.

The pope speaks of the relationship between the ministerial priesthood and the priesthood of all the faithful. He sees the former as "different, not simply in degree but in essence" (no. 22, p. 571), and as having responsibility "to form and to rule the latter," while being "ordered to the service of the entire people of God" (no. 22, p. 571). The pope is firm in making the distinction, but equally firm in stressing complementarity, mutuality, and interrelationship and the need for mutual acceptance and acknowledgement, since the church's mission "is realized not only by the ministers in virtue of the sacrament of orders, but also by the lay faithful; indeed, because of their baptismal state and their specific vocation, in the measure proper to each person the lay faithful participate in the priestly, prophetic and kingly mission of Christ" (no. 23, p. 571). John Paul then urges pastors to foster ministries, offices, and roles typical of lay life and founded in baptism, and when necessary should entrust to lay faithful, additional ministries connected with their own pastoral service, where allowed by canon law. In the latter case even when dealing with "the various ministries, offices and roles that the lay faithful can legitimately fulfill in the liturgy," the laity ought to exercise them "in conformity to their specific lay vocation" (no. 23, p. 572).

Our own times see a fruitful manifestation of charisms, distributed by the Holy Spirit for the benefit of the church. John Paul II insists that the authenticity of these charisms is to be discerned by the church's pastors (no. 24, p. 572).

Lay faithful who participate in various ways in the life of the church need a "precise vision of the particular church with its primordial bond to the universal church" (no. 25, p. 573). Thus aware of their "catholic spirit" and sense of belonging, lay faithful are called to share collaboratively in their diocesan and parish church, to contribute their unique gifts, and to work together with others in lay groups. Regarding the last mentioned form of lay responsibility the document insists that "the freedom for lay people in the church to form such groups is to be acknowledged. Such liberty is a true and proper right that is not derived from any kind of 'concession' by authority, but flows from the sacrament of baptism" (no. 29, p. 575).

This freedom, exercised in communion, is based upon personal call, a sense of responsibility for the faithful, authentic communion with pope and bishops, conformity to the church's primary evangelizing role, and a commitment to be a genuine ecclesial presence in society. After urging pastors to encouragingly foster lay groups, the section ends by affirming "communion leads to mission, and mission itself to communion" (no. 31, p. 576).

Part 3 deals with the co-responsibility of the lay faithful in the church's mission to build up its own communion and to proclaim the gospel to a world in need of reevangelization. Lay faithful can overcome the separation of the gospel from life, and individually and communally reevangelize their own ecclesial communities and the world. They can challenge them to respect human dignity and rights, fostering growth in the family, solidarity in charity, and dedication to justice through public service for the common good. They should place the needs of individuals at the center of socio-economic life and participate in the transmission of the culturally enriching values of humanity.

Part 4 speaks appreciatively of the rich variety of vocations among the lay faithful: "Every one of us possessing charisms and ministries, diverse yet complementary, works in the one and the same vineyard of the Lord" (no. 55, p. 588). Part 5 addresses the formation of lay faithful as a continual process to discover and live one's vocation and mission as a dimension of a totally integrated life. "Formation is not the privilege of a few, but a right and duty of all" (no. 63, p. 591).

The exhortation is a positive affirmation of the lay faithful's contribution to the communion of the church and its mission of outreach. Lay faithful gain their life, participatory rights, and specific ministerial functions through the sacraments of initiation, charisms from the Holy Spirit, and mutual intervocational challenge. While there is the usual Vatican emphasis on the need to control, it is somewhat toned down in this document, which is a remarkably positive affirmation of lay life.

CONCLUSION

The whole direction of the life of the present pope has been toward implementing a vision of a collaborative church. He has always held broad views of ministry, as we saw in his own priestly and episcopal life. Moreover, he came to his present universal ministry with similar vision and determination. However, he once confided, "I am afraid that the Curia and the administrative problems of this Vatican machine will take so much of my time that nothing will be left.... I am sure... [it was not the] intention of previous Popes... but rules prevailed. Certainly it is not God's doing!"[77] John Paul's fear was well founded, and his initial efforts to strengthen a collaborative vision of church soon yielded to a prevalence of dominant structures and rules. However, while the pope has been unable to change the structures around him, his teachings remain masterly proclamations of a call to communion and collaboration.

After the attempt on his life, the pope told those around him that he had rearranged his priorities. Now he focuses less on institutions and more on personal conversion. He exhorts all to a collaborative church life in communion, rarely giving any practical suggestions, but rather trusting that groups know their own needs. His focus is less on ministerial needs because of a lack of priestly vocations; rather he stresses personal holiness and evangelical transformation that lead to ecclesiological renewal in deeper communion. From this he is confident there will result the integral renewal of modern life.

In reviewing his many sermons and writings we have discovered seven common components of his theology of collaboration: (1) the importance of the recognition of the dignity of lay life; (2) his insistence on the proper rights of laity; (3) the importance of the lay condition as determinative of all aspects of lay life; (4) respect for the interdependence and mutuality of all vocations in the church; (5) a vision of the church as communion; (6) an emphasis on those ecclesial ministries that are specific to laity; and (7) the nature of ecclesiastical mission and responsibility of the hierarchy.

These common components also help explain the pope's vision of the mutual empowerment of the faithful within ecclesial communion. He frequently addresses the relationship of laity to the hierarchy, the need for collaboration between them, the importance of sacramental life as a source for the common call to ministry, and the emphasis on the hierarchy's ordering of the communion of the faithful.

Every vision must eventually be institutionalized if it is to maintain its prophetic influence. Neither the universal church nor the institutions over which Pope John Paul has immediate authority have implemented his vision of a collaborative church. Rather it remains our common calling, the focus of our communal conversion, and the object of the credibility of the church.

6

CHARISM, POWER, AND COMMUNITY

Bernard Cooke

That something revolutionary is occurring in the exercise and structuring of authority and power in the church is obvious. Indeed, for some time now there have been references to the "crisis of authority" in the church, particularly though not exclusively in the Roman Catholic Church. While this situation was reflected in some of the shifts in attitude that marked the proceedings of the Second Vatican Council, the council was not the source of the change that marks the present life of the church. Rather, the source lies in the complex social developments that came to a head in the years around World War II, years that made evident the decay of many of the authority/power structures of European or European-derived society.

There is nothing new, of course, about a power struggle taking place in the church. The past two millennia have witnessed a constant attempt by one or other group in the church to seize power that they had not previously possessed and an equally constant effort by those already in power to resist the efforts of the new claimants. Bishops have struggled with presbyters, deacons with presbyters, religious orders with bishops, bishops with popes, patriarchs among themselves, and even occasionally some groups of laity with church officials. Given this history, there is a general tendency today to interpret what is occurring in the church as another challenge to established authority, more specifically a claim of the episcopacy to greater independence vis-à-vis the papacy and a claim of the laity to greater initiative and autonomy in determining and carrying out the discipleship that derives from baptism.

It is true that such power shifts are taking place and rightly so, but that is not the heart of the crisis. What is occurring, to some extent at least as a result of recovering the deepest traditions of Christianity, is a revolutionary appraisal of the very notions of power and authority as they apply to the Christian community. While the social forces at work in the shifts that have marked the middle half of this century triggered this reappraisal, more recent influences, especially the emergence of feminist thought, have had a major impact on bringing the issue to a head. Drawing from the fundamental distinction between "reaction" and "revolution" that Hannah Arendt details in her book *On Revolution*, one might say that whereas in the past the same ball game was being played with the sides changing from time to time — the dialectic of master and slave described by Hegel and then Marx — what is now occurring is a whole new ball game. (Given the propensity in governmental and business circles to describe ruthless exercise of power as "playing hardball," the metaphor of a ball game to describe the changing context of power today seems quite appropriate!).

POWER IN THE EARLY CHURCH

Perhaps the most important catalyst in the present change of understanding of "power" as it applies to the church has been the modern study of Christian origins. New Testament scholarship in particular presents us with an approach to authority and power that is much different from the view that has been dominant for most of the past two thousand years. That latter view has spoken of the "jurisdiction" proper to those who occupy official positions in the church. The very term implies the application of a political model for thinking about the Christian community, with authority and power in the church considered, therefore, as realities that can be satisfactorily explained in terms of political scientific analysis and exercised legitimately as elements of *Realpolitik*. One need only examine the historical development of papal ecclesiology that followed the Council of Constance to discover the categories of modern theological reflection that reflect this political model.

Even the notion of *potestas ordinis*, which presumably referred to an exercise of power quite different from *potestas jurisdictionis*, was part of a worldview that saw society and the church stratified in a hierarchical pattern that distinguished those who possessed the power to save from those whom they were empowered to save. The faithful were to be saved by the ministrations of the ordained, i.e., those placed officially in one of the higher orders, since these ordained had been given the power to transmit the saving grace that made eternal life possible. As the idea became accepted that this *potestas ordinis* was exercised specially in sacramental rituals, the very character of liturgical activity changed basically: whereas in earlier centuries sacramental liturgies were something that Christian communities *did* as active professions of their faith, the sacraments now became something that ordained celebrants did *to* and *for* the relatively passive faithful. One spoke now about "administering the sacraments."

What made this modeling of the church so influential was the fact that it was not recognized as an *interpretation* of what had occurred in Jesus, and so the possibility of its being recognized as at least partially a *misinterpretation* did not exist. Instead, this hierarchical arrangement was considered to be the way that God had structured the universe and human society; it was by "divine institution" and obviously not to be tampered with by those tempted to change. While the detailed picture of a hierarchically arranged creation, both heavenly and ecclesiastical, which was provided by Pseudo-Dionysius, was not accepted in its entirety, its widespread, centuries-long influence testifies to the unquestioned acceptance of the patriarchal/hierarchical view that has reigned relatively unchallenged for centuries.

It is this worldview, this understanding of authority and power, that the New Testament literature challenges. The heart of the challenge lies in the transformed meaning given to "the kingdom of God" by Jesus and then by earliest Christianity. Enough careful research has been done to justify the position taken by Norman Perrin in his *Jesus and the Language of the Kingdom*, namely that Jesus used the term "the kingdom of God (heaven)" as a tensive symbol whose referent was the ruling activity in history of Israel's God. That divine activity had, of course, been interpreted for centuries prior to Jesus, interpreted for the most part in terms of the culturally-accepted notion of "ruling" that was associated with the kingships of the ancient Near East and particularly kingship going back to David in Israel's own history. In the religious expectations of Jews in Jesus' day that divine ruling was one day to work through a human figure, a Messiah, to achieve the restoration of Jews to the glory that supposedly had once been enjoyed under the rule of David himself.

Jesus saw himself called to initiate the definitive stage in the establishment of God's reign, but not in the political terms prevalent in popular hopes. Instead, his was a prophetic call and prophetic activity; in him power and authority worked in ways quite contrary to ordinary human exercise of power. This had already been stated in Isaiah 55: "My ways are not your ways, says the Lord; for just as the rain and the snow come down from heaven and do not return until they have watered the earth... so shall the word which comes from my mouth prevail." That power of God's Word, the Word that according to the priestly account of creation brought the universe into being, the Word that placed on the lips of the great prophets had power "to build or to destroy, to plant or to uproot," was what Jesus experienced working through him in his public ministry. This meant that he did not see himself as empowered with *official* power or authority — he had no official credentials. He was tempted to use the power of wealth and ruling position as a means of fulfilling his messianic role (the third temptation in the desert in Matthew's account); but he refused it.

When his disciples, having finally come to recognize him as Israel's Messiah, argued among themselves as to how they would share in the power of the kingdom, Jesus pointed out to them their radical misinterpretation of his messianic role: "The Lords of the Gentiles dominate their subjects [i.e., rule by ordinary political power] but it is not so in my kingdom; for I have come not to be served but to serve and to give my life for the redemption of many" (Matt. 20:25–28). The reference of this saying to the fourth of the Servant Songs in Deutero-Isaiah leads us to a concatenation of texts whose theological perspective is a mind-boggling upending of all our established views of authority and power and of how they are meant to unify and activate human society.

The presence of these texts in the New Testament writings makes it clear that the early Christians who produced this literature had had to face the task of claiming "Messiah" for Jesus despite the fact that the manner of his crucifixion ruled him out as the Messiah commonly expected by the Jews of his day. In doing so, they went back to Jesus' own self-perception as eschatological prophet and consciously used it to give a meaning to God as "king" that for the most part we have overlooked for the past two millennia.

Very briefly, what is the "new" meaning of God's kingship that was sacramentalized in Jesus' public ministry and above all in his death and resurrection? It is that God rules by sharing divine selfhood with humans through the offer of friendship; for if humans accept this offer in freedom, their vision of what life is all about will be basically altered, they will be transformed in their affective motivations by this divine love, they will be led to unexpected levels of personal freedom, a sequence of human actions will ensure what would not otherwise have been possible, and a community of persons, human and divine, will emerge as "the kingdom of God." Even more mysteriously, the death of Jesus, undertaken in love for his human sisters and brothers and in witness to the truth of his Abba's self-revelation, sacramentalized the suffering servanthood of Jesus and, because he embodies the divine Word, sacramentalized the suffering servanthood of his Abba.

Obviously, this understanding of authority and power is contrary to our prevailing notions. So much so, that it seems unrealistic to see such "servant power" as able to provide structure and effectiveness to our economic, political, social, and even religious activity. Yet, the outlook of the New Testament is unmistakable, even as it recognizes — e.g., in Paul's statement to the Corinthians (1 Cor. 1:22–25) — that this wisdom of Christianity is a stumbling block to "the

Jews" and sheer nonsense to "the Greeks." And it has remained a stumbling block and nonsense for most Christians up to our own day.

To make some sense out of this contention that "servant power" is actually the salvation of humanity, let us push a step further in its analysis. What we are dealing with as one examines the biblical texts more closely is the divine creative power that we have come to call "the Holy Spirit," the Spirit of God that is also the Spirit of Jesus as the Christ. To structure our discussion we might follow the two-stage pattern of Luke/Acts, i.e., the Spirit moving Jesus and the Spirit moving the church.

THE SPIRIT IN JESUS AND THE CHURCH

While all the Gospels and Paul speak of God's Spirit working in and through the ministry of Jesus, it is the Lukan Gospel that treats the theme in most detail. Indeed, remembering that for Jewish thought at the time of Jesus as well as for earliest Christianity the Spirit of God is the Spirit of prophecy, the perspective that dominates Luke's redaction is that of God's Spirit working in Jesus the eschatological prophet. It is through the Spirit, God's own creative power, overshadowing Mary in a way reminiscent of the origin of the universe, that the human existing of Jesus begins. This same Spirit inspires the canticles of Mary and Zachary and leads Simeon and Anna to the Temple for the presentation of Jesus. The Spirit leads Jesus to the Jordan to be baptized and then to the desert for trial; and Jesus upon leaving the desert "in the power of the Spirit" begins his ministry by preaching in the synagogue in Nazareth where he identifies himself as prophetic in terms of Isaiah 61, "The Spirit of the lord is upon me...."

Both Jesus' teaching and charismatic healing flow from the Spirit, the divine *dynamis* that accompanies the authority, the *exousia*, he possesses as the Son of Man. It is because the Spirit works through him that his words are effective commands that rid people of the demons that cripple or bind them. Like a Jeremias endowed with the word that "builds or destroys, plants or uproots," Jesus' words are life-giving to the daughter of Jairus but destructive to the unproductive fig tree. And when some of the Jewish leaders refuse to listen to his preaching, Jesus accuses them of sinning against God's Spirit, which is working through him.

Overshadowed at the transfiguration by the bright cloud, a theophanic manifestation of the Spirit, Jesus undertakes his *exodos* toward Jerusalem and his death and resurrection. To understand the early church's insight into the Spirit's role in Jesus' resurrection we turn from Luke to Paul, who understands the risen existence of Jesus as a mystery of en-spiritment. It is God's Spirit that had animated and guided him in his earthly career that now finds full expression in the new life that flowers from the seed sown on Calvary. So fully does the Spirit find expression in this new unending life of Jesus that Paul can say that Jesus has "become living spirit." With this complete possession of the Spirit common to himself and his Father, Jesus becomes fully the Christ through sharing this Spirit as source of unending life.

Both Luke and Paul retain an essentially communitarian dimension to the Spirit; even Jesus' possession of and by this Spirit takes place within the mystery of his "headship." There are not many Spirits; there is only the one unlimited Spirit of God from which flows that ultimate personal life, the inheritance of Jesus in which his human brothers and sisters are invited to share. Men and women are able to possess this Spirit precisely by their participation in that community of faith that is the not-yet-totally-realized kingdom of God on earth. While this "kingdom of God on the way" is more extensive than the church, the church is meant to play a special role of discipleship in achieving the full realization of the kingdom. Individual Christians become enlivened and empowered by this Spirit of Christ as they enter the Christian community, and they are meant to become increasingly enspirited as they are progressively socialized into this community.

Within the church certain members are empowered by Christ's Spirit to perform functions required for the community's survival or well-being or for the effective carrying out of its mission. As Paul points out to his Corinthian converts, such charismatic gifts are not given for the sake of the individual who is so gifted; rather, their purpose is the "building up" of the church that is the Body of Christ (1 Cor. 14:1–5). This charismatic endowment, the response of Christ's Spirit to the needs of the community itself and of the humans the community is meant to serve, is the source and the norm of all truly Christian ministry.

However, these special charisms, important as they are, are neither the most basic nor the most potent empowerment granted Christians for the implementation of their discipleship. More essential, indeed indispensable, are the gifts of faith and hope and charity that are intrinsic to the new life being given by the risen Christ in a continuing pentecost. It is the new vision of reality, the new motivation coming from that vision and from the love relationship offered by God through his Christ, and the peace-filled trust in the fidelity of this love that provide a new level of living and of creative activity. Other gifts of the Spirit enhance, nurture, support, and safeguard the life of faith, hope, and love; but it is the community's sharing in the new life flowing from Christ's Spirit, God's creative love, that is *the* charism beyond all others.

What all this says is that the New Testament model for thinking about power and authority in the church is not a political or organizational model but a "life" model, the model of a *living* social reality. This organic model is in continuity with Jesus' own parables that consistently use metaphors drawn from living, growing things. The power operative in the church is life-power, the power of Christ's life-giving Spirit; the authority proper to the Christian community is that which flows from the possession of the God-given life of faith, hope, and love and from the special charisms granted to further this life in the community. Only because it possesses this life can the Christian community share it with other humans; the life itself is what empowers Christians in their ministry to the kingdom of God.

As was already mentioned, individuals receive their basic empowerment insofar as they share in the life of the community. This sharing is intertwined with the process of initiation that traditionally has been associated with the liturgy of baptism. Without denying a special role of baptism in Christian initiation, we are once more becoming aware that initiation is a much lengthier — actually a life-long — process. In the case of an adult initiate, the early stages of the catechumenate are already the beginnings of sharing the worldview and activities of the community, and the baptismal ceremony is meant to lead to increasing involvement in the worship and ministries and mutual caring of the Christians who form the receiving community for the new member. In the case of one baptized in infancy, the years of growing into adulthood should be a gradual introduction to the faith and life of the family.

One cannot become a Christian simply by the baptizing action of an ordained minister. The person himself of herself must *become*. The individual must learn and believe and experience and love and minister and hope, and in this way become increasingly Christian. This cannot be done apart from the community of believers, for the learning and believing have to do with that explanation of human life that is the heritage of Christian tradition. Obviously, one cannot identify oneself as a Christian committed to discipleship without the experience of sharing in the ministries undertaken by the community. Nor can one continue creatively in Christian faith and ministry without the support of others whose own hope in the face of frustrations and difficulties gives promise that the idealistic goals of the gospel are humanly attainable.

All this is to say that it is in sharing the faith life of the church that an individual is empowered to become Christian and to participate in the Christian task of bringing Spirit-life to other humans. Socialization into the church, becoming a Christian, receiving the Holy Spirit are in concrete reality one and the same process, which is liturgically celebrated in the rituals of baptism, confirmation, and Eucharist, but by no means exhaustively expressed in these sacramental actions. In these ritual moments, if they are enacted as they should be, i.e., as truly human shared professions of faith, an individual becomes more en-Spirited by experiencing more intensely than before the Spirit of Christ, which animates the church.

Unfortunately, in the course of the centuries our attention came to focus too exclusively on the symbolism of water in the liturgy of initiation. Along with that came a lopsided concentration on "removal of original sin" and the view that something totally supernatural and mysterious called "sanctifying grace" was granted as the ground for gaining heaven. As a result, the immediate and all-important symbolism of *entering and being received by a community of Christians* was overlooked in the ritual itself and in its catechetical explanation. Basically, the baptismal liturgy was still an action of a person becoming a member of a particular group of Christians, but the absence of that group — except for the sponsors and the baptizing minister — made it impossible for one to experience baptism as *being welcomed* into the community. Whatever thought was given to "empowerment," and in most cases there was no awareness of the initiate's empowerment for discipleship, was in terms of a mysterious reception of "grace." Even the venerable notion of "sacramental character" as the root of Christians' evangelical mission was largely forgotten in recent centuries.

Given this semi-magical understanding of what happened to the new Christian in baptism, it is no wonder that there was little, if any, appreciation of the fact that this liturgy was but a moment in a lifelong process of initiation into the life of the church. Add to this the alienation of most Christians from active participation in ministry as ordained clergy established a virtual monopoly of discipleship. The resulting experience of most Christians was, then, that of receiving salvation through clerical mediation. Even the sacramental character of baptism was considered in theological reflection as the ability to profitably *receive* other sacraments. As far as life in the church was concerned, most men and women were powerless and without authority, something that is still reflected in the church's canon law.

Fortunately, this distorted theology of Christian life and liturgy has been contested and to some extent corrected in recent decades. As twentieth-century theologians, both Catholic and Protestant, began to reappraise the nature and role of sacraments, they gradually rediscovered what was called "the ecclesial dimension" of these ritual actions. The individualism of previous catechetical instruction about sacraments has not vanished, but to a large extent it has been modified by a realization that the Christian community, both the local community and "the great church," is somehow involved in any liturgical action. Along with this, the notion of "the priesthood of the faithful" has been theologically reexamined with less of the contentiousness that marked the debates of the sixteenth and seventeenth centuries; and the result has been a realization that priesthood is essentially a characteristic and function of the community, for it is the community and not any individual that is "Body of Christ."

As the discipleship of the entire community and its prophetic/priestly character are being recognized anew, the questions about authority and power inevitably come to the surface. If again, following the insights gained by contemporary biblical study, we use a "life model" in thinking about the church, then the power that nurtures and intensifies the community's life is not viewed as coming "down from above" through levels of clerical mediation but as flowing from the immanent presence of Christ's Spirit to the community. Whatever endowment or empowerment is granted individuals in the community comes from the community itself and more radically from its indwelling Spirit.

What is occurring in our theology is a simultaneous revision of our ecclesiology, our pneumatology, and our christology. Because — to express it graphically — we have no longer in our religious imagination sent the risen Jesus to heaven to await the parousia, but instead are regaining the early Christian awareness of the continuing presence to us of the risen Christ, we can revivify the Pauline notion of "Body of Christ" and become aware once more of Christ's Spirit empowering the whole community for its mission of transforming human history. What this requires, however, is a painful abandonment of those forms of authority and power that are incompatible with such a church, exercises of authority and power that may fit organizations directed to achieving wealth and domination and earthly glory but that have no place in a discipleship of equals.

THE ORDAINED MINISTRY

In some ways the theological test case is the explanation of the power exercised by the ordained celebrant of the Eucharist. This has become a critical issue in many portions of the Catholic Church where the shortage of ordained men has severely limited the availability of eucharistic liturgy and where, as a consequence, the need for such an ordained person is being questioned. What power does the ordained person possess that makes him indispensable in the eucharistic celebration, if indeed he is indispensable?

For centuries the response to such questions has been conditioned by the assumption that the ordained celebrant was the one who performed the liturgy. He did it within the context of the community, for the sake of the community, but it was *he* who did it. He alone was able to do this, because the necessary power of transforming the elements of bread and wine had been given him in his ordination. Of course, the primary agent of the action was in some fashion Christ himself, for the celebrant acted *in persona Christi*. Since this was so, it was the celebrant who sacramentalized Christ; it was in seeing the celebrant that the faithful at Mass were in him to see the risen Lord whose surrogate he was. That the ordained celebrant stood in for Christ and acted in Christ's name and by this power was most evident at the consecration of the Mass when the celebrant pronounced Jesus' own words of eucharistic transformation, "This is my body; this is my blood."

Today this theological explanation is being questioned and possibly revised. Instead of regarding the ordained individual as the agent of the liturgy, we have become more aware that it is the entire community that celebrates Eucharist. Christ, present as the risen Lord, is truly *the* agent of Eucharist, but he is this in and through the gathered community that is his Body. Because it is "Body of Christ," the community can sacramentalize and speak for the risen Christ; because it is "Body of Christ," its activity, and in a distinctive way its symbolic activity, is truly activity of the risen Christ. Because it is Body/sacrament of Christ and animated by his Spirit, the community is empowered to make continually present in history the saving reality of Jesus' death and resurrection. So, in eucharistic celebration it is the community that is acting *in persona Christi*.

What, then, is the role of the ordained; is it in any way distinctive and grounded in power that he alone possesses? For the moment, our best response to that question seems to be that the ordained presides over and catalyzes the activity of the celebrating community. Functioning as a sacrament within a sacrament, his faith is meant to reflect and animate the faith of those present, his formulation of belief and prayer is meant to give unified expression to the worship of the group; in other words, he acts *in persona ecclesiae*. What comes with his ordination is the ability to function not just in the "person" of the local community but also in the "person" of the worldwide church, for his public commission to ministry by a bishop in ordination has established him as one whose teaching and ritual activity is linked with the collegial witness of the episcopacy.

Aided by one who in this way embodies the charisms of liturgical presidency, the community (including this charismatic leader) can give expression to the Spirit of Christ, which — as Paul wrote to the Galatians (4:6–7) — empowers them to cry out "Abba, Father" in acknowledgement of God as revealed in Jesus. To praise God in this fashion is, however, only one aspect of the mission of Christ's Spirit to the community. Inseparably linked with liturgical rituals is the community's covenantal acceptance of the call to discipleship.

The church is empowered by its Spirit, which is the Spirit constantly shared with it by its risen Lord, in order to bring about in history the reign of God, that community of divine and human persons that is the goal of creation. No power short of God's own power is able to achieve this purpose, but that power of God is not power as ordinarily understood — at least as understood in the prevailing official ecclesiology. God's power to create, along with human co-creation, is the paradoxical power of self-giving servanthood. If God and God's Christ work with this kind of authority and power, there is no other kind of power that is proper to Christian ministry, whether that ministry be exercised within the community itself or in the community's efforts to bring human life to its fulfillment.

However, all that has been said so far is challenged by the claims of "practicality." Is it humanly possible to have a unified grouping of humans, no matter how idealistically Christian they might be, without some organization? Is it possible to avoid chaos and consequent ineffectiveness in ministerial activity unless there is some authoritative direction? The response to both questions is an obvious "no." Among the charisms given to individuals by Christ's Spirit for the sake of the community's life and mission is the charism of *governance*, a clear recognition that able administration of the structured elements of the church's life is a gift to be cherished. This means that those who are in directive positions must possess the power and authority needed to guide and unify the community, and to some extent at least this involves something like jurisdiction.

This practical demand for administrative power can be reconciled with the New Testament ideal of servant-power, if in considering ecclesiastical administration one retains the life-model (instead of a political/organizational model) for thinking about the church. In this model, the community's own life force, its Spirit, remains always the source and norm for any governance; those who govern do not legitimately function as a group *above* the rest of the faithful, but as representatives and agents *of* and *for* the community whose members they themselves are. The charism of governance that such administrators exercise is not itself the power to Christianize; that power is Christ's Spirit nurturing faith and love within the community and its individual members. Like others in the church, those in official positions are meant to help transform the lives and persons of their fellow humans by sharing their own Christian faith and hope and love. In some cases their public prominence might even suggest that their ability and responsibility to exercise discipleship is greater. But what they do as mediators of "salvation" they do by virtue of being Christian rather than by virtue of official jurisdiction.

One final remark: Clearly, the thrust of this essay raises a critical issue to be faced, namely, the relationship (which historically became the coincidence) of governance and liturgical presidency. Though this issue is central to any resolution of the present "crisis" of authority and power in the church, it is too large and important a matter to be here treated incidentally; it demands its own full examination.

7

EMPOWERING LAY LEADERSHIP IN THE CHURCH: CHALLENGES AND RESPONSIBILITIES

Robert F. Morneau

A pressing, contemporary question in the church: do ordained presbyters have the responsibility to empower the laity for leadership in the church? An affirmative answer seems so obvious that the question becomes almost rhetorical. Yet, as recently as 1975, we find the following "job description" in the brilliant apostolic exhortation *Evangelii Nuntiandi* of Pope Paul VI:

> A mark of our identity which no doubt ought to encroach upon and no objection eclipse is this: as pastors, we have been chosen by the mercy of the Supreme Pastor, in spite of our inadequacy, to proclaim with authority the Word of God, to assemble the scattered People of God, to feed this People with the signs of the action of Christ which are the sacraments, to set this People on the road to salvation, to maintain it in that unity of which we are, at different levels, active and living instruments, and unceasingly to keep this community gathered around Christ faithful to its deepest vocation.[1]

Simply because the duty to empower lay leadership in the church is not mentioned in the above listing, we cannot draw the conclusion that empowerment is not a responsibility. Other documents provide ample evidence that ordained ministers have both a responsibility and marvelous challenge of assisting lay people to exercise appropriate leadership within the ecclesial community.

In this essay I will make ten assertions regarding the empowerment question. However, before giving my propositions, I would like to offer a context for them by quoting at length a reflection by Pope John Paul II in his postsynodal apostolic exhortation *Christifideles Laici*. This document addressed the vocation and mission of the lay faithful. Although the issue of empowerment is not specifically dealt with, the implications are obvious:

When necessity and expediency in the church require it, the pastors, according to established norms from universal law, can entrust to the lay faithful certain offices and roles that are connected to their pastoral ministry but do not require the character of order. The Code of Canon Law states: "When the necessity of the church warrants it and when ministers are lacking, lay persons, even if they are not lectors or acolytes, can also supply for certain of their offices, namely, to exercise the ministry of the word, to preside over liturgical prayer, to confer baptism and to distribute communion in accord with the prescriptions of the law." (Canon 230.3) However, the exercise of such tasks does not make them pastors of the lay faithful: In fact, a person is not a minister simply in performing a task, but through sacramental ordination. Only the sacrament of orders gives the ordained minister a particular participation in the office of Christ, the shepherd and head, and in his eternal priesthood. The task exercised in virtue of supply takes its legitimacy formally and immediately from the official deputation given by the pastors as well as from its concrete exercise under the guidance of ecclesiastical authority.

The recent synodal assembly has provided an extensive and meaningful overview of the situation in the church on the ministries, offices and roles of the baptized. The fathers have mentioned a deep appreciation for the contribution of the lay faithful, both women and men, in the work of the apostolate, in evangelization, sanctification and the Christian animation of temporal affairs as well as their generous willingness to supply in situations of emergency and chronic necessity.

Following the liturgical renewal promoted by the council, the lay faithful themselves have acquired a more lively awareness of the tasks that they fulfill in the liturgical assembly and its preparation, and have become more widely disposed to fulfill them: the liturgical celebration, in fact, is a sacred action not simply of the clergy, but of the entire assembly. It is therefore natural that the tasks not proper to the ordained ministers be fulfilled by the lay faithful. In this way there is a natural transition from an effective involvement of the lay faithful in the liturgical action to that of announcing the word of God and pastoral care.[2]

The mission and ministry of Jesus is one of reconciliation and fullness of life. Every disciple of the Lord, male or female, ordained or nonordained, young or old, has been given a participation in this singular mission through baptism, confirmation, and the gift of Eucharist. Though members of the church have been given different roles, all share in the same life-giving Spirit. A contemporary challenge in the life of the church is to clarify the uniqueness of each role and to encourage all to share more deeply in the work of evangelization and sanctification.

Necessarily our discussion will deal with one of the key realities that is found in every social grouping, whether secular or religious. That reality is one of power. The Second Vatican Council used a vocabulary that, for some twenty-five years, we have attempted to understand and implement. This includes such terms as "delegation," "co-responsibility," "collegial spirit," "consultation," and "subsidiarity." Admittedly, all has not gone well. Empowerment has not been realized because some have refused to delegate their power. In other circumstances, abdication has resulted in chaos and confusion. Consultation has turned into a democratic caucus for some. And subsidiarity, rather than fostering decision-making, has caused paralysis when people have not been properly trained.

But there are success stories. Empowerment has taken place and has furthered the mission of the church. With proper theological formation and the development of practical skills, the whole church has grown through the appropriate sharing and exercise of power.

ASSERTIONS

1. Empowerment is the process by which an individual or a community is enabled to bring about change by the possession and exercise of power.

> Empowerment is about a basic human need that mentoring can help fulfill; it is about helping each one of us name and claim our gifts — not for our self-aggrandizement, but for building up the Kingdom of God. Empowerment as the dictionary defines it is giving power or authority to someone.[3]

In John's Gospel we are told that Jesus came to bring life, life to the full (John 10:10). The implication underlying this mission is the necessity of growth, of positive change. The development of potential is one means of growth, the turning from evil to goodness is another. Whether we speak of development or conversion, change is necessary; through it we move from one stage or condition to another if life is to be fully lived.

According to Rollo May, power is concerned with the ability to bring about or prevent change. Powerlessness means that people are in circumstances preventing them from realizing their full potential. The consequence is waste: waste of time, waste of energy, waste of gifts, waste of life itself. In her recent novel *Breathing Lessons*, Anne Tyler writes about a family in which the father, Ira, sees his son as simply wasting his life. The book articulates the reality that unless people are empowered, waste abounds.

Presbyters have a unique opportunity and an urgent responsibility to follow the mandate of Jesus that life reach full maturity. The principle of sacramentality, whereby God mediates grace, love, and mercy through human and natural channels, draws us to realize that people (community) are a primary means of reconciliation and wholeness. Presbyters must empower people to become disciples, to become instruments of peace and servants of the mysteries of God. Failure to recognize how the Spirit is working in people and negligence in encouraging people to use their talents for building God's reign, lead to waste and great deprivation. Empowerment is not an option. It resides at the center of responsible leadership.

2. Empowerment becomes an obligation of the ordained clergy because lay people, whom they serve, play an essential and necessary role in the church's mission of salvation.

> The lay faithful have an essential and irreplaceable role in this announcement and in this testimony: Through them the church of Christ is made present in various sectors of the world as a sign and source of hope and of love.[4]

> Indeed, pastors know how much the lay faithful contribute to the welfare of the entire church. They also know that they themselves were not established by Christ to undertake alone the entire mission of the church toward the world, but they understand that it is their exalted office to be shepherds of the lay faithful and also to recognize the latter's service and charisms that all according to their proper roles may cooperate in this common undertaking with one heart.[5]

The old Latin adage holds true: *In omnibus respice finem* ("In all things, look to the end"). Empowerment is a contextual concept and cannot be understood outside its relationship to the mission of the church. Jesus came to bring about union with the Father and unity among people. He came to proclaim the good news of divine love and mercy, to manifest in time and space the will of the Father, to participate in the sufferings and joys of others, to lead us through suffering and death to the glory of the resurrection. Jesus' work continues today. There is only one ministry and mission and through baptism all the people of God are given a share in the work of salvation.

But if people are given a mission, they must also be given the necessary power to fulfill the responsibilities of that task. At this point theology is of the utmost importance. A proper understanding of who has the mission of salvation must be articulated. If that mission is perceived to be in the hands of the ordained clergy, then empowerment of the laity is not even a question to be discussed. But the teaching of Vatican Council II and the tradition of the church remind us that the laity play "an essential and necessary role in the church's mission of salvation." The corollary quickly follows: power must be given to people to fulfill their Christian duty of building up the Body of Christ, of making Christ present and manifest in the world.

Focusing is important. The end dictates the means. Created in God's image and likeness, all of us are called to share in the gift of eternal life. Yet that destiny can be thwarted. Sin separates us from God and one another. Our mission is to counteract sin by participating ever more deeply in the life, death, and resurrection of Jesus. We do this through our sacramental life, hearing the word of God, and Christian service. Empowerment is a means by which we participate more fully in the paschal mystery and the mission of our Lord.

3. Empowerment of the laity takes place at two levels: in being missioned to permeate the world with gospel values and in the building up of the ecclesial community itself.

> The various ministries, offices and roles that the lay faithful can legitimately fulfill in the liturgy, in the transmission of the faith and in the pastoral structure of the church ought to be exercised in conformity to their specific lay vocation, which is different from that of the sacred ministry. In this regard the exhortation *Evangelii Nuntiandi*, that had such a great part in stimulating the varied collaboration of lay faithful in the church's life and mission of spreading the gospel, recalls that "their own field of evangelizing activity is the vast and complicated world of politics, economics as well as the world of culture, of the sciences and the arts, of international life, of the mass media. It also includes other realities which are open to evangelization, such as human love, the family, the education of children and adolescents, professional work and suffering. The more Gospel-inspired lay people there are engaged in these realities, clearly involved in them, competent to promote them and conscious that they must exercise to the full their Christian powers, which are often repressed and buried, the more these realities will be at the service of the kingdom of God and therefore at the service of salvation in Jesus Christ, without in any way losing or sacrificing their human content, but rather pointing to a transcendent dimension which is often disregarded."[6]

> The lay faithful have their part to fulfill in the formation of these ecclesial communities, not only through an active and responsible participation in the life of the community — in other words, through a testimony that only they can give — but also through a missionary zeal and activity toward the many people who still do not believe and who no longer live the faith received in baptism.[7]

Professor Belden C. Lane, of St. Louis University, published an excellent study of American spirituality entitled *Landscapes of the*

Sacred: Narrative and Geography in American Spirituality (Paulist Press, 1988). Lane contends that story and place mediate the presence of God. As we look at the question of empowerment, a specific question arises regarding the "place" of the laity in the church, the "place" of the laity in the world. *Where* lay persons minister qualifies the type and degree of empowerment that is to be given them.

The first quotation above gives a series of *places* where they are to do ministry: (1) the complicated political world; (2) the economic world; (3) the world of culture; (4) the worlds of science and art; (5) international life; (6) the arena of the mass media; (7) the domain of human love; (8) the family; (9) the education of children and adolescents; (10) the professional world; (11) the experience of suffering. Given this extensive list, one wonders whether or not any area has been left untouched. The second quotation above adds an additional "where." The laity are to be empowered in the ministry of formation of the ecclesial community and in their missionary zeal. Ministry takes place in a specific time and place. Those who are called to ministry, that is, all the baptized, must be given not only the responsibility flowing from their participation in the life of Christ but also the "power" to complete their task.

While the tradition has emphasized that the primary ministry of the laity is "in the world," not primarily in the formation of the ecclesial community, today the situation calls for a deeper appreciation of this latter responsibility. The shortage of ordained personnel, the diminishment in the number of religious, and the increased theological training of many lay people are all factors that contribute to the necessity of involving many more laity directly in the building up of the faith community. The important distinction between ministry *ad intra*, that is, nurturing the development of our own ecclesial life, and ministry *ad extra*, that is, reaching out to the needs of the broader world, must not be used to subvert the empowerment question. To say that the ordained and religious will do the *ad intra* ministry and that the laity are to do the *ad extra* ministries is too narrow and unrealistic given the new circumstances of the church.

God mediates the divine presence in time and space. Whether that is within the walls of the church or on the streets, all the baptized are to assist in that mediation, in telling the story of God's redemptive love.

4. Empowerment involves a correct understanding and fitting implementation of such "power words" as "delegation," "subsidiarity," "co-responsibility," "consultation," and "collegiality."

The possession of power naturally tends to the dissolution of mutual trust and intimate fellowship.[8]

Power without genuine responsibility is a dazzling-clothed impotence.[9]

...power is the mediation of God only insofar as it is love and service; otherwise it turns into sin.[10]

Language describes reality; sometimes it defines it. Our vocabulary has a significant influence on behavior and on our understanding of reality. When we speak of power and its role in human life, it is important to recognize that there are different ways of understanding power and different ways of exercising it. At times power can be manipulative and exploitative; at other times it is life-giving and liberating. We speak of delegation when power is given to another; subsidiarity when power to make decisions is exercised at the lowest possible level; co-responsibility that calls people into mutual ministry; consultation that allows all facets of an issue to be reflected upon; a collegial spirit whereby a spirit of cooperation and mutual regard characterizes the exchange within a community.

Empowerment of the laity by the ordained finds practical expression in the above listing. A case in point would be the parish council. When empowerment is exercised properly, the members of the council will sense that they, along with the pastor and other professional leadership personnel, are mutually responsible for the education, worship, and stewardship programs of their faith community. There will be an atmosphere of collaboration whereby no important decision will be made without the input and deliberation of the council. People will be urged to take the initiative to make decisions if the issue is within their competency. A significant factor in the area of empowerment is the "attitude" on the part of the ordained and nonordained. If people have sufficient self-confidence not to be threatened by others who seek to share in power and if individuals do not aggressively seek "power positions," empowerment will probably be felt as a graced reality.

5. Empowerment faces a series of obstacles: abdication, usurpation, authoritarianism, misplaced energy, religious disintegration.

At the same time, the synod has pointed out that the postconciliar path of the lay faithful has not been without its difficulties and dangers. In particular, two temptations can be cited which they have not always known how to avoid: the temptation of being so strongly interested in church service and tasks that some fail to become actively engaged in their responsibilities in the professional, social, cultural and political world; and the temptation of legitimizing the unwarranted separation of faith from life, that is, a separation of the

Gospel's acceptance from the actual living of the Gospel in various situations in the world.[11]

Psychologists and spiritual directors are continually reminding us that gifts can become weaknesses, blessings can turn into curses. This happens when something good is misdirected or is used inappropriately. Empowerment is not exempt from turning sour, of moving from life to death. The postsynodal document on the laity points out two areas of temptations that relate to the empowerment question. First, there is the temptation to move away from the messy and complex secular issues of life that daily press upon so many people: fiscal responsibilities, parenting, seeking justice, searching for simplicity of life. Weariness or doubt, discouragement or fear can drive people into the "safe" refuge of church life. Even more dangerous is the failure to integrate faith with the Monday-through-Saturday aspects of life. Religion becomes privatized and rests comfortably in the forty-five minute slot on Sunday morning. Authentic empowerment, while not excluding church ministry, enables people to permeate all of life with gospel values and simultaneously to link everyday life with God's word.

John Courtney Murray's *The Problem of God* sketches out various forms of atheism that afflict our minds and hearts. In writing about the denial of God, Murray states: "The denial is not of the theoretical order. It has the sense of an active ignoring of the presence of God, a refusal to abide his judgments."[12] Thus we do our academic work, our economic transactions, our political deciding without reference to the transcendent. This pragmatic atheism isolates humanity from the source of its existence, from its true destiny. Empowerment must reverse this tendency of godlessness and help people to link every aspect of their life — school, marketplace, legislatures — to the judgments and priorities of God.

Other obstacles to empowerment need to be noted. At times, because of frustration, laziness, or incompetency, ordained leaders abdicate their responsibilities and simply turn over "the shop" to the laity. Then there is the power play (à la trustee-ism) whereby aggressive individuals seek power inappropriately in order to control the parish according to their own "lights." Authoritarianism, a third obstacle, simply refuses to involve the community in decision-making and accountability. Since Vatican Council II all three forms of anti-empowerment activities and attitudes have shown their ugly faces.

6. Empowerment must be done in conjunction with theological formation as well as training in professional skills necessary for all leadership roles.

Since formation for the apostolate cannot consist in merely theoretical instruction, from the very beginning of their formation the laity should gradually and prudently learn how to view, judge, and do all things in the light of faith as well as to develop and improve themselves and others through action, thereby entering into the energetic service of the Church.[13]

In this dialogue between God, who offers his gifts, and the person, who is called to exercise responsibility, there comes the possibility, indeed the necessity, of a total and ongoing formation of the lay faithful as the synod fathers have rightly emphasized in much of their work. After having described Christian formation as "a continual process in the individual of maturation in faith and a likening to Christ, according to the will of the Holy Spirit," they have clearly affirmed that the formation of the lay faithful must be placed among the priorities of a diocese. It ought to be so placed within the plan of pastoral action that the efforts of the whole community (clergy, lay faithful and religious) converge on this goal.[14]

A number of Catholic hospitals and universities have moved into the area of mission effectiveness. Members of the board of trustees as well as management people are attending retreats and workshops in which the mission of the sponsoring bodies is explained. Basic gospel values, e.g., the dignity of the human person, the sacredness of life, reverence for truth, are shared in the context of what each institution is all about. Board members and management personnel, already empowered through life experiences and professional competency, are given theological formation so that the hospital or school might be true to its existential purpose.

The adage "the roots determine the fruits" has considerable validity. The quality of ministry (fruits) will be radically conditioned by the spiritual and theological training (roots) that people receive. It is unfair to ask financial experts to sit on parish councils or school boards and to expect them to make wise economic decisions, without giving them an ecclesiology that informs all Christian decisions. A wise decision made on Wall Street is not necessarily a good decision regarding use of monetary resources in the church. Empowerment alone is not sufficient. A vision of God's reign and concerns must accompany the sharing of responsibility and power.

The teaching and prophetic roles of the ordained in the church come into play here. Without a vision, without theological principles, confusion reigns. Our Catholic tradition and values must be transmitted in coherent and intelligible ways — such is the task of theology. Here a concern needs to be acknowledged. Has pragmatism (being productive, useful, etc.) become so predominant as to downplay if not negate the value of the intellectual life? Put more boldly:

Is there an unconscious anti-intellectualism afoot that makes theological formation a mere option if not a waste of time? The question is worthy of reflection.

7. Empowerment bears fruits and can be evaluated in terms of a community's vitality flowing from full, conscious, and active participation of its members.

> The fundamental criteria mentioned at this time find their verification in the actual fruits that various group forms show in their organizational life and the works they perform such as: the renewed appreciation for prayer, contemplation, liturgical and sacramental life, the reawakening of vocations to Christian marriage, the ministerial priesthood and the consecrated life; a readiness to participate in programs and church activities at the local, national and international levels; a commitment to catechesis and a capacity for teaching and forming Christians; a desire to be present as Christians in various settings of social life and the creation and awakening of charitable, cultural and spiritual works; the spirit of detachment and evangelical poverty leading to a greater generosity in charity toward all; conversion to the Christian life or the return to church communion of those baptized members who have fallen away from the faith.[15]

Are there standards to evaluate Christian maturity? According to Evelyn and James Whitehead, "Religious growth will be charted in terms of an adult's maturing sense of identity (discipleship), the ability to love and give of oneself (charity), and the capacity for responsible care (stewardship)."[16] Similarly, it is possible to identify characteristics that point to successful empowerment. The postsynodal document *Christifideles Laici* lists seven elements, ranging from a renewed appreciation of our sacramental life to evangelization, to indicate ecclesial vitality. A vibrant, empowered parish and diocese should be able to demonstrate deep participation by a large segment of its membership. Periodically, it would be wise for the parish community to assess the quality of its prayer and contemplation, liturgical and sacramental life, vocational awareness (especially regarding priesthood and religious life), catechetical instruction, spiritual and corporal works of mercy, social justice programs, evangelization and ecumenical endeavors, stewardship practices and educational strategy.

The ideal of full, conscious, and active participation must deal with maladies that perennially afflict the human spirit and ecclesial community. One is apathy, a haunting indifference that causes procrastination at best, paralysis at worst. Jesus attempted to empower ten lepers to return to full communion. We know the sad ending to the story. A second factor threatening the achievement of the ideal of full participation is ignorance. Not knowing our identity or destiny, not knowing the mystery of God's love and mercy, not knowing our potential and the possibilities of fresh alternatives minimize the effectiveness of empowerment. A third inhibiting element to full and active participation is fear. Unless we can trust that the responsibilities that come with power are life-giving and not death-dealing, fear will hold us captive. People who live in fear, the darkness of ignorance, the debilitating realm of apathy, seldom are capable of being empowered no matter how often or how effectively empowerment is offered.

8. Empowerment focuses upon two elements: gifts and needs. Leadership potential is perceived and then nurtured in structured ways.

> Spiritual gifts are worthless in themselves unless they help to build up the community and are inspired by authentic love.[17]

> We will never believe that we have anything to give unless there is someone who is able to receive. Indeed, we discover our gifts in the eyes of the receiver.[18]

> What is not used is but a load to bear.[19]

Ministry is a complex reality, a polyvalent concept. Without being reductionistic, we can point out two elementary ingredients in the ministerial formula: ministers are gifted people and ministers perceive and address others' needs. In the same breath, we must add that a basic mutuality exists in ministry since those who are "labeled" ministers are also ministered to by those whom they serve. In fact, it is difficult at times (as in spiritual direction) to know who is the director and who the directee.

Empowerment is a process by which gifts are recognized and carefully nurtured. Empowerment is not for its own sake but focuses on meeting the needs of the afflicted. Ordained ministers have the responsibility of not only using their own gifts to meet the needs of others (hands-on ministry) but are also mandated to enable members of the entire community to participate in the mission and ministry of Jesus. According to Romano Guardini, that mission involves some specific tasks:

> The young creature in the stall of Bethlehem was a human being with human brain and limbs and heart and soul. And it was God. Its life was to manifest the will of the Father: to proclaim the sacred tidings, to stir mankind with the power of God, to establish the Covenant, and shoulder the sin of the world, expiating it with love and leading

mankind through the destruction of sacrifice and the victory of the Resurrection into the new existence of grace. In this accomplishment alone lay Jesus' self-perfection: fulfillment of mission and personal fulfillment were one.[20]

Baptism calls all of us to use our talents to follow in the way of Jesus.

Lest empowerment become haphazard or arbitrary, structured programs are needed to insure its accomplishment. Realistically, some ordained presbyters lack skills to facilitate empowerment. Diocesan programs will be necessary to supplement the work of the clergy at the parish level. Fortunately, many dioceses have lay ministry programs that are well designed and well staffed to further the development of gifts and to assist in the work of making disciples of all nations.

9. Empowerment is rooted in God's grace working in the depth of every individual. Through the sacraments of initiation, all share in unique ways in the power and wisdom of Jesus.

> There should be no surprise, therefore, that the Catholic possesses such high regard for earthly things. Family and friendship, human work and human artistry, imagination and intelligence, meal taking and journeying, laughter and learning — all things are sacramental. Through such events God comes. In such events the Catholic believes that people can know, as well as one can in this life, the presence of God. Because of the incarnation, any moment in a person's life can be a graced moment, brimming with meaning for those who have the eyes of faith.[21]

> The principal lesson of community is a principal lesson of the kingdom — namely, that God breaks in at the weak places. God's Spirit is active in the most unlikely places — the poor, broken, and humble places. The power of God is most realized at the point of our vulnerability, our risk-taking, and our letting go. To be vulnerable means to be available to the power of God's love.[22]

Jesus is the power and the wisdom of God. Through the sacraments of initiation and through our sacramental life, all the baptized, confirmed, and nourished people of God share in that singular wisdom and power. The life of grace is dynamic and permeates every dimension of life. We are sent forth in faith as an evangelizing community to build the reign of God, a reign of justice and love, of freedom and charity, of truth, goodness, and beauty.

Grace is the radical source of empowerment, and ordained presbyters, in a unique way, are stewards and ministers of the mysteries of God. Through word and deed, Christ is again made present and unleashes the fire that enkindles the earth. To stir the baptismal flame, to empower people to share the grace they have received, is a central element of priestly ministry. Grace as divine power brings about transformation on both a personal level, resulting in individual sanctification, and at a social level, establishing a just and ordered society.

10. Empowerment must foster holiness. If not, it poisons all those who possess it and are touched by it.

> Thus it is evident to everyone that all the faithful of Christ of whatever rank or status are called to fullness of the Christian life and to the perfection of charity. By this holiness a more human way of life is promoted even in this earthly society. In order that the faithful may reach this perfection, they must use their strength according as they have received it, as a gift from Christ. In this way they can follow in His footsteps and mold themselves in His image, seeking the will of the Father in all things, devoting themselves with all their being to the glory of God and the service of their neighbor.[23]

> To be able to discover the actual will of the Lord in our lives always involves the following: a receptive listening to the word of God and the church, fervent prayer, recourse to a wise and loving spiritual guide, and a faithful discernment of the gifts and talents given by God as well as the diverse social and historic situations in which one lives.[24]

The purpose to the church is to foster union with God and unity among people. Ordained ministers are to employ every means at their disposal in seeking this twofold goal. At times they will foster a spirit of prayer, encourage people to simplicity of life, advocate detachment and sacrifice, always with the same goal in mind: communion. Empowerment must foster holiness or we miss the whole meaning of the church's mission.

In what sense is empowerment a means to holiness? By enabling people to share who they are and what they have with others, community is formed. Central to empowerment in ministry is assisting people in putting on the mind and heart of Christ. Through the administration of the sacraments, by means of preaching the Word of God, through the building up of God's family, through the art of listening and loving, presbyters facilitate growth in holiness and in the fulfillment of Christian duties.

Holiness has to do with listening and loving. Insofar as ordained ministers are good listeners and Christian lovers, they will be effective in fulfilling all their priestly duties, including empowerment. A poet, Jessica Powers, summarizes well what it means to live with the Spirit of God. A living of this poem might well be the secret to empowerment for all of us:

TO LIVE WITH THE SPIRIT

To live with the Spirit of God is to be a listener.
It is to keep the vigil of mystery,
earthless and still.
One leans to catch the stirring of the Spirit,
strange as the wind's will.

The soul that walks where the wind of the Spirit blows
turns like a wandering weather-vane toward love.
It may lament like Job or Jeremiah,
echo the wounded hart, the mateless dove.
It may rejoice in spaciousness of meadow
that emulates the freedom of the sky.
Always it walks in waylessness, unknowing;
it has cast down forever from its hand
the compass of the whither and the why.

To live with the Spirit of God is to be a lover.
It is becoming love, and like to Him
toward Whom we strain with metaphors of creatures:
fire-sweep and water-rush and the wind's whim.
The soul is all activity, all silence;
and though it surges Godward to its goal,
it holds, as moving earth holds sleeping noonday,
the peace that is the listening of the soul.[25]

CONCLUSION

Leon Bloy states in his novel *The Woman Who Was Poor* that "there is only one sorrow and that is not to be a saint." Sanctity is a central goal of our faith journey but perhaps there is a second sorrow: that people who are gifted and given responsibility to transform the world fail to do so because they lacked power.

Empowerment deals with this second sorrow, one that is felt keenly in our times because power is not adequately shared or exercised. But this need not continue whether we speak of political, economic, cultural, social, or religious matters. People can and must be empowered in order that their humanity and the common good might be fully realized. Ordained clergy have a unique and privileged responsibility to see that these tasks are accomplished.

When we become saints and full citizens of the church and of the world a new joy will spread across our planet. It will be the joy marked by the unleashing of the Spirit who dwells within each of us. Only then will love be felt and peace embraced. Empowerment furthers God's reign by enabling us to achieve our vocation to be God's people.

8

PRIESTS AND LAITY: MUTUAL EMPOWERMENT

Roger M. Mahony

The church throughout the world is struggling to exercise its participation in the priesthood of Jesus Christ. And though no one theme can capture the full import of the Second Vatican Council, central to its understanding of the church and to the reform it inaugurated has been precisely this effort to realize the full breadth of the continuing priestly ministry of Christ.

Two dimensions of this priestly ministry are especially clarified by the council. First, conciliar teaching urges the church to express more adequately the fact that all the baptized participate in Jesus' priestly ministry. Secondly, the council underscores the belief that nothing of human life lies beyond the scope of Jesus' priesthood.

The fullness of participation by all the baptized in the priesthood of Jesus was perhaps most pointedly articulated in the council's *Dogmatic Constitution on the Church*,[1] the *Constitution on the Sacred Liturgy*,[2] and the *Decree on the Apostolate of the Laity*.[3] The theology of these documents, further reflected in the revised code of canon law, draws from tradition the identity of all the baptized as members of the people of God, the Body of Christ, a priestly people.

Any distinctions among the members of the church, any special roles, arise only in this context and take nothing away from this basic fact that all those baptized in Christ are baptized into a share in his priestly ministry. All offer spiritual sacrifices to the Father and all share Jesus' condition of being both priest and victim: it is our own lives that we offer to God.

The full scope of Jesus' priesthood, extending to all of culture and society, indeed to all human joys and sorrows, is perhaps more pointedly expressed in the *Pastoral Constitution on the Church in the Modern World*[4] and in the *Decree on the Church's Missionary Activity*.[5] Here the church's relationship to culture and society is acknowledged and described. The church's evangelizing and teaching works require that the ministers of the church respect and be open to

the experiences and insights of the world[6] and share in the struggles
to humanize the world.[7]

THE CATHOLIC IDENTITY

This broadening of the scope of Jesus' priestly ministry and of our
participation in this ministry has had a powerful impact on the life
of the church in the past quarter century. Furthermore, shifts in the
socio-cultural situation of Catholics in the United States have intensified this impact. From the middle of the nineteenth century to
the middle of the twentieth, the minority status of U.S. Catholics
fostered the kind of protective solidarity in which hierarchical authority tended to reduce the responsibility of individual members of
the church. In addition, the parallel system of educational and welfare
services we felt compelled to establish to care for ourselves tended to
separate the church from the broader culture and society.

Now that U.S. Catholics have been accepted as full members of
the society, relationships within the church and of the church to other
social institutions have become somewhat ambiguous. The stance or
mission of the church in relation to U.S. culture and society has become more diffuse, and the scope and distribution of responsibility
within the church have been shifting in ways that relate both to the
intent and effects of the council.

This narrowing of the "social distance" that once separated clergy
from laity, and church from society, inevitably leads to questions of
"identity." As the gap between clergy and laity has been reduced —
a gap that entailed different levels of education as well as different
degrees of responsibility for the life of the church — some ordained
priests have begun to wonder about their specific and distinct role.
At the same time, some people in the church, eyeing the increased
involvement of laity in ministerial roles, express concern about the
potential "clericalization" of the laity.

This "problem of identity" is not restricted to clergy-laity relationships. It arises as well when the church community is less isolated
from the rest of society. The more that individual Catholics find
themselves in leadership positions in business and government, education, social welfare, and the arts — outside the ambit of church
structures — the specific responsibility of the Christian in the world
becomes a more complicated question. The theology and practice of
the "apostolate of the laity" need renewal if lay people are to fulfill
their share in the mission of Christ in and through the use of their
talents and opportunities in the world of human affairs.[8]

In various parts of the world, this search for understanding Christian leadership in secular structures has led to the formation of new
movements and the revival of others. One thinks, for example, of

Communione e Liberazione, founded in Italy, or *Opus Dei,* founded in Spain, each of which has its own way of articulating and organizing the Christian mission of the lay person in the world. The church in the United States, while hospitable to almost all movements, is essentially more pragmatic and less movement-oriented than that. We will address these questions more through parish-based programs than movements, in the pluralist context of normal pastoral structures rather than the single-minded commitment of movements. Nonetheless, we have barely begun to take up this concern, to ask the question about a "secular spirituality," a way of thinking and a set of practices that help to mediate the relationship between Christian discipleship and secular leadership.[9]

But by closing the gap between church and world, we have raised questions of identity not only for the individual Catholic but also for Catholic institutions. As Catholic hospitals are required to meet the criteria of both government and the health professions, as Catholic colleges adopt prevailing academic standards and practices, as Catholic welfare institutions accept public funds for the provision of human services, as Catholic organizations promote justice in public policy, the church in these institutional forms is faced with questions of identity: what is distinctively Catholic about the church's practice in these institutions and how does the church balance its distinctive role with its readiness to be a partner in a pluralist society?

With these major shifts in understanding, identity, and role, we are required to keep searching for an apt expression of both what all those who work for the common good and share Jesus' priestly ministry have in common, and of what remains distinct in their roles. I present all this as the context for my comments here and as a case for modesty regarding what we can hope to achieve at this point in history. I wish to address specifically the relationship between clergy and laity in two parts. First, I want to suggest some features of the general and ministerial relationships between clergy and laity. Secondly, I want to take up, not the question of the clergy's "empowerment" of the laity, so often discussed these days, but the reverse: how the laity enable ordained priests to exercise their ministry more aptly and more adequately. How does the living out of the priesthood of all the baptized enrich rather than impoverish the priestly ministry of the ordained, broaden not narrow the scope of ministry of the ordained?

My concern is not to respond to the defensiveness of some few priests who feel that their role and identity are in danger of becoming what is "left over" after laity and religious assume various responsibilities in the life of the church.[10] My object is more positive than that: how and why is the expanding ministry of the laity an enhancement of the ministry of the ordained priest?

ORDAINED MINISTRY:
EVOLUTION IN RECENT HISTORY

Many good studies of ministry and of ordained minist have appeared in recent years. These trace the establishment and ordering of various ministries in relation to each other in the early years and centuries of the church, the shifts in what people expected from priests as the church spread across centuries and cultures, the developments in the theology of ministry and of orders, and proposals for clarifying various ministerial positions in the church. All these studies underscore both some essentials in the ministry of the church and enormous differences in the roles of ordained priests.

At certain times in history, the priest was such a central public figure that his work extended far beyond the ministry of word and sacrament. At other times, when there were far more priests than were needed for the pastoral care of local communities, some priests were ordained simply to fulfill the commitment of Masses for the deceased. At certain times the authority of the clergy extended to many areas of people's lives; at other times, the clergy were almost completely subject to the authority of lay princes. It is neither my purpose nor my competence to review that history. I do want to note, however, a few developments in the more recent life of the church in the United States that affect our understanding of the life and ministry of the priest in relation to the laity.

As the combination of immigration and high birth rates led to the geometric expansion of the church in the United States from the late nineteenth century to the mid-twentieth century, and while Catholics for the most part remained in a minority status, the life of the church and the authority of the priest were extensive. The church and priest provided an assurance of order, a way of looking at the world and acting in the world, that helped people make sense of their lives. The teaching of the church through the priest especially offered a picture of the universe — of this life in relation to the beginnings and end of life — in which we could all find a place, and an honored place, as a member of the communion of saints.

This view of the universe found expression in the art and architecture of the church, as well as in the baptismal naming of each new Catholic. The sacramental structure of every life, from birth, through marriage, to death was then assured. This order of the world was described in theology, expressed in forms of church life and piety, and organized in clear rules of moral behavior. But this pattern of piety was also "fleshed out" in a broad range of church community aids to human development. Schools, works and institutions of charity, and networks of support all made the church a way of life. In this setting the ordained priest was a central guide and support for life. To be sure, the priest exercised the ministry of word and sacrament, but his work was far broader than the strictly sacerdotal. His "profession," if you will, was not so much priesthood as church, i.e., priests were assigned to any activity that built up the local church.

In a revisionist history, we can regard this as a kind of usurpation by the priest of responsibilities that belonged to the whole church, and, in the long run, we would have done better to engage more of the laity in these works of leadership. Nonetheless, that critique could be anachronistic and it may be that priests, and I should quickly add sisters, took on these responsibilities so that people could be free for the arduous tasks of family and work. It may also be true, as one theologian has suggested, that we have overloaded the priest with the works of administration that are more properly episcopal, and those of service that are more properly diaconal, with the result that the properly presbyteral ministry of word and sacrament received inadequate attention and Christ's faithful did not adequately share in these other ministries.[11]

Priesthood and Professions
It may also be useful to remember that these developments were occurring at a time when "professions" were developing: the establishment of specialists in any number of disciplines, who could authoritatively assume responsibility for areas of knowledge and practice in society. Ordained priesthood was becoming one of the professions. The priest was the one learned in doctrine, moral teaching, and worship; the people were the "clients" who could count on the priest for proper administration of these matters.

There were positive aspects to this, such as the improvement of the criteria for admission to orders and of the education of priests. In the late 1950s, a prominent Jesuit was heard to say disparagingly of seminaries that they were the equivalent of "theological barber schools" preparing men to carry out simple functions with little intellectual or spiritual development. More recently, the academic standards of these schools have been improved, they have secured certification by accrediting associations, the granting of academic and ministerial degrees has become standard, and more attention has been paid to pastoral ministry formation. Nonetheless, priesthood is a profession only by analogy. And the laity are not clients to be treated only in terms of their "needs"; they are members of Christ's priesthood who together carry on the work of the reign of God.

As we come to the end of the twentieth century in the United States, theological developments regarding church and ministry, and cultural developments regarding both American Catholics and the place of professionals in our lives, converge to call for and substantiate new patterns of relationship between clergy and laity. Theological and ministerial trends in the church stress the sharing of all the baptized in the priesthood of Jesus, and cultural trends fight against the dangers of professionalism by stressing the individual's and the community's right to retain responsibility for their own lives: their education, their health, their welfare. These theological and cultural trends call for: respect for the people's responsibility for their own individual lives and their communities, trimming back of the authority and work of "professionals" so as to respect the contributions "lay persons" can make, a style of service by "professionals" that will encourage people to share responsibility for their lives and communities.

Some have chosen to call this style of leadership "servant leadership," a term that has its roots in the Last Supper, when Jesus demonstrated the quality of Christian leadership with the symbol of washing the feet of the Apostles. This shift is not a political shift, a strategy of adapting to people's demands for participation. It is a *theological shift*, a way of realizing and respecting the fact that the Spirit works throughout the church, that the work of Christ requires engagement of the full Body of Christ.

Furthermore, we approach the question of the relationship between clergy and laity, not from the frantic framework of a shortage of ordained priests, but from the confident context of God's providing throughout the church all that the church needs in wisdom and grace for its community and mission. We approach the question with no disparagement of past patterns, but with a wonderful sense of the confluence of factors in church and culture that promote new patterns of shared responsibility for the building up of the church. In this context, the ministries of the church will have much to learn from the skills of collaboration developed in business, education, and other arenas of life. Leaders in these realms of life should have much to learn from the church community about the deeper communion of life we all share and the sacred quality of all persons.

Priests, Lay People, and Ministry
If the past was shaped by the convergence of theology, the social experience of U.S. Catholics, and cultural development of professions, and if the present likewise benefits from convergence of theological, social, and cultural factors, a key objective of the present situation is to achieve a balance between recognizing what laity and clergy have in common and how they are distinct. I would like to make a few remarks about this balance.

As I have mentioned, in a time when the theological, social, and educational gap between laity and clergy has been narrowed, we can become preoccupied with the danger of overlaicizing the clergy and overclericalizing the laity. And both dangers exist. Nonetheless, I am convinced that one of our problems is that we still do not take seriously enough how much the clergy share the conditions of life and ministry of all the baptized. This can happen when we try to speak about the laity as employers or employees, as consumers or citizens, as active and passive participants in culture, as if priest or religious did not share these roles.

Thus, we can talk about programs to help lay people relate their faith and work, as if this is not almost as great a challenge for clergy, or preach about the demands of community and citizenship as if priests were exempt from these demands.[12] The council's *Dogmatic Constitution on the Church* and the code of canon law make clear in their organization that we are all first and foremost baptized Christians, sharing what that means in terms of discipleship and apostolate.[13] The more we recognize our common call and how difficult it is for all of us to be faithful to that call, the more we will avoid false distinctions, the kinds of distinctions that can lead to clericalism. Clericalism can be promoted by clergy or laity to the extent that claims of special entitlement, of exaggerated competence, or of special exemptions from certain obligations are attached to the clerical status.

It can happen when laity abdicate their responsibility for their own conscience or relegate to the clergy care for the least among us. We would do well often in speaking and writing about discipleship and apostolate to avoid the term "laity" altogether and to speak of the people of God or Christ's faithful,[14] in imitation of council and code, for what we are addressing are the conditions and requirements of discipleship affecting all members of the church. This became evident in the U.S. bishops' recent work on the moral dimensions of economic life, for we could not speak about the obligations of employers without acknowledging and addressing our own obligations as employers.

To ensure that we speak of the opportunities and obligations common to all Christ's faithful is not to underestimate the distinct role of the ordained or even the teaching that this distinction is one of kind, not degree. In fact, as I had occasion to stress in my remarks to the Synod of Bishops in 1987, to note that the distinction is one of kind is to state that it is not one of degree; the clergy are not less or more baptized than the laity, not inevitably less or more holy, not less or more bound by the common demands of discipleship.[15] We are all graced and obligated by the demands of discipleship; we are all equal before the Lord, but those ordained have a specific charism for the good of the church whose distinctiveness is undoubtedly clarified and strengthened the less it is misplaced. The clearer we are about what all the members of the church have in common, the entitlements and obligations consequent upon Christian initiation for all of us, the clearer we will be about the specific role and ultimate goals of ordained ministry.[16]

To misplace the distinction between all the faithful and the ordained, either by arrogating too much to the ordained or by exempting the ordained too much from the obligations of all the faithful, is to leave the relationship open to ideology, fads, or self-interest. It can also lead to exclusions of lay people from the very many ministries of the church that do not require ordination.

Just as we can be so preoccupied with the distinctions between laity and clergy so we can be overly defensive about the clericalization of the laity. In recent years, a growing number of lay people have committed themselves to the formal ministry of the church in parishes and diocesan offices, on campuses and in prisons, and in almost all the settings of church ministry. They are not members of religious orders and have not received the sacrament of holy orders.

Nonetheless, a kind of "order" of ministry is emerging. In fact, Pope John Paul II has expressed concern that a kind of parallel structure to that of holy orders may be emerging.[17] It appears in the term "lay ministry," which has come to refer primarily to those who work within the structure of the church to help the whole church further its communion and mission. This is distinct from the laity who exercise a form of "ministry" in their families, work places, and local communities. It is in regard to those in "lay ministry" that cautions are voiced regarding "clericalization of the laity."

It was to this issue that I addressed some comments in my presentation to the Synod of Bishops, comments which, I fear, were misunderstood. At that time, I proposed that the term "lay minister" might be an oxymoron, an internal contradiction. For, while we all can and must minister to one another and there are innumerable ministries that require no further authentication than our baptism (see Gal. 3:23–29), for someone to give her or his life to *be* a minister is, in some respects, to be separated from among all of Christ's faithful for service to the community of Christ's faithful.[18]

My purpose in suggesting this is not in any way to diminish or discourage the incredible expansion of what we call "lay ministry," the commitment of lay people to formal ministries in the church community. On the contrary, my concern is to protect both these dedicated people and the ministerial work of the church. At present a kind of "free-lance" ministry has developed: women and men obtain formation for ministry in a seminary or other program so that they can make a fruitful and long-term commitment to the ministry of the church. They then seek to be hired for a position in a parish or other church institution. In this process, they are subject to the vicissitudes of changing pastors and administrators.

At the same time, pastoral leaders of the church have not participated in formulating an appropriate formation and certification process to ensure that these new ministers are well prepared for ministerial responsibility. In such a situation, both dioceses and lay ministers risk the dangers inherent in the absence of mutual commitment. The diocese could "use" these ministers as long as it is convenient without affording them protections appropriate to one who is committed to church ministry. On the other hand, the lay minister could expect the entitlements of ministry without making the commensurate commitments necessary for authentic and faithful ministry.

To ensure that we provide for these persons adequate formation and conditions for exercising ministry, the bishops must take a more active role. Some form of mutual or reciprocal commitment on the part of the bishops and these ministers seems called for to protect these persons who are committing themselves to either a lifetime, or at least an extended tenure, as minister, and to protect the ministry of the church community entrusted to these persons. To some extent, of course this involves "clericalization," if by that we mean recognition of a formal status to act in the name of the church and for the sake of enabling the church community to fulfill its mission, with all the safeguards and assurances this requires.

Negative reactions to this may derive from attaching to the word "clergy" the excesses of clerical*ism*, though I do not think we have suffered too greatly in this country from either clericalism or anti-clericalism. On the other hand, failure to acknowledge that in some way those lay people have become church *ministers*, have been "set aside," can back the church into the kind of parallel "order" Pope John Paul II warns against. Furthermore, life as a minister that is subject solely to academic certification and employment processes risks making ministry a job rather than a vocation, a vocation that is mediated through the community of the church. In fact, the Holy Father states quite clearly that a person is not a minister simply in performing a task, but through sacramental ordination.[19] It is for this reason that I urged at the Synod of Bishops consideration of more "orders" or offices of ministry as reflective of the vocation and responsibility of these new ministers.[20]

Finally, by not acknowledging adequately the distinction between Catholics committed to lives as church ministers and the majority of God's people who are not so committed, we also risk misdirecting our efforts to promote this special group rather than all of Christ's faithful who are trying to be faithful disciples and apostles. My concern is not to strip lay ministers of their lay status so much as it is to respect what it means to the church and to the individual to give one's life as a minister of the church.

By way of summary, full participation in responsibility for the communion and mission of the church by all of Christ's faithful and the appropriate assignment of specific responsibilities within the church will be enhanced to the extent that we fully acknowledge the clergy's share in the opportunities and obligations of all of Christ's faithful; that we are clear about the full incorporation of new ministers into the structures of church ministry; and that we see all of formal church ministry in service to the Body of Christ and its priestly ministry to all the concerns of the human community.[21]

CHRIST'S FAITHFUL EMPOWER THEIR PRIESTS

Now I would like to address my second concern, namely, how do Christ's faithful enable those who are ordained priests to serve the priestly mission of Jesus? What is it that the whole community of the church can provide as context, cooperation, and support for the ministry of the ordained priest? I think there are many ways this happens.

Using All the Gifts of the Spirit

First of all, as I have reiterated from conciliar teaching, all of Christ's faithful fill out the meaning and ministry of the priesthood of Jesus. In biblical and theological terms, the Spirit of God has provided gifts to all the members of the church, different gifts to different members, for the good of the church. In purely human terms, this means that the members of the church possess an enormous variety of talents and great diversity of expertise, and each of us is called to be a good steward of our talents, contributing these to the service of others and the good of the church.

On the one hand, the priestly ministry of Jesus is not fully exercised if these gifts of the Spirit are not exercised for the community and mission of the church, if church leaders do not provide opportunities for the exercise of these gifts and call forth their exercise within the community of the church. On the other hand, each of us is a poor steward of our gifts if we do not see these as gifts to be given, talents to be used for the sake of the human community and, in that way, for the full mission of the church.

This does not mean that only within the circle of formal church structures are such gifts used or is such ministry carried out. No, this extends to family, work, and world. It does mean, however, that there is an obligation also to contribute these talents to the formal mission of the church. It also means that the priest should not assume or claim that he has only his own gifts to work with. One lesson to be learned from the process of writing the pastoral letters of the U.S. bishops is that the church spoke most fully, called most fully on all the gifts of the Spirit, when the entire church was called on to contribute to those pastoral letters, each speaking from his or her own area of competence and concern, all ordered to a faithful and pertinent contribution to contemporary issues by the bishops.[22]

The priestly ministry of Jesus needs the contribution of all those who are part of Jesus' priesthood, and the ordained priest needs both to call forth the full ministry of the Body of Christ and find support and cooperation in this sharing of responsibility.[23]

Broadening the Perspective and Scope of Priesthood
A second way in which Christ's faithful contribute to the ministry of the ordained priest is both by broadening the perspective within which that priestly ministry is conducted and by extending the priestly ministry into more areas of life.

First, engaging the members of the church in planning and preparing the ministries of the church, whether this is in the form of parish councils or in liturgy preparation groups, preaching preparation, adult education that involves considerable discussion, or other special planning groups, is to broaden the perspective within which these works are planned and conducted. A certain maturity, a certain breadth of vision, a certain fresh pertinence can be achieved when the diverse experiences and insights are brought to bear on the conduct of church life. Since Catholic priests are male, the inclusion of women brings an essential dimension to pastoral understanding and practice. Since priests are celibate, this also means that Christ's faithful can ensure consideration of the more typical perspectives and experiences of married life when the gospel is interpreted and taught. Family people can help the church to see how all that it does can help or hinder the development of strong family life. But the same broadening of perspective applies to other realms of life as well: for example, work and play, ethnic differences and occupational challenges. It is by including Christ's faithful in the planning and performance of ministry that the full range of human experience is acknowledged and addressed.

Another consequence of drawing on the experience and expertise of all the faithful is that the ordained priest who is expected to help articulate the sacred and moral dimensions of life's complexities may be more emboldened to take on this task. Having the assistance of people who are more familiar with the intricacies of economics or the nuances of marital relationships can help the priest as preacher and teacher to venture into areas from which he might otherwise shrink. Being able to reflect with the other members of the church on the links between faith and the many realms of human life can give the preacher the insight and courage to make preaching pertinent.

Enlisting the members of Christ's faithful to share responsibility for the community and mission of the church also makes it possible to increase the varieties of ministry within the church community and to extend the mission of the gospel into all corners of culture. The many aspects of people's lives that need creativity or healing, and the many ways in which the community needs to "bear one another's burdens," can only be developed if the entire church community shares the responsibility of the priesthood.

Also, we will not avoid the "burnout" of the ordained priests by trying to turn back the clock on the scope of parish ministry and adopting a "What has this to do with me or thee?" approach to various needs among the people. We have a tradition of parish life in this country that makes the parish an appropriate forum for almost any concern, a partner in almost any local community initiative. The priest who tries to protect himself from overextension by denying any parish responsibility for these areas of human need will not be able to do so. It is clear that we cannot maintain this tradition unless we expand the number of people who share this responsibility for the entire parish community.

The involvement of the whole Body of Christ in planning and performing the priestly ministry of Jesus in our time not only ensures that the full range of human experience helps shape that ministry and that it is possible to minister to a wide variety of needs and opportunities in the Christian community, but it also enables the ministry of the church to reach into all corners of culture and society. To the extent that all Christ's faithful recognize the priestly power and obligation they share in Christ, our approaches to government and commerce, to consumption and community will be affected. The possibilities of grace in all human situations can be harvested. But if Christ's faithful do not exercise their baptismal share in Jesus' priestly ministry, ministry could be virtually restricted to those matters of personal and home life, or the ordained could feel obligated to take on positions in business or politics or other "worlds" because they think this is the only way to bring the transforming word of the gospel to bear on these situations. To put this in other terms, if evangelization is to mean more than reaching out to alienated Catholics and is to mean bringing the message of the gospel to all of human affairs, all the members of the Body of Christ must see themselves in the evangelizing ministry of bringing "new meaning" to the culture and the priestly ministry of transforming the society.[24]

Strengthening Presbyteral Ministry

Again and again, I have heard from priests who have shared with parishioners responsibility for the life of the parish that the more people are involved the more they want the priest to be the priest. While in some very rare occasions a kind of competition for influence or control over parish life can arise in parish councils or among those who share the ministry of the parish, the more typical experience is that when people find their views and talents respected, they are more willing to acknowledge their need for the particular leadership and special ministry that the ordained priest contributes to the church community.

But the ordained minister is often burdened with responsibilities that should be carried by others, and this takes time and priority away from his specific ministry of preaching, teaching, and the celebration of the sacraments. The more fully Christ's faithful become involved in sharing the ministry of the church the more the priest is able to focus on his presbyteral ministries. In fact, it may well be that increased involvement of Christ's faithful in the ministry of the church will encourage the community to mediate the Spirit's call to young people to give themselves to a life of ordained ministry.

It also seems to me that the more fully Christ's faithful share in the priestly ministry of the church, the more the priest can be himself, acknowledging his own needs and limitations. For we then avoid distorting expectations that Catholic priests are privately endowed "gurus" on whose personal holiness and revelation depend the ministry of the church. That is not our tradition and teaching. A priest is called, prepared, and expected to be faithful guardian and instrument of the holy, of the gospel and sacrament, and thereby must feel in an especially acute way the demands of discipleship. But he must make no claims of exemplifying in a special way the achievement of holiness. The priest, with his specific status and responsibility, is fellow pilgrim with all of Christ's faithful, constantly trying to grow in discipleship as he exercises his apostolate. Proper sharing by all of Christ's faithful in Christ's priestly ministry allows the priest to admit his own needs for ministering.[25]

Admittedly, the increased involvement of the members of the church in the activities of the church does bring new demands on the time and talents of the ordained. We cannot be naive about this. Consequently, for broadened participation by God's people in the ministry of the church to help the pastors and priests to exercise their proper ministry, it will be important that they be helped with the matters of administration and pastoral (or diaconal) care that now consume their time. It is not helpful, for example, to provide new lay parish ministers for the works of liturgy development, teaching, and preaching, i.e., for those works that are most properly presbyteral, while leaving the ordained priest with no help for the administrative and diaconal works of the community.

We cannot overestimate the importance of freeing priests to be priests, for we cannot overestimate the importance of the ministries of word and sacrament. If Christ's faithful are to realize all that Christ's priesthood means, we must give much greater attention to the quality of our performance of worship in the Eucharist and all the sacraments, as well as to the quality and pertinence of our preaching and teaching in all its forms. Yet, this is not likely to happen unless we are realistic about the work expected from priests. It will not do to urge them to give more attention to the ministries of word and sacrament while increasing their burdens of administration and pastoral care. We will enhance the priestly ministry of the church not only by increasing the participation of the laity but also by organizing this greater participation to ensure that priests can focus on their properly presbyteral ministry.

Increased Responsibility and Support

It is axiomatic that the more people feel a sense of participation and responsibility — what in current jargon is sometimes called a sense of "ownership" — the more they are willing to support that enterprise. Studies have indeed found that people will give more of their time and money to the church the more they feel that their views and talents are respected and called upon. A major issue for the church of the future will be whether we can afford the ministry we need. Will the members of our church community provide enough financial support for the ministers we need, the ministers that will not only serve the community but enable the community members to serve one another? It will be to the extent that the members of the church actively share responsibility for the life of the church that they will provide support for that life.

In some respects, this means recognizing the adult consequences of baptism. Because most Catholics are initiated into the church shortly after birth, the clergy can act as if the rite subjects the baptized to parenting by the ministers of the church. To bring Christ's faithful into full responsibility for their own lives and for the lives of one another is to treat them like adults. Conversely, to the extent that people feel that they are being treated like children (or like clients), they will not assume mature responsibility for supporting the work of the church community.

To share the priestly ministry of Jesus is to assume adult responsibility for ensuring that the community has the resources it needs to fulfill its mandate as a community of disciples.

CONCLUSION:
FULFILLING THE PRIESTLY MINISTRY OF JESUS

Christ's priesthood and the church involve a great paradox. Christ's priesthood is, as described in the Epistle to the Hebrews, unique and completed once and for all in the sacrifice of his life to the Father. On the other hand, as Peter teaches in his epistle, we who are baptized into Christ have become a royal priesthood: we share in the priestly ministry of Jesus, a ministry in which the Spirit through the Body of Christ that is the church transforms all of life so that God's power and glory may be revealed. On the one hand, all share in the priestly ministry of Jesus, but there are distinct vocations, distinct ministries within the community of disciples. One of these we have come to call priest, which is to help the priestly people fulfill their baptismal charism and call. On the other hand, when Christ's faithful fulfill their baptismal charism and call, they enable the ordained priest to fulfill his proper ministry for the church.

The paradoxical nature of these relationships means that we will never work them out without the guidance of the Holy Spirit, deliberately sought when we come together to share the ministry of the church. It also means that we will have to be consistently careful and reflective about our mutual and respective gifts and responsibilities in the church if we are to respect and support each other's ministry. It means that we should establish clear structures, policies, and processes for the sharing of priestly ministry that will honor the beliefs and values we hold as disciples of Jesus. Such structures are required for the sake of justice, justice to all the individual ministers involved and justice to the demands of the gospel and ministry. It further means that we need to acquire the skills of community, the ability to turn our beliefs into daily practice.

9

FROM PATERNALISM TO EMPOWERMENT

James R. Jennings

November 1988 marked a major shift for the Catholic Church in the United States on the subject of empowerment. That month the bishops voted to make the Campaign for Human Development a permanent program of the United States Catholic Conference. For nineteen years, the USCC had maintained an *ad hoc* relationship with the campaign, a program aimed at empowering organized groups of poor and low-income people to participate more fully in decisions that affect their lives. The bishops' vote ended one of the longest temporary arrangements in the history of the conference.

An unresolved question during those years of *ad hoc* status was the appropriateness of the direct involvement of the church as an institution in the empowerment of the poor. The purpose of the following overview is to explore some of the historical factors that contributed to this lack of resolve and those that led ultimately to the resolution.

The two subjects implicit in this essay, power and empowerment, do not find a comfortable reception in the parlance of the general public, especially among Catholics. The aphorism of the nineteenth-century British Catholic Lord Acton, "Power tends to corrupt and absolute power corrupts absolutely," has become part of the conventional wisdom. Even before Acton, the British poet Percy Shelley wrote,

> Power like a desolating pestilence,
> Pollutes whate'er it touches.

To frame this overview, a definition of terms is in order. The conventional definition of power is the ability to act. An additional nuance needs to be added: Power is the ability to decide to take a course of action and then to have the capacity to act upon that decision. The two components — deliberation and action — are essential ingredients of the meaning and exercise of power.

To decide to act without the capacity to act is frustrating, and while it may lead to an exercise of power, it is likely to lead to violence or, more often than not, to apathy, alienation, or disengagement. The capacity to act without a deliberate, rational decision to take a certain course of action can also be chaotic and destructive. Power, then, is the ability to decide to do something and to have the capacity to act upon the decision.

Webster's definition of empowerment also reflects a non-nuanced view of the process. According to the dictionary, to empower is to give power, or to permit. The paternalistic character of this definition is striking. The one who gives power or permits another to act may at a later time decide to retract the gift or the permission. In the following treatment of empowerment, paternalism has no place. To empower others, persons in authority provide the space, the latitude, and the environment for those without power to participate in increasing degrees in the decisions that affect their lives. The gift is not of power or permission to others; it is space for persons to exercise their God-given human capacities.

The following overview of the evolution of the church's engagement with empowerment of the poor begins with a brief survey of the formulation of the church's social teachings beginning with Pope Leo XIII, followed by a review of some of the pressures in the 1960s that reshaped the church's worldview. The concluding section focuses on the U.S. bishops' nineteen-year "experiment" with empowerment.

LEO XIII BREAKS NEW GROUND

The first of the modern social encyclicals, *Rerum Novarum*, issued by Pope Leo XIII in 1891, clearly marked a watershed for the church's involvement in the social order. Pope Pius XI's commemorative encyclical, *Quadragesimo Anno*, in 1931, claimed that Leo's encyclical was "the Magna Carta on which all Christian activities in social matters are ultimately based."[1] In its time, Leo's encyclical raised both hackles and hopes. It was not universally well received, as is evident by Pius XI's frequent references to its critics, including Catholics, who feared it was socialistic or revolutionary.[2] In the United States, pro-union Catholic leaders found it to be a great ally in their drive to gain support for their cause.[3]

It is clear that Leo was aware of the interrelationships in the exercise of power upon the powerless. "On the one hand, " he wrote, "is the group which holds the *power* because it holds the wealth.... On the other side is the needy and *powerless* multitudes..." (emphasis added).[4] In the interest of redressing this imbalance, Leo cited the formation of workers' associations and noted with gratification the formation of large numbers of associations "with workmen alone."[5] "Mixed" associations, composed of workers and employers, were viewed with suspicion among workers on the continent. His acknowledgement of strikes by workers is further evidence of awareness of the need for collective action by otherwise powerless individuals, "isolated and defenseless" workers against the "callousness of employers."[6]

It must be noted, however, in the context of reviewing the evolution of the church's position on empowerment, that Leo's endorsement of worker associations is perhaps the best that can be attributed to him. This is not to denigrate his great contribution to Catholic social thought. To be critical of his views, or their absence, on empowerment is falsely to enjoy the benefits of a century of hindsight. His call for state intervention in the economic life, in an environment dominated by *laissez faire* capitalism, is notable, as is his encouragement of the formation of the associations of workers. These two high points alone are sufficient to earn the encyclical "its place as one of the major social documents of modern times."[7]

Donal Dorr maintains that while Leo had a keen interest in changes in society, the preferred model was "change 'from the top down' rather than 'from the bottom up.' "[8] Leo's worldview was dominated by an organic understanding of society that persisted in the social teachings until the 1960s. In this view, society was seen as an organically united social body, composed of classes, all integrated in a cooperative network. The role of the public authority was to remain above the potential conflicts of the classes, mediate their differences, maintain the status quo, and protect the poor from the exercise of the power of the rich.[9]

Among the factors that shaped the contours of Leo's social thought two are especially relevant for this overview of empowerment. The first is the traditional relationship between the church and the state, which resulted in what has been called "concordat Christianity."[10] The second factor that influenced Leo's social thinking was paternalism. These two factors are captured in a single paragraph of *Rerum Novarum*, First, the role of the state: "It is the duty of the public authority to prevent and punish injury, and to protect each person's possessions." Second, regarding the powerless in the state: "The poor and the helpless have a claim to special consideration...wage-earners who are among the weakest should be specially cared for and protected by the commonwealth."[11]

Here the ambivalence of Leo's worldview is disclosed. First, his political conservatism was evident in his prejudice in favor of the state as provider of redress and the maintainer of social equilibrium.

Second, his biblical radicalism was reflected in his predisposition toward the poor. On this point perhaps his phrase about the poor's "claim to special consideration" contains the notion, in embryo, which some ninety years later was formulated as "the preferential option for the poor."

Leo's insistence on the importance of the state reflects the "concordat-Christianity," noted by Hanson, that embodied a hierarchical view of social systems. Distinct social classes are the norm, and the parties are called to conversion of heart leading to social harmony. This hierarchical style was reinforced by concordats, legal treaties between the church, i.e., the Vatican, and the co-signing head of a nation state. The arrangements guaranteed Catholic privileges (e.g., Catholic status as the exclusive religion in the nation) in return for ecclesiastical political support. Dorr's thesis is that while *Rerum Novarum* set forth a challenge to some features of the economic order, Leo's political realism favored maintaining the political status quo.[12] Otherwise the church might be viewed as encouraging the disruption of the social order. Therefore, for Leo, change "from top down" was the appropriate mode.

The second factor that informed Leo's social thinking was paternalism. Oswald von Nell-Breuning, credited as the principal drafter of Pius XI's encyclical *Quadragesimo Anno*, said that Leo XIII wrote as a "father and lord, in the tone of paternal benevolence."[13] This tone is reflected in *Rerum Novarum*. For example, Leo seemed to be suspicious about the capacity of poor people to control their lives. His description of employers' responsibility in this regard is instructive: "The employer is bound to see...that the worker not be exposed to corrupting influences...nor led away to neglect his home and family or to squander his wages."

He counseled the workers not to do anything that might "outrage an employer" and to avoid "people with artful promises that raise false hopes which usually end in disaster." He reminded the poor that the church has taken measures "to spare them the shame of begging" by providing support systems so that no suffering "was not visited and relieved." He warned workers that the rest from work on Sundays and festivals "is not to be the occasion of spending money and a vicious excess, as many would desire."

He urged that the authority of the law be used to protect workers, to intervene in workplaces and factories where they may be exposed to conditions that endanger their morals such as "the mixing of the sexes or any occasion of evil."[14]

In *Rerum Novarum* he wrote, as a first principle, that humanity must remain as it is. It is impossible to reduce human society to a single level:

There naturally exist innumerable and important differences among mankind; people differ in capability, in diligence, in health, and in strength. And unequal fortune is a necessary result of inequality in conditions. Such inequality is far from being disadvantageous either to individuals or to the community.... Each man [sic], as a rule, chooses the part which peculiarly suits his case.... The pains and hardships of life will have no end on this earth.... To suffer and to endure, therefore, is the lot of humanity.[15]

This compound of a static view of society and a strong sense of paternalism is aptly reflected in the passage where Leo offers the model of Jesus for the poor:

Jesus displays the tenderest charity to the lonely and oppressed. These reflections cannot fail to keep down the pride of those who are well off and to cheer the spirit of the afflicted; to incline the former to generosity, and the latter to tranquil resignation.[16]

With such a worldview it was unlikely that change could come "from the bottom up."

AN ERA OF RISING EXPECTATIONS

According to Joseph Gremillion the "status quo model of society... blemished and bemused" the church's social teachings, from Leo XIII until the 1960s.[17] By the 1960s several major phenomena had occurred that provoked a shift of the church's worldview. For one thing, the era of the concordats had virtually dissolved. While the Vatican in the nineteenth century had extended the number of concordats with nation states, the effective force of those agreements had waned significantly by the mid-1900s. Although many of these treaties had not been revoked, the Vatican's relationships with nation-states has become more independent than in the concordat era.

The appointment of bishops was one of the cornerstones of traditional concordats and a source of potential intimidation for the Vatican.[18] The Vatican Council's Decree on the Bishops' Pastoral Office reflects this concern, and marks a distinct shift on the subject. It claimed for "the competent ecclesiastical authority" exclusive power to appoint bishops, asked civil authorities to waive any provisions in this matter that they enjoyed from existing agreements, and expressed the intention no longer to concede this right in the future.[19]

With the demise of the traditional concordats, the church gained an independence from nation-states not previously enjoyed that has enabled it to speak to social and political issues with greater frequency and candor. The emergence, for example, of human rights on the church's agenda in the 1960s marks this shift.

Perhaps another measure of this phenomenon is the appearance over the last hundred years of papal documents that address social issues. The recent Vatican guidelines for the teaching of the church's social doctrine in the formation of priests features nine such publications.[20] Two documents from the period 1891 to 1931 are cited; an average of one every twenty years. For the period 1961 through 1987 seven documents are cited, an average of one every four years!

Another phenomenon, the diminution of paternalism, was noted by Pope John XXIII in 1963 in his encyclical *Pacem in Terris* in a section called "Signs of the Times." He wrote that the present era was marked by the rising expectation among workers who "bluntly refused to be used at the arbitrary disposition of others.... Women are becoming more conscious of their human dignity and will not tolerate the treatment to which they had been traditionally subjected." "In our day," John XIII summarized, "in many human beings the inferiority complex which endured for hundreds of thousands of years is disappearing." Even more remarkably, he stated that when people become aware of their rights, they have "the duty to claim those rights as marks of their dignity, while others have the obligation to acknowledge those rights."[21] The notion of the empowerment of the poor begins to emerge.

The movement of the church in Latin America in the 1960s is especially notable. Long associated with the ruling oligarchies in the region, the bishops at their 1968 conference in Medellín, Colombia, broke new ground. In the Medellín documents, the notion of the empowerment of the poor begins to emerge with further clarity. Dorr's summary of the bishops' treatment of conscientization is instructive: "People become responsible for injustices by remaining passive, by failing to take courageous and effective action for fear of the sacrifice and personal risk involved in doing so."[22]

As an antidote to passivity, the bishops endorsed "organizations of the popular sectors which are capable of pressing public officials who are often impotent in their social projects without popular support."[23]

It is noteworthy here that the Latin American bishops underscore the need for political action to remedy social disorders. In this regard, they foreshadowed a papal shift from Leo's aversion to address the political order to Pope Paul VI's announcement in *Octogesima Adveniens* that in the present time "the need is felt to pass from economics to politics... the ultimate decisions rest with political power."[24]

By 1979, the Latin American bishops at Puebla, Mexico, according to Dorr's analysis, were able to sustain the key elements they had adopted at Medellín, despite political and ecclesiastical pressures. Their prize achievement was framed in one of the documents in a chapter bearing the controversial title, "A Preferential Option for the Poor," in which they "affirm the need for conversion on the part of the whole Church to a preferential option for the poor, an option aimed at their integral liberation."[25]

It remained for Pope John Paul II to place the empowerment of the poor firmly on the church's agenda. For him the 1971 Roman Synod's call to action on behalf of justice was to be focused upon the "powerless" poor. Less than four months into his papacy, the Holy Father told impoverished Mexican Indian peasants in 1979 that they had the right to be respected and not be deprived "through manipulation and outright theft of the little that they have."[26]

During his first tour of Brazil, again within months of his ascendancy to the papacy, he addressed dwellers in a shantytown near Salvador de Bahia. "You must struggle for life," he said, "do everything to improve the conditions in which you live....Do not say 'It is God who wills it' that you remain in these conditions of poverty....These are contrary to your dignity as human persons." To masses of Filipinos in a waterfront slum in Manila, he said that the Beatitudes tell people in poverty that they can change their conditions if they pool their determination to be the authors of their own progress and development. To impoverished Guatemalan Indians he said, "Organize associations for the defense of your rights and the realization of your own goals."[27]

Perhaps the best summary of the Holy Father's endorsement of the exercise of power by the poor to change social conditions is found in his encyclical *On Social Concern:*

> Those who are weaker...should not adopt a purely passive attitude or one that is destructive of the social fabric. But while claiming their legitimate rights, they should do what they can for the good of all. Positive signs in the contemporary world are the growing awareness of the solidarity of the poor, their efforts to support one another and their public demonstrations on the social scene which, without recourse to violence, present their own needs and rights.

To this endorsement of the actions taken by empowered poor people, the Holy Father calls the church "to take her stand beside the poor, to discern the justice of their requests and to help satisfy them."[28]

A U.S. EXPERIMENT

The U.S. church was not immune from the winds of change that swept society in the 1960s. The nation was beset with social turmoil. While the U.S. economy in the twenty years after World War II succeeded in providing a remarkable standard of living for most of its citizens, the nation suffered from the paradox that millions of Americans were caught in poverty. Urban riots swept across the country, and the public's attention was focused on the social blights of racism, poverty, and minority tension.

Fresh from the exhilarating experience at Vatican II, the U.S. bishops, energized by the spirit of church renewal and the council's call to "read the signs of the times," established in 1969 the Campaign for Human Development, "aimed at eliminating the very causes of poverty." The task force which was assigned responsibility for the campaign's design by the U.S. Catholic Conference relied heavily on the model program that Cardinal John Dearden, archbishop of Detroit, then president of the NCCB/USCC, had put in place in his diocese. His directive to the designers bears repeating: "We do not intend to set up a program in a patronizing or paternalistic way that tells people what they need and provides it for them. We want to know what they need.... They will tell us what they need."[29]

In the resolution that established the campaign, the bishops acknowledged that past efforts of charity by the church have been exemplary, but too often they dealt only with the effects of poverty. Because of the magnitude and complexity of the nation's social problems they felt a new initiative was called for. The resolution read in part: "There is an evident need for funds designated to be used for organized groups of white and minority poor to develop economic strength and political power in their communities."[30]

The following November, in 1970, the bishops, in reaffirming their decision of the prior year, called for an annual collection for the Campaign for Human Development to fund the organizing efforts of people in poor and low-income communities. The resolution states: "In our time the legitimate aspirations of the poor for self-determination cannot be ignored."[31]

A set of criteria for funding was approved that specified grants were to be made to organizations controlled by groups of people from poor, low-income communities with plans to attack causes of their poverty by effecting institutional changes. Projects that provided direct services to the poor or that were controlled by government or church agencies were excluded.

Thus, the bishops launched an experiment in empowerment. For the first time, the Catholic Church in the United States would be an active promoter of the process of empowerment of the poor. The process did not envision that the church would exhort persons in authority to give those in need better opportunities or conditions, either through their benevolence or their good will. The empowerment process intended to enable poor, low-income communities to share in the decision-making processes that affect their lives, and thereby participate more fully in the nation's political and economic life.

The premise upon which the campaign was built was virtually untested at the time. Groups of poor people in the United States, organized in an empowerment mode, were rare. The federal government's War on Poverty, introduced during the 1960s, had a good track record, but the element of empowerment, central to CHD, was absent.

According to John McKnight, professor of urban affairs, Northwestern University, "To the degree that the War on Poverty attempted to provide services [to the poor] in lieu of power or income it failed.... You cannot service somebody to freedom and liberty. In our society these come from income and power, and unless something happens to change the quantum of these two things, poor neighborhoods won't change."[32]

As the campaign grew, community-based organizations of poor and low-income people working to change the conditions that affect their lives also grew in numbers, strength, and effectiveness. Over the ensuing two decades, the campaign has become the nation's largest program devoted exclusively to funding the empowerment of poor people. To support the policy of empowerment, the U.S. bishops have disbursed more than $150 million from the voluntary contributions of Catholic parishioners.

The experience of CHD has not been trouble-free, and this has perhaps contributed to the tentative treatment given to it by the USCC, reflected in its *ad hoc* status for almost twenty years. Over the years, the campaign has been subjected to what Bishop Francis Mugavero of Brooklyn called "nagging right-wing criticism."

In the second year of the campaign, a Catholic municipal judge falsely charged that millions of dollars of CHD funds had gone to or was scheduled to go to organizations that participated in abortion and birth control programs. Periodically the campaign's funding criteria have been criticized for not including such worthy projects as Catholic schools and direct service agencies.

In 1984, a widely circulated anonymous essay charged that the campaign supported "leftist political activists" plotting "to destroy our economic system." One critic labeled the campaign "a program disguised as a bumper sticker."[33] Reminiscent of some Catholic critics' charges of Leo XIII's drift to socialism, a group of Catholic laymen recently charged that "the Campaign for Human Development has been unobtrusively seeking to enhance communitarian socialism in the United States."[34]

The campaign received in 1979 its supreme vote of confidence. That year, during John Paul II's first visit to the United States, he commended the bishops for "their wisdom and compassion in establishing the Campaign for Human Development...aimed at supporting self-help projects...removing the causes and not merely the evil effects of injustice." He thanked American Catholics for their positive support for the program and prayed that "God gives you strength, courage and wisdom to continue to work for justice." Despite this accolade and its source, the campaign continued on its experimental course as an *ad hoc* activity of the NCCB/USCC.

It must be acknowledged that from the very beginning of the campaign the bishops' commitment was not unconditional. While the initial resolution in 1969 called for "A National Catholic Crusade Against Poverty" aimed at eliminating the very causes of poverty, the commitment to raising the funds was not open-ended. The bishops agreed "to commit the Church to raise the sum of $50 million over the next several years." When that amount was reached by 1977, extensive discussion ensued on the floor at the bishops' May meeting in Chicago.

After lengthy debate, a motion to extend the campaign's collection at least five years was not acted upon. A substitute motion limiting the collection to one year was approved. By November, a number of bishops, led by Cardinal Terence Cooke of New York, who argued that the collection was needed more than ever, expressed their concern about the decision that had been made in Chicago. After extended debate, the bishops voted to override the Chicago decision and to continue the CHD collection for an indefinite period of time. The status of the campaign did not come formally before the full body of bishops again until 1985.

In the bishops' November meeting of that year, a recommendation was placed on the agenda calling for a change in the status of the campaign from *ad hoc* to standing. Several questions from the floor were raised about the appropriateness of making the campaign's collection a permanent entity in the Conference in view of the uncertainty among some bishops about CHD's value. After several bishops spoke to the merits of the recommendation, including Bishop James Malone, then president of the NCCB/USCC, it was withdrawn, because of the uncertainty about the depth of the bishops' commitment to the policy of empowerment as incarnated in the campaign.

Subsequently, Malone named an eleven-member bishops' committee, chaired by Bishop Joseph A. Fiorenza of Galveston-Houston, to evaluate the experience of the campaign and assess its future. The first action of the Fiorenza committee was to mail a questionnaire to the bishops to determine their individual views about the campaign. The overwhelming majority of the respondents expressed their strong endorsement of the practice of funding organizing efforts of poor, low-income groups to root out institutional causes of poverty. One of the key questions included a summary of CHD's funding criteria and asked: "In your opinion, are the Campaign for Human Development's goals appropriate to the Church's mission to the poor?" Of the respondents, 172 bishops answered in the affirmative; one answered in the negative!

It is important to recall that coincident with the assessment of CHD, the bishops had been reviewing, periodically since 1984, a series of drafts of a projected pastoral letter that addressed conditions in the U.S. political economy, especially as they affected the poor. By November 1986, the bishops adopted the final version of the pastoral, *Economic Justice for All.*[35]

It is clear in the letter that the subject of empowerment takes a high position. For example, the pastoral maintains that "the principle of participation leads us to the conviction that the most appropriate and fundamental solutions to poverty will be those that enable people to take control of their lives." Supplementing the participation principle, the bishops endorse a policy of empowerment: "We believe an effective way to attack poverty is through programs...oriented toward empowering the poor....Poor people must be empowered to take charge of their lives." Toward the concluding section of the pastoral the bishops reaffirm the good judgment and vision of their brother bishops who established CHD: "Our experience with the Campaign for Human Development confirms our judgment about the validity of self-help and empowerment of the poor."[36]

Two years after the passage of the pastoral, Fiorenza presented to the full body of bishops his committee's report of the two-year study of the campaign. Based on the findings of the study, the report recommended that the Conference no longer maintain the *ad hoc* status of the campaign. In his presentation he said, "With the past nineteen years behind us, the successful experience of the Campaign is a matter of record. I believe that record of accomplishments enabled us to overwhelmingly support our landmark pastoral letter, *Economic Justice for All.*" In adding his conviction that "the Campaign is a truly remarkable achievement in the life of the Catholic Church in this country," he said he hoped his fellow bishops concurred. They did; they voted overwhelmingly to accept the recommendation. The experimental period ended; a new chapter for empowerment began.

SUMMARY REMARKS

Over the last one hundred years, the church's efforts to address human concerns have evolved along a twisting trail from paternalism to the poor to the empowerment of the poor. Leo's response, as well as those of his immediate papal successors, was shaped by a culturally imbedded paternalistic/hierarchical worldview. In addition the papacy was beset by ambivalence. On the one hand the Vatican had become strongly allied with the ruling powers in many of the nation–states. On the other hand it was drawn by the gospel imperative to respond to the needs of poor people.

A historic breakthrough occurred with the papacy of John XXIII, who acknowledged that workers, women, and victims of colonialism refuse to be treated in the paternal patterns imposed upon them that disregarded their human rights. He further asserted that they have the duty to claim those rights! Clearly the church had begun to view its role in society in a way fundamentally different from Leo's day.

John Paul II added a new dimension to the church's message. No longer was it limited to an exhortation exclusively directed to those in authority to undergo a change of heart and then to reform inequities in society. He commended the movement of solidarity *among* the poor and urged others to join in solidarity *with* the poor when they exercise their power to change the conditions that affect their lives.

Finally, the U.S. bishops, in a style characteristic of American pragmatism, expanded the church's message to include not only exhorting the powerful to be charitable to those in need. The U.S. church instituted a program to empower the powerless — a shift from preaching about power to enabling groups of people to exercise power. These groups with their grievances and their plans have successfully confronted city officials, state and federal authorities, private financial institutions, corporate executives, health providers, administrators of public education — the list is virtually endless — in their efforts to participate more fully in the decision-making processes that affect their lives. In this way they experience the human development implicit in the campaign's title: a human development that enables individuals to gain a new sense of self-respect and personal dignity.

In the years ahead, the church will face many new challenges in its perennial mission to bring glad tidings to the poor. As it shapes appropriate responses to the changing conditions, the church's past hundred-year experience of moving from paternalism to empowerment will serve as a valuable lesson and a rich legacy.

10

LITURGY AND EMPOWERMENT: THE RESTORATION OF THE LITURGICAL ASSEMBLY

Bob Hurd

In what follows I wish to explore the liturgy as a political phenomenon and, specifically, as a site of empowerment. In the language
of Vatican II's reforms, this empowerment goes by the name of the
restoration of the liturgical assembly.[1] "Assembly" is a relatively new
word in the vocabulary of Roman Catholics, and for good reason.
The paradox we have faced in twenty-five or so years of trying to
implement the liturgical reforms is that these reforms presume a political unit, the assembly, which has not existed in the church's life
for centuries. A quite different organization of people at worship —
the differentiated priest/congregation pair — has predominated since
the Middle Ages.

Liturgical reform turns out to be much more complex than it first
seemed. If we imagine the liturgy as a picture, then reform initially
seemed a matter of changing and reorganizing some of the figures in
this picture: turning the altar around, putting the language into the
vernacular, clarifying the component parts of the liturgy, restoring a
number of liturgical ministries, recovering some ancient customs, reorganizing the lectionary cycle, and so forth. But the significance of
the restoration of the assembly lies in the fact that the very frame
of the picture, the very horizon within which these particulars of the
reformed liturgy are implemented, is also to be transformed. Consequently, full implementation is not just a matter of retrieving some
customs once practiced in the early liturgy, but of reclaiming the political and ecclesial self-understanding that these customs signified
for the ancient worshiping community. Not only the particulars, we
might say, but also the politics of the liturgy were changed by the
reforms of Vatican II.

The crux of the matter is that unless both aspects are addressed,
the reformed liturgy will not work. The presider's role, as described
in the *General Instruction of the Roman Missal*, simply cannot be

fulfilled if the community is not really gathered and does not really act as an assembly. In practice, the presider is all too often forced to compensate for the "missing assembly," that is, for the congregation that is not yet an assembly. The result is an unexpected and ironical one. The new liturgy was supposed to restore the participation of the people and de-center the priest as the sole celebrant. But the combination of the "missing assembly" with the fact that the priest now faces the people and speaks directly to them actually places undue emphasis upon the presider. The presider's role becomes distorted into something like that of a talk-show host whose ability to inspire and entertain either makes or breaks the liturgy. Some enjoy playing this role, others find it a demoralizing burden. But it is not the role that the *General Instruction* envisions for the presider.

A similar pattern has emerged with regard to other leadership roles such as that of the liturgical musician. In our postconciliar time, liturgical music has gone through a veritable death and resurrection. It is a commonplace that good music means good liturgy. If the presider experiences reprieves from the spotlight during the liturgy, this is because the music group shares the burden of "entertaining the troops." If the music inspires and moves, then the liturgy is considered a success, even when the presider's style is mediocre. Again, some musicians enjoy this role, others find it a hardship. Granted that music at liturgy should always be inspiring and beautiful, the role of the liturgical musician is not to provide aesthetically pleasing experiences to an audience.

Needless to say, if those with leadership roles (presiders, musicians, readers, and so forth) exercise them in the distorted ways described above, the rest of the community will exercise its role in a correspondingly distorted fashion. Vatican II's profound call for the active participation of the people tends to be realized in the form of an audience that is attentive rather than inattentive, that dutifully makes token verbal responses instead of remaining silent. Under such conditions a good experience of parish liturgy is one in which the congregation/audience feels moved or nourished by what is offered to it by those who "do" the liturgy (i.e., the presider, readers, musicians, etc.). But this is not the role the reforms envision for the people of God. Unlike the talk show or the concert hall, there is no audience, not even a very intelligent and attentive one, in the reformed liturgy.

All of this indicates that while the particulars of reform have been implemented fairly quickly, its political meaning and implications are far from being realized. Much of our effort at reform has been undercut and trivialized because unwittingly we have been pouring new wine into old wineskins. We have been fitting the new particulars of the reforms into the political framework of the older liturgy. To put it succinctly, most parish liturgies continue to be *priest-centered liturgies with congregations* instead of *assembly-centered liturgies with presiders*. What is the difference? What exactly is meant by the restoration of the liturgical assembly? Finally, what is the connection between this restoration and the politics of empowerment?

THE POLITICS OF LITURGY

Coming to grips with these questions requires a willingness to view the liturgy as a political reality, as an event in which power relations are displayed. I suspect that for most people this goes against the grain. Power is one of those heavily charged words — like "self" — that are open to vicious as well as virtuous interpretations. It almost immediately suggests vices such as arrogance, domination, coercion, and even violence. Power corrupts, absolute power corrupts absolutely. Power is one of the temptations Jesus overcomes in the wilderness. God is praised for casting the powerful from their thrones and raising up the lowly. One gets the idea that power is not a particularly good thing to have. But implicit in this negative assessment of power is the affirmation of power, albeit along different lines. For the lowly who are raised up are not only freed *from* power, they are freed *into* power. Freed from the oppressor, they are empowered to exercise an agency and autonomy previously denied them: "that we might serve you without fear, in holiness and righteousness all the days of our lives," as the Canticle of Zechariah says. One is thus brought round to the elemental notion of power as a perfection, as proper to human persons and communities. To have or realize power is to actualize our capacities, not only as human beings but also as graced partners of the God who liberates.

It is a great mistake, therefore, to think or even wish that liturgy, the font and summit of our partnership with the God who liberates, could somehow be a politically neutral phenomenon. It is not and never has been. In any collective human endeavor power relations are lived out. In any ritual in which a given culture explicitly celebrates its self-understanding, a social paradigm of power is displayed, contemplated, and affirmed. When people gather for worship, whatever their particular theology, they assume roles and postures vis-à-vis each other and God. These modes of relating bespeak a certain distribution of power and project an ideal of collective life, a sort of *micro-polis*.

But in addition to this anthropological constant, the theme of power lies at the very heart of the gospel itself, and so has a christological root as well. Coming to terms with power and power relations in communal life is intrinsic to the celebration of the paschal mystery. How could it be otherwise? At liturgy we gather in the name and stand in the person of Christ Jesus. This is the Jesus who "does the will of the Father" freely rather than slavishly and who thus stands in a specific type of power relation to the Most High. If we take seriously the solidarity of the Father-Mother with the Crucified, then a specific type of power relation to creation, finitude, and human history is displayed: God, whom we so readily call the "All-powerful" and "Almighty" One throughout the liturgy, is paradoxically the Most Lowly and Vulnerable One. Like Rachel of old, God is the parent who suffers when her child suffers and whose power consists precisely in complete identification with suffering without repression or aloofness or false consciousness. Jesus himself comes to serve, not to be served. Those who would call him Lord must do the same. For those baptized in Christ there is no Jew or Greek, slave or free, male or female. Social structures that discriminate against persons on the basis of race, class, or gender are incompatible with acceptance of Christ and his message. The salvation that comes to us in Christ is a liberation from the tyranny of principalities and powers so that we may know the freedom of the children of God. We cannot be in right relation to God whom we do not see if we are not in right relation to the neighbor whom we do see. These are but a few random examples of what might be called "the politics of the paschal mystery." How we will be with each other and with God — these socio-political questions are *simply* the fundamental religious issues of the gospel. Understanding and applying the politics of the paschal mystery must in principle ever remain an unfinished task, but that there is such a politics is undeniable. Gandhi once said that every truly religious act is a political act. We may add that no truly Christian liturgy can be apolitical.

Power as an anthropological concern, power as a christological concern — these, then, are the two intertwining roots of the liturgy as a political reality. That they are intertwining, that they have an ongoing dialectical relationship, should be noted. The gospel is not a cultureless content that only subsequently interacts with this or that culture. It emerges within a culture and is passed on in varying cultural contexts. Consequently, any given community always sees and appropriates the politics of the paschal mystery through the lens of its own cultural presuppositions. This simultaneous unity and distinction of gospel and culture is inescapable: our own graced history and life experience, culturally situated and determined, is the hermeneutical key we bring to the paschal mystery. And conversely, this paschal mystery throws light back upon our own experiences and issues.

This is true not only for us but for those who first experienced the Christ-event. The process whereby christological titles — "Messiah," for example — came to be applied to Jesus displays this dialectic of previous religious and political categories of power with what is radically new in the revelation of God's power in Jesus. The early church interpreted the power and authority of Jesus according to the diverse religious and political symbolisms of its time. But this horizon of understanding was held in tension with the uniqueness of Jesus. Even while trying to apply titles such as "Messiah" to Jesus, Scripture (and so, too, the early church) preserves his ambivalence toward them. To some extent they give access to the mystery of Christ but they can also obscure and mislead if they are not critically adjusted in light of the Christ-event itself. Jesus is Messiah, but not without a radical rethinking and transformation of this inherited category.

A similar dialectic of culture and gospel is at work in the history of the liturgy. The politics of the liturgy at any given time is never just the politics of the gospel. Rather, the paradigm of power projected in the liturgy in any historical period always reflects a culture's specific appropriation of the politics of the paschal mystery in light of its own self-understanding. This appropriation may not only benefit from but also critique and transform the very cultural models it draws upon. On the other hand it may reduce the gospel to something that uncritically serves and legitimizes them. Clearly, then, the issue is not whether there is an interfacing between gospel and culture in liturgy — there always is — but whether this interfacing is self-possessed and critical. And of course we must take into account our limitations as historical beings: the best that one age or even one generation can accomplish in the way of critical attunement between gospel and cultural paradigms may not be good enough for a succeeding age. As Vatican II teaches, one must be guided not only by past decisions and pronouncements but also by the "signs of the times." Critical revision is thus an ongoing theological and pastoral task of the church. On a grand scale, Vatican II provides us with the most recent instance of critical adjustment.

HISTORICAL PATTERNS

Examples of the precarious and yet inescapable interplay between cultural paradigms of power and the politics of the paschal mystery abound in the history of the church and its liturgy. A review of this history, at least in broad outline, will serve to clarify the political significance of the present shift from the priest-centered liturgy to the assembly-centered liturgy. But the story is a complicated one. In some periods, the worship of the church distances itself from reigning cultural paradigms, in others it adopts and absorbs them.

In the New Testament period, for example, there was a conscious, deliberate move away from patterns of cult and priesthood traditional to some forms of Judaism as well as to the religions of Rome and Greece. The early Christians had no priesthood in the sense of a special group set apart from the rest of the community to perform religious acts on their behalf. The term "priest" was reserved for Christ alone and "priestliness" attached to the whole people of God as the Body of Christ. Though a variety of leadership roles emerged within worship (and church life), liturgy was the work of the whole gathered people rather than the special preserve of a priestly caste. In other words, the early church effected a significant redistribution of power and social agency in the liturgical sphere: the agency of the worship leader was an expression and function of the agency of the whole people. The foundational unit of liturgical action was not the polarized *priest/congregation* pair, but the single reality of the *assembly* that included the presider, other leading ministers, and all present. It was this one assembly, the local church — manifesting itself in a diversity of roles and symbolizing the entire church — that performed the liturgy. The locus of the holy was no longer a special caste or special places such as temples and shrines or even the cosmos, but the people of God themselves.[2]

In the patristic and medieval periods, however, this early desacralization and declericalization of worship gradually gave way to a reassertion of the older categories. Old Testament patterns of priesthood, transcended in the early church, were now increasingly invoked to explain episcopal and presbyterial ministry. As Christian worship moved from households to large public buildings or basilicas, the distinctly Christian notion of the gathered people themselves as the *ecclesia* began to be eclipsed by the idea of the church building as a sacred site or temple. At an earlier period Minucius Felix (*fl.* 218–35) had boasted, "We have no shrines and altars."[3] But this boast was rendered inaccurate by the gradual transformation of the early church's table of fellowship into an altar of sacrifice.[4] We can detect the shifting distribution of liturgical power and agency in St. John Chrysostom's description of the eucharistic prayer:

> The eucharistic prayer is common; the priest does not give thanks alone, but the people with him, for he begins it only after having received the accord of the faithful.... If I say that, it is so that we learn that we are all a single body. Therefore let us not rely on the priests for everything, but let us, too, care for the Church.[5]

On the one hand, Chrysostom reaffirms the early church's assembly-centered model of worship. That he has to make a point of it, however, suggests that change is in the wind. He has to remind his people of their status as co-agents of the liturgy as though this self-awareness were beginning to slip away from them.

Along with the resurgence of these older religious models of power, the church also received the impress of Roman imperial culture. The religious and political world of Jesus envisioned the power of God by analogy with human kingship. Within this framework, the religious art that emerged in the Middle Ages shows how the risen Lord's "lordship" came to be specified by Roman imperial power. Christ in glory became a thinly veiled Roman imperial judge of the universe. And those who stood *in persona Christi* at liturgy inherited these same imperial characteristics. When the Catholic Church became the state religion under Constantine, the honors, privileges, and powers accorded to church authorities — bishops in particular — mirrored those given to Roman secular authorities such as judges. It is quite amazing just how much of the traditional liturgical symbolism of the bishop's power and authority is an essentially *secular* import from the court ceremonial of Roman times. Theodor Klauser provides the details of this cultural overlay:

> Since for the most part the bishops were made equal to the highest dignitaries in the land, the *illustres*, they received in addition a number of insignia such as the *lorum* (the *pallium*), the *mappula* (a ceremonial napkin), the *campagi* (a special kind of footwear), the *camalaucum* (a distinctive headgear), and probably also the golden ring. In the same way, they held certain privileges such as the right to a throne whose height and design were carefully prescribed, the right to be accompanied by lights and incense, and the privilege of being greeted with a kiss of the hand.[6]

If I may anticipate a little, it is not difficult to see the critical issues for contemporary worship that are posed by such a transformation. For the present-day worshiper need not be explicitly aware of all these historical details to be affected by them. To this day many of our churches still look more like palaces, courts, and even courtrooms than places where people gather to share a meal. The entrance of the presider, particularly if that presider is a bishop, more often than not has the feel of royalty about it, especially when accompanied by that triumphal type of music that has become customary on such occasions. Behind these apparently superficial and harmless nuances there lies the deeper question of what sort of social paradigm of power is set up between the gathered people and their leaders by such imagery. Is the presider's chair a throne, a seat of judgment? Is the presider a kind of spiritual prince, a higher being whose actions determine the spiritual histories of his subjects, precisely because he has powers that they lack? If so, what will the role and status of those gathered before this royal court be? Does such imagery invite and support their collaboration in the liturgical action that is to take place?

Or does it, at least subliminally, reinforce a social paradigm in which they are reduced to an audience? But more on this later.

As the Roman *imperium* gave way to the feudal order of the Middle Ages, the dichotomy between those few who had social agency and the masses of people who did not heightened. The primary social agent in the medieval world was the feudal lord. His serfs were his patients, his dependents. In this same world the primary agent of social-ecclesial action — including liturgical action — was the lord bishop (assisted by his clergy), and the laity were his patients, his dependents. It was in this atmosphere that the liturgy developed into an exclusively clerical action. As the ordained representative of the bishop, the priest was the dispenser of grace to the laity. He had official powers and knowledge that ordinary folk did not have.

The laity for their part were understood to have neither competence nor authority in matters sacramental and liturgical. Everything that had formerly evinced their co-responsibility for the liturgy — "the work of the people" — disappeared from worship. In the liturgy of the early church there had been an ongoing dialogue of prayer between the presider and the gathered people. During the Middle Ages, however, ordinary worshipers came to be voiceless while the priest and his assistants said all prayers on their behalf. The ancient prayer of the faithful, a prayer of the whole gathered people, was eliminated in the interest of reducing the time the liturgy took. The presentation of the gifts, in which the people brought forward the bread and wine for the Eucharist as well as gifts for the poor and for the church, fell out of use. The eucharistic prayer, originally a dialogue between the people and the presider, came to be said by the priest alone with significant portions in silence.

Whereas the earliest worshipers had been called *circumstantes* because they *stood around* the eucharistic table with their presider, the lay worshipers of the Middle Ages were pushed farther and farther away from the table. Architecturally speaking, a division was introduced between the space around the table, which became the *sanctuary*, and the space where the laity congregated — the *nave*. In our own modern churches the communion rail (visible or perhaps now removed but invisibly still very much in place) is a relic of this medieval distinction between the inner sanctum reserved for the priest alone and the outer precincts reserved for the laity. Music played a role in this distancing of the gathered people from their presider and the liturgical action, as Robert Cabié recounts:

> Chanting became an increasingly complex matter and therefore the prerogative of canons, trained bodies of singers, and cantors, as the "choir" replaced the congregation. This element of substitution

was aggravated in cathedrals and abbeys by the installation of rood-screens, which, from the fourteenth century on, often became more or less opaque partitions between the faithful and the few individuals who were the sole agents in the Eucharistic celebration. All these factors turned the laity into onlookers so passive that the liturgical books no longer even mentioned their presence.[7]

Ordinary worshipers, no longer able to see the eucharistic action or take any real part in the ritual, gave themselves to private devotions or listened to the trained choir during the Mass.

In the early church those who gathered to make Eucharist naturally partook of the eucharistic bread and wine. But in the Middle Ages matters reached the point where the faithful were discouraged from receiving communion at all. A number of factors were at work here: people were intimidated by the requirement that they go to confession before receiving; married people were required to refrain from sexual relations as a preparation for communion. Often, when people did approach the table to receive, they were urged to make an act of spiritual communion instead of actually receiving the Eucharist. Finally, some of the liturgical theology of the time suggested that since the priest received communion on behalf of the whole people, it was not necessary for them to receive.[8] The priest-centered liturgy, in which the priest became the sole performer of the liturgical action, displaced the more ancient pattern of the assembly-centered liturgy, in which the Eucharist was understood to be a collective action of the gathered people under the leadership of their presider. The historical decline and finally disappearance of the whole assembled people as the single, unified *agent* of the liturgy reveals a tendency well worth noting. Initially, leadership roles in the liturgy evoked and facilitated an action belonging to the whole community. But with time and the influence of the feudal paradigm of power these roles came to take the place of the community's action. In consequence, while the gathered people might be *patients* of liturgical action they could not be *agents* of it.

These liturgical developments matched and expressed concurrent trends in ecclesiology, ministry, and christology. In the ecclesiological sphere, the one people of God had been, in effect, split into two camps — the *church agent* (the clergy) and the *church patient* (the laity) — a dualism that has only begun to be dismantled with Vatican II. The problem with such an ecclesiology, which represented a departure from the self-understanding of the early church, may be put as follows. The church is the historical extension of Christ's agency as sanctifier and liberator. If I am without agency, if I am merely a passive object of someone else's agency, then I am not really "church."

I am an *object*, perhaps, of the church — but I am not the *subject* of the church.

This dichotomization also entailed a departure from the early church's understanding of ministry. The ancient pattern, remnants of which survived up to the twelfth century, was as follows: the one who presided at liturgy was the one who actually stood in the role of empowerer to the local community.

The presider's "powers" evoked and expressed the power of the local assembly as church and made no sense outside of this relationship. In other words, the priest's power was not only a gift *for* the people of God — it was at the same time a gift expressing the power *of* the people as church. Ministry was not only for the local community but from it.[9] This was so much the case that an ordained person who had no pastoral charge, who did not preside over the upbuilding of a particular church community, could be returned to the lay state. Hervé-Marie Legrand plots the shift from this ancient pattern to the one we are all familiar with today, and quotes Yves Congar by way of summary: "While for the ancients it is existence in the body of the Church which makes it possible to perform the sacraments, after the twelfth century there emerged a theology of self-contained powers: if one personally possesses them, one can posit the sacraments."[10] No wonder that in the medieval era the primary symbol of the church was the cleric, for it was the cleric who exercised agency in liturgical and sacramental matters. This agency no longer reflected the agency of the whole people as church, but the agency of a class differentiated from the people.

Not surprisingly, this is also the era in which Christ as salvific agent is understood as a mostly divine figure who comes from above to perform mediating actions for those far below him. Though medieval orthodoxy gives a fairly nuanced bow to the humanity of Christ, in the end this humanity is all but absorbed into his divinity, as the various treatises on the knowledge of Christ demonstrate.[11] Christ's being *for* the people (a descending christology) is at the forefront. Christ's being *of* the people (an ascending christology) is all but absent. Consequently, sacramental/liturgical agency — ultimately the action of Christ — is something done *for* the people, not *by* the people. It follows that those who stand *in persona Christi* in liturgy do something *for* but not *with* the people. Thus according to the imperial-feudal paradigm of power and leadership, which survived in Catholic life and worship right up to Vatican II, the priest's role was paternalistic rather than collegial. The community leader, whether secular prince or lord cleric, was *the* social agent and his subjects were essentially passive and dependent.

The reforms of the present have to be read in the light of this history. One of its lessons is the foolishness of claiming an apolitical status for the church and its liturgy. Every now and then some church official says that the church is not a democracy, implying that it must remain aloof from politics if it is to preserve its essence and identity. Whatever grain of truth there may be in such statements, they betray a strange historical amnesia. For insofar as the church is not democratic it is surely something else — monarchical? patriarchal? imperial? feudal? — and this "something else" is just as indebted to the history of human political order as the democratic ideal is. From this history, in fact, two models of worship have emerged, one assembly-centered and the other priest-centered. Each embodies a different politics, a different bringing together of cultural patterns with the politics of the gospel. The priest-centered model presupposes a foundational distinction between those who have liturgical power and those who do not. The assembly-centered model begins from the supposition that liturgical agency — indeed, responsibility — belongs to each member of the assembly and that particular leadership roles evoke, express, and focus this collective agency of the people of God. The restoration of the liturgical assembly mandated by Vatican II and formalized in the *General Instruction* is thus a call to overcome the centuries-long ingrained habit of the priest-centered liturgy as well as the politics it implies.

The sources of this reform are both ancient and new. On the one hand, it retrieves the church's most ancient politics of worship; on the other, it does so with an eye to "the signs of the times." That is to say, contemporary reform is no more exempt from the dialectic of gospel and culture than any other age. Undoubtedly, the liturgical and ecclesial reforms of Vatican II, counterbalancing a historically exaggerated hierarchicalism with such notions as collegiality, collaboration, and the common priesthood of the faithful, are influenced by the general secular development of democratic institutions. From this perspective, the *General Instruction* is a document of empowerment because it makes the assembly-centered model the norm. Without in any way diminishing the distinctive leadership role of the ordained presider, the document reiterates throughout that the primary agent of the liturgy is the assembly.[12] Its political substance is basically democratic in the sense that it envisions every human person as a co-responsible agent of salvation history. There is room all round for giving and receiving, for serving and being served. But persons are not to be reduced to mere objects, patients, or consumers in their own religious histories. The council judged such a reduction to be a disempowering distortion of the true nature of Christian life and liturgy.

PASTORAL IMPLICATIONS

The practical difficulty is that, despite Vatican II's call for the restoration of the assembly, a confusing mixture of both models is still at work in most parish liturgies. The result is that contradictory expectations are placed on both presiders and assemblies. In order to sort through this confusion, it might be useful to place these models side by side in diagrams and compare them. Both charts employ the restored ministries in order to demonstrate how each model is to some extent operative in contemporary parish liturgy.

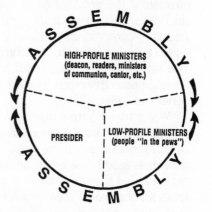

I. PRIEST-CENTERED MODEL

PRIEST & ASSISTANTS
(deacons, readers, cantors, etc.)   CONGREGATION

AGENT	◄	►	PATIENT
MINISTER	◄	►	MINISTERED-TO
PROVIDER	◄	►	CONSUMER
PLAYER	◄	►	SPECTATOR
CELEBRANT	◄	►	AUDIENCE

II. ASSEMBLY-CENTERED MODEL

ASSEMBLY

HIGH-PROFILE MINISTERS
(deacon, readers, ministers
of communion, cantor, etc.)

PRESIDER | LOW-PROFILE MINISTERS
(people "in the pews")

ASSEMBLY

In both models the priest is the agent of the liturgical action. But in the second (assembly-centered), so too are the gathered people — they are co-agents with their presider. The priest as the presiding member of the assembly guides and enables what is supposed to be an action of the whole gathered people, much as a conductor leads the musicians of an orchestra in the playing of a symphony. The shared, ecclesial nature of this action is indicated by the fact that all present (from the most prominent member to the least) belong to the circle of the assembly. No one stands outside it, either as incompetent spectator or independent cult agent.

In both models the priest is an *alter Christus* whose actions are a service and a grace to others. But in the assembly-centered model, the remaining members of the assembly are also *other Christs* whose presence is a ministry, and a *liturgical* ministry at that. This is true not only of those who have a specific, high-profile ministerial role such as reading or giving communion. It is also true of those people "in the pews" whom we habitually regard (and who probably regard themselves) as having no liturgical ministry. Not everyone presides or reads or leads the singing, but everyone has by baptism the calling, responsibility, and competency to perform the service of the liturgy with their presider. Not every member of the orchestra has the role of conductor or first violin, but all help to make the symphony happen.

That is why the *General Instruction* describes the prayer of the faithful, for example, as a moment in which "the people exercise their priestly function by interceding for all" humankind (chap. 2, 45).[13] That is why the *Constitution on the Sacred Liturgy* stresses the fact that the gathered people offer the Eucharist "not only through the hands of the priest but also together with him" (chap. 2, 48).[14] That is what the plural pronoun "we" signifies in the presider's prayers: ultimately, the presider never says "I" because it is the assembly who celebrates and never a lone minister.[15] This also explains why the assembly-centered model has no congregation, if what is meant by that is a body of people set off from those who are liturgical ministers. The assembly-centered model has no role for mere patients. There is no audience. Everyone is part of the orchestra, though there are a variety of roles.

While there is no congregation in the assembly-centered model, it is striking that there is no assembly in the priest-centered model. That is, there is no sense of co-agency on the part of all gathered. The common priesthood that all share by baptism does not come into play in the liturgical sphere. Instead, a dualism as old as the medieval model splits up the world into two theaters of operation. Laypeople are to lead good lives and set good examples out in the secular/temporal world, for that is their sphere of activity. Clergy (and to some extent religious) have their agency in the spiritual/sacramental/liturgical world. Laypeople enter the sacramental world as patients and consumers to have their spiritual needs taken care of, much as one goes to the doctor for medical attention. Hence, although on paper the words "assembly" and "congregation" are synonymous, in reality they are not. In historical context, congregation means those who do not minister but are ministered to, those who are not agents of the liturgy but patients, those who are not *the celebrant* but rather *the people*. In short, the "sub-text" of the word "congregation" is *non-agent*. There is a political difference between the priest-centered liturgy with a congregation and the assembly-centered liturgy with a presider.

It would be a useful exercise for liturgists, musicians, planners, and presiders to review their present liturgical style with the following question in mind: Which political model is really operative in the way liturgy is typically conducted — the priest-centered or the assembly-centered one? Here I can only give a brief indication of what such an exercise might reveal.

Let us examine the introductory rites. According to the *General Instruction* (chap. 2, 24) the purpose of these rites is the formation of the assembly. Before anything else can successfully happen at liturgy, in other words, the political unit that is to enact it must be constituted. Now the *General Instruction* clearly names the whole gathered people as this political unit. So the introductory rites should be conducted in such a way that the people come to recognize their status and role as the assembly: when they gather they are the Body of Christ. But is this what typically happens? As the gathering song begins and the presider with a few other ministers comes forth from the rear of the church, is not our focus immediately shifted from the assembly as collective agent to these few individuals, especially the presider? The processants do not emerge from the gathered body as members of it, coming forth to perform the service of leadership. Instead they arrive from outside as players or performers who have come to provide something to a waiting audience. In this case the gathering song no longer functions as a communal action forming everyone present (including the presider and other ministers) into a celebrating community. Rather it is distorted into ceremonial accompaniment for the entering presider — "traveling music" for Father. How common it is, too, for presiders to follow up a full-blown gathering song and procession with the words: "Let us now *begin* our liturgy *In the name of the Father...*" as though the song we have all just sung is not yet a real beginning to the liturgy but something outside it. If people do not sing with much conviction or interest, perhaps it is because they accurately perceive that their contribution really doesn't count for much in the ritual. Here, then, is a practical illustration of how the persistence of the medieval paradigm undercuts the intentions of the reformed liturgy. Since, according to the priest-centered model, the priest is *the celebrant* of the liturgy, the point of the introductory rite is *his* entrance.

There is nothing wrong with a procession as such, but the way in which it is conducted can evoke quite different political paradigms. With a little imagination, a procession could be arranged that would both heighten the focus on the assembly as collective agent and underscore the presider's role as enabling leader. For example (and this is only one of many possibilities), let us imagine the presider "in place" at the presidential chair as the liturgy begins, clearly a member of the assembly. As the music starts, the presider calls the people to unity in the Spirit while processants with incense bowls come down the various aisles of the church and incense the assembly. The community answers this call by singing the refrain of a gathering song with a text affirming the dignity of the Body of Christ (for example, Marty Haugen's "We Are Many Parts, We Are All One Body").[16] After the incensing and singing, the music quiets down and the presider invites the assembly to open itself once again to receive God's Word. The lector then processes in with the book, accompanied by a candlebearer. The assembly responds once again with the refrain of the gathering song. As the book is placed, the song is sung through to the end with verses added. The presider's greeting, the penitential or sprinkling rite, and the opening prayer follow.

To take another example, what is communicated in the usual manner of presenting the gifts? People from the assembly approach the table with the bread and the wine. Presider and gift-bearers meet in a collaborative action. That is the good news. The bad news is that the presider (with deacon and/or servers) usually "intercepts" these gift-bearers at the foot of the altar, approximately where the communion rail used to be. What is being said about the assembly's relationship to the eucharistic table in this practice? Whose table is it? What is being said about the action that will unfold at this table? Whose action is it? Who will offer the great table-prayer?

Interestingly, the *General Instruction* says only that the gifts are to be received "at a suitable place" (chap. 2, 49).[17] Why have we instinctively, as it were, assumed that the only "suitable place" is outside the old sanctuary? Are not the assembled people themselves the true sanctuary? Citing Ephesians 2:21–22, the introduction of the *Constitution on the Sacred Liturgy* says that the people of God are "a holy temple of the Lord, a dwelling-place for God in the Spirit."[18] Why do we act as though we do not really believe this when it comes to liturgy? Common sense suggests that if the gifts are to be brought *to the table*, then perhaps the giftbearers should bring them *to the table!* In any case, these instances illustrate how the vision and rhetoric of the reforms are undercut by the unconscious persistence of the medieval political paradigm. What we say ("please join in — you are a priestly people") is contradicted by what we do ("but you can't come to the table").[19]

Obviously, it makes a great difference which model guides those who plan liturgy from week to week. If one subscribes, whether consciously or unconsciously, to the priest-centered model, then the reforms appear to urge the "congregation" to participate by being more attentive, receptive, and responsive to the actions of those who are ministering to them, particularly the priest. But once one has grasped the significance of the gathered people — including their presider — as *assembly*, then the reforms seek to heal this splitting of the liturgical assembly into two parts: the priest who "does" the action on the one hand, and the "congregation" that is "done to" on the other. Healing this split is a work of empowerment.

11

"HE HAS PULLED DOWN THE MIGHTY FROM THEIR THRONES, AND HAS EXALTED THE LOWLY": A FEMINIST REFLECTION ON EMPOWERMENT

Susan A. Ross

Luke's recounting of the reversals of the Magnificat sets the tone for this reflection on women and empowerment for leadership in the church today. The tone is both one of judgment and promise, for in many ways, the mighty still occupy their thrones and the lowly still await their exaltation. Women's very real lack of power in the church today stands as an indictment of the "power structures" as they exist. The church as an institution has stood squarely in the way of women's access to decision-making power by its opposition to women's ordination. As Anne Carr has expressed it,

> The question of ordination to the priestly ministry represents an important symbol of the lack of the presence of women in the official life of the church, a symbol of women's exclusion from all significant decision-making and practical policy formation, a traditional exclusion that is historically based on the inferiority and subservient status ascribed to them.[1]

The scandal of women's exclusion from power cannot be overlooked. Therefore any discussion of the empowerment of women must be juxtaposed with our lack of political and symbolic power and the failure of the leadership of the church to rectify this scandal. Throughout this essay this aspect of the powerlessness of women will function as an undercurrent, continually reminding us of the structural failure of the church as an institution to empower women fully as Christians.

At the same time, however, it is equally important to recognize that the empowerment of all persons, and especially of women, does not consist solely in access to institutional forms of power. Christians are empowered by God through the grace of baptism, not ordination. Ordaining women would not solve the problem of women's access to power; it would only complicate it. Yet ironically the situation of women on the margins of power enables us to imagine new and more creative forms of empowerment. We need, then, to broaden and even transform our understanding of power so as to be more fully aware of its productive and destructive workings.

My discussion of women and power will be both a critical and constructive one. It is inspired by Luke's image of Mary reflecting on the transforming power of the lowly. My comments will be critical of one-sided conceptions and uses of power, which limit it to power that is possessed by one over and against another. This unilateral form of power is all too often coercive and destructive and has been used historically to limit women's exercise of power. It will also be self-critical of naive idealizing as unrealistic; in other words, while we may be critical of unilateral forms and exercises of power, we cannot ignore their existence or their necessity in certain circumstances. Drawing on not only theological but also philosophical and social-scientific works in feminist theory, this essay will also be constructive insofar as it will attempt to describe forms and uses of power in ways that will enhance the dignity of all human beings and promote the transformation of self and society. If the goal of a Christian understanding of power is the empowerment of all God's people, we will need to be attentive to power in all its demonic and graced forms.

WOMEN AND POWER

Women's relationship to power is an admittedly complex one. On the one hand, women have traditionally "lacked" power. Especially when power is conceived in terms of physical force, women have been generally viewed as far less powerful, subject to the superior power of men. Until 1920, women lacked the power of the vote, and women's wages still do not have the economic power that men's wages have. Yet women are not without some power, at least in popular conceptions: the "power behind the throne," the "powerful mother," the power of the seductive woman are all familiar images of the power that women are said to wield over men. None of these images, however, is unambiguous: each suggests a weakness on the part of the man to whom this "powerful woman" is related; her power is a power that ought not to be. As Judith Andre notes, "Female power is considered inappropriate and even dangerous."[2] She develops this assertion by noting that women may have *power* over men, but they do not have *authority*.[3] And power without authority robs a person of autonomy:

> Nothing is more central to human functioning than autonomy:
> the sense of oneself as able, indeed obligated, to make responsible
> choices about one's life. The person who is denied authority, how-
> ever, constantly receives the message that she has no right to make
> such choices.[4]

The operative conception of power in this essay is one based in relationship: to self, to others, and to God. The work of such thinkers as
Jürgen Habermas in critical theory,[5] Michel Foucault in the dynamics of power,[6] Bernard Loomer in process theology,[7] and Elizabeth
Janeway in political theory[8] has shown that power is not an abstract
concept but a complex relational reality. "Power" exists between and
among human beings: political leaders, constituents, friends, spouses,
parents and children, pastors and parishioners. These power relationships can be competitive, dominating, cooperative, protective,
abusive; how these relationships are described stems from the basic
understanding of the self at work in the relationships. That is, how the
person in relationship conceives of the self and other(s) determines
in large part the nature of power. By the same token, a society that
values certain qualities (e.g., competition and autonomy) will reward
and empower these qualities in people. An individualized, separated
understanding of the self will see the "other" in different terms than
the vulnerable or dependent self.[9]

It should be no surprise that the predominant understanding of
power in the Western world is the unilateral one of "power over":
that of ascendency and control over others. But the increasing concern
for a broader and more "horizontal" notion of power — "empowerment" — is evidence of a changing sense of the self and of the self's
relation to others. This concern is reflected in the work of feminist
theologians on the human being's relation to self, others, and God and
drives feminist theology to develop new models of these relationships.
The concepts of the "connected" self[10] and of God as Mother, Lover,
and Friend[11] are some examples that suggest different conceptions of
the self and of God and therefore of power itself.

The nature of women's empowerment in society and in the church,
as I will develop it here, revolves around five principles basic to feminist thought: solidarity, marginality, embodiment, knowledge, and
transformation.[12] These principles arise out of women's own experience as created in the image of God and as called to exercise
power in the personal, political, and religious spheres of life. My
reflections are also inspired by the example of the most powerful
one, whose power did not coerce and manipulate but was shared;
it was a power that transformed. It is in the complex interweaving of
these principles that a fuller understanding of the empowerment of

women can be gained and steps taken to empower women in concrete ways.

SOLIDARITY

To place solidarity in the center of the empowerment of women is to highlight the relational nature of power. The woman alone is almost always the powerless woman, but women in solidarity constitute a powerful group.[13] This solidarity constitutes a threat to existing systems of power because women have traditionally understood identity as being bound up in relationships with men and children and have looked to men for validation of power. But the power of women in solidarity comes from each other and is not bestowed upon women by men. This understanding of power comes from a conception of the self as relational and from a basic sense of the worth of women.

Much has been written in recent years regarding women's self-understanding as fundamentally relational, in contrast to the individualistic patterns of male selfhood predominant in our culture.[14] Women do not experience the self as a solitary entity but as a related one. Western society's prevailing definition of the self is highly individualistic, a conception based primarily upon the experiences of men who find their identity in autonomy and separation, because they have been raised by women, from whom they must separate to become men. In this male-oriented conception of the self, power is possessed by one over and against the other.[15] The development of the nuclear family in postindustrial Western society and the development of a highly individual and self-centered self has had the effect of defining power in unilateral terms and locating power in places where women have been absent or few in number. Women, therefore, "lack" power.

With the growth of the women's movement in the 1960s and 1970s, women began to discover common strengths as we came to see what we had in common, that our perceptions of reality were accurate, and that we shared many similar experiences. Especially among white, middle-class women, consciousness-raising groups in which women came together to share their experiences became sources of validation and of empowerment. These groups' mode of operation was dialogical and nonhierarchical; each woman had the opportunity to speak without being interrupted. What resulted was a realization on the part of many women that their experiences were not unique or isolated (and therefore without power) but shared. This common experience has been revealed as a powerful force: the power of solidarity and community.

There has been some criticism of this conception of "women's experience" by black, white, Hispanic, and other women who lack the privileges of the white middle-class.[16] The claim has been made that women of privilege have the luxury to reflect on the validity of their own limited "experience" without needing to be concerned about having enough income, food, education to survive. This is an important and valid critique. I would, however, point to the literature of and by women who are oppressed not only by sex, but also by race and class, which demonstrates that community and solidarity remain crucial to women's empowerment.[17]

The relational power of solidarity can be further characterized as nondualistic and appreciative of differences. As nondualistic, women's power of solidarity rejects a unilateral or "zero-sum" conception of power. In a unilateral understanding of power, there is a limited amount of power. If one has more, the other has less. Power is not shared, but is a prize to be grasped by one over the other. But the power of women's solidarity is a power that increases as it is shared. The recognition that one is not alone, that women working together can accomplish what one woman alone cannot, is a strengthening experience, not a weakening one. The growth of economic power in women's agricultural and sewing collectives illustrates this point.[18]

It should be noted, however, that this experience of solidarity and of recognition is not always a happy one. It is frequently the case that women recognize the validity of experiences that have been depreciated, ignored, or even dismissed by patriarchal culture. Recognizing the validity of these experiences may bring relief, but it often also releases long pent-up anger. The power of women's anger (to be discussed in more detail below) is an important resource and is not to be passed over easily in favor of a quick resolution. It is often a necessary step in the process of personal and social transformation.

The power of solidarity is also open to and appreciative of difference. The immediate experience of the power of solidarity is that of identification: we realize that we are not alone, that there are others "like us," that "we too" have had the same experience. Not unlike romantic love, this initial experience serves to bond us with others, and we overlook any differences at first as unimportant. But, inevitably, differences arise. Poor women and middle-class women have different problems to solve. Black women and white women find that their experiences are not always similar. Latin women and Asian women find that descriptions of "women's" experiences are inadequate to describe their own. The power of solidarity recognizes the strength in diversity and difference. It is not necessary to have only one understanding of experience, to insist that "all" women experience sin, or God, or community in only one way. A recognition of difference is an appreciation of ambiguity, of unsettledness, a willingness to live with shifting notions of power. Where unilateral forms of power seek certainty, power as solidarity is a moving power, not settling into one fortified place for its exercise, but willing to share, to be silent, and even to be temporarily powerless when the situation may call for it.[19]

The power of solidarity in its relationality, nondualism, and differentiation runs counter to the strains of individualism, hierarchy, and uniformity in the church today. But the potential rewards of developing solidarity are great.

MARGINALITY

The power of women is a power that recognizes its own ambiguous position. As a power on the margins, it is always a voice from both inside and outside since the position of marginality is neither wholly "inside" nor entirely "outside." Even as women may be "insiders" in institutions, women remain — with few exceptions — outsiders even as we are insiders. Marginality connotes both a situation of little importance and also a situation on the borders.[20] Thus marginality means that women's alliances may shift; women of color, for example, may recognize a closer alliance with men of color than with middle-class white women concerning socio-economic issues, but may align with other women on issues concerning family violence. Since women have not historically occupied positions of power, women possess the "epistemological privilege of the oppressed":[21] the identification of a particular place — the oppression of women — from which to reflect and act theologically. The particularity of women's marginal position is recognized and not subsumed under a false generic conception of "man's situation."

The marginal voice of women is a critical voice that seeks to expose abuses of power and from this marginal position draws its strength. As Marsha Hewitt so clearly puts it, "The aim of a feminist critical theory should be to expose the dehumanizing, authoritarian forces which increasingly threaten foreclosure of every possibility for individual and social transformation."[22]

In her paper on women and power to the Catholic Theological Society of America, Sandra Schneiders draws on the passion narrative in the Gospel of John. Focusing on the three main actors in the drama — Jesus, the Jewish leaders, and Pilate — Schneiders shows how women find their situation portrayed by Jesus, since women are " 'powerless' even though they possess the only genuine authority, the power to appeal to the conscience of their oppressors with the truth of their claim."[23] The power of the truth is an important but also dangerous form of power. As women and other oppressed groups are all too aware, the truth does not reside in any one person or institution but is that to which all human beings are subject. The dangerous power of the truth of women's equal personhood cannot be absolutized by women over and against men nor against others whose powerlessness takes different forms such as the poor and people of color.

This crucial dimension of power comes, ironically, from women's marginal position. The concern for freedom and liberation is a concern from the underside of history, the power of the oppressed. The truth of the claim that Schneiders mentions above is that of the fundamental equality of men and women as Christians.[24] As the institutional structures of the church continue to deny this equality under the guise of "complementarity,"[25] women and men continue to expose and to criticize this injustice. Marginality here constitutes a privileged position. But at the same time, the "epistemological privilege" of the marginalized must always incorporate its own self-critical process, lest it become another ideology, which mistakes a partial expression of the truth for the truth itself.[26] The strength of this marginal position is that it is a critique of all structures of inequality and domination and therefore is open to judgment by its own criteria.

There is also another kind of power that accrues to the powerless: that is, the power of freedom from ties to structures. The power of rejection of structures of authority, in overt and in covert ways, is a source of power because of the relational nature of power itself. Subversion, resistance, confrontation, even women's "manipulation" of men, are all ways of using the power of the marginalized to resist structural forms of power.[27] This power of resistance inevitably brings conflict. Covert forms of resistance have long been the stock-in-trade of oppressed groups and are ways of forcing overt expressions of power. These conflicts can expose otherwise hidden uses of power and therefore can serve a critical function.

Marginality also suggests a positive form of power. Women on the margin are free to develop new ways of being, alone and in community, that are not determined by those at the center. The kind of communities that Rosemary Radford Ruether envisions as "Women-Church" are some examples of this freedom on the margins.[28] The Exodus community of Women-Church offers women alternative understandings of the self, of community, of ritual, that can energize women to continue in the struggle for full equality — not a false equality imposed by others, but one defined by women and men together.

The power of marginality as ambiguous, critical, sometimes covert, and free suggests the inherent instability of power. Power as a relational reality can never be entirely tamed but is always subject to the movement of the Spirit. As marginal, this aspect of power will continue to exist as the place for self-reflection on the part of individuals and institutions and serves as a constant point of caution to any exercise of power.

EMBODIMENT

The third aspect of women's empowerment is embodiment. Women's "closeness" to our bodies and to nature has been a long-held cultural and religious conviction.[29] Traditionally, this has meant that women are less intellectual than men, especially in cultures that hold to a dualistic understanding of the person as a mind controlling a body. The tie to nature has also emphasized women's greater emotionality, especially in cultures that regard emotional expressiveness as a sign of weakness. The early women's movement tended to deemphasize women's bodiliness in its effort to secure "equal rights" for women and held to a modern, "Enlightenment" understanding of the person that stressed human rationality and autonomy.[30] More recent discussions of women's (and of men's) embodiment have emphasized the dualistic underpinnings of these conceptions of the person and have sought to develop a more wholistic attitude toward embodiment, stressing the power of the body and of nature. The power of female sexuality, so often depicted as demonic, and its alliance with the powers of nature, is a positive source of power and needs to be more fully understood.

Some forms of feminism have accepted and affirmed the traditional association of women's bodiliness and nature as an expression of women's special appreciation of and kinship to the natural world. While there are valuable insights from the goddess-centered[31] and creation-centered[32] forms of spirituality, to embrace uncritically the tie to nature without recognizing the historical and cultural dimensions of women's bodiliness is dangerous.[33] An appreciation of the embodied character of human nature recognizes its complex historical-cultural roots. The power of the body has long been recognized in cultural and religious prohibitions concerning bodily functions. Here it is especially important to understand the cultural traditions before immediately condemning any and all ascetic practices. As scholars such as Peter Brown and Carolyn Walker Bynum have brilliantly shown, many of the historical practices of bodily discipline have sought to tap into the enormous religious and cultural power of the body.[34]

The complexity of the historical treatment of the body notwithstanding, far too often women have been uncritically identified with the body and its functions and relegated to positions of social and religious inferiority because of the perception that women are "closer" to our bodies than are men. Even the first draft of the recent bishops' pastoral on women's concerns, while finally recognizing the sinful character of sexism, nevertheless still quotes approvingly papal writings that describe women almost entirely in terms of our real and potential motherhood.[35]

Women's recognition of bodily power is not an uncritical identification of our bodiliness as defined by centuries of sexism nor is it an embrace of our intellectual capacities as they are defined by men, but rather a critical awareness of the integrity and complexity of the embodied person. Women are in the process of developing a language and practice of the body that celebrates the uniqueness and power of women's biological experience, that also recognizes the ambiguity of bodily experience, and that unambiguously rejects the objectification and denigration of women's bodiliness by the dominant patriarchal culture. Violence against women has been based on an implicit cultural permission given to men to have power over women's bodies.[36] Physical and emotional abuse of women is the sinful use of male power in maintaining the powerlessness of women. The exposure of these abuses of power and their legitimation by secular and religious culture and the education of women and men to the beauty and power of the body are central to an understanding of the embodied power of women.

Embodiment, however, refers not only to individual bodies but also to the larger bodies of the church and of the world. To speak of the church as the "Mystical Body" of Christ is to recognize that Christ is really present in the community. But this embodiment has not been fully nurtured; indeed, it has been malnourished. The radical love of which Jesus spoke and which he lived, the inclusion of *all* in the community of the church, the need to *make present* Christ in the church — all of this speaks of the embodiment of the spirit of God in the world. In addition, the recognition that we as human beings are rooted in the physical world means attending to the fragile character of our embodiment and the responsibilities it entails.[37]

The power of embodiment entails putting into practice — embodying — the goodness of the body, especially women's bodies. This means recognizing and educating ourselves to the goodness of sexuality[38] and committing the church to incorporate the power of human embodiment in worship, teaching, and in practice.

KNOWLEDGE

The power of women is tied to women's increasing knowledge of self and of the world. This means access to education in the traditional sense but it also means an appreciation of the knowledge women have gained in our struggles and of forms of knowledge that may otherwise be dismissed by the dominant patriarchal culture.

As women have gained access to educational, social, and political institutions, we have become increasingly aware of how our "ways of knowing" can be both helpful and detrimental to "educational success."[39] Education is a political activity, and the mode of knowledge as developed in the Western, post-Enlightenment world is a knowledge based on an understanding of the self as a rational and autonomous individual and this individual's power to "grasp" and possess the objects of its knowledge. A feminist conception of knowledge seeks to expand and even transform knowledge, incorporating the knowledge of groups as well as individuals, and incorporating as well the power of the emotional as well as the intellectual.

The power of the consciousness-raising group has already been mentioned as a source of knowledge and validation for women. In addition, the knowledge possessed by nondominant individuals and groups in our cultural traditions, as expressed in writings by women and groups that have not received the baptism of canonicity,[40] as well as the knowledge gained in solidarity with nondominant groups, provides valuable insight. This is a practical, not a purely theoretical knowledge, and its power is ultimately expressed in transformative action.[41]

Feminist scholars have also recently turned our attention to the very conception of knowledge itself and questioned the role of the emotions in the act of knowing. Usually regarded as "clouding" the possibility of "clear" and "objective" knowledge, emotions are in fact valuable sources of knowledge. What Alison Jaggar terms "outlaw emotions,"[42] what Beverly Harrison describes as "the power of anger in the work of love,"[43] are crucial ways of coming to a new awareness of the power of women's knowledge. These "outlaw" emotions, such as anger, allow women and men to see injustice, react to it not "intellectually" — coolly and abstractly — but with passion. Knowledge then becomes more than a storehouse of intellectual ideas; it becomes as well the basis for action. Knowledge is able to move from its isolation in academia to the workplace, the home, and not least of all, the church. As Alison Jaggar remarks:

> I suggest that emotions are appropriate if they are characteristic of a society in which all humans (and perhaps some nonhuman life, too) thrive, or if they are conducive to establishing such a society.[44]

The power of being connected bodily and emotionally is an ethical power, as Beverly Harrison puts it, and she further maintains that "all power, including intellectual power, is rooted in feeling."[45] These feelings are what empower us to act; their power cannot be dismissed or ignored.

The knowledge of women represents a powerful resource for the church. While women's educational power has long been used to educate the young, it has not been recognized — indeed, it has been feared — in educating adults. Drawing upon women's knowledge and encouraging women to develop intellectually and emotionally will only increase and enlarge human knowledge, as will encouraging women and men alike to expand our approaches to knowledge and education.

TRANSFORMATION

All of the above — solidarity, marginality, embodiment, and knowledge — lead ultimately toward transformation: of the self, the family, the church, society. Women's power is a transformative power in that it is a moving, and even unstable, force[46] that seeks to unseat the forces of domination and injustice. At the same time, it seeks to empower all to full and equal discipleship in the church. Like the religious term "conversion," transformation (which I have chosen to use here because of its wider — social — connotation than conversion) is a recognition that the present structures are unjust and sinful and that we need to transform ourselves and society in the light of the gospel.

In his powerful essay "Messianic or Bourgeois Religion?" Johannes Baptist Metz contrasts the "messianic" religion of the poor, oppressed, and disenfranchised with the "bourgeois" religion of the comfortable and powerful. "Bourgeois" religion needs no future, since it already possesses one: it is an extension of the present in which the bourgeois have all they need. "Messianic" religion, on the other hand, has a different future: it is one that "disrupts," reverses, transforms.[47] Based in the gospel call for conversion, the power of transformation is the call for justice, for radical love. At the same time, however — and this is what distinguishes the call for religious transformation from a secular call for change — there is the recognition that no human structure will ever fully embody the gospel message. This is what makes the power of transformation a shifting power: it is a call for patriarchal religion to repent from sexism, but also a call to white feminists to repent from racism and classism[48] and a call to black male liberation theologians to repent from sexism.[49]

Paula Cooey develops this understanding of transformation in relation to power: "If power is understood in a broad sense as vitalizing energy rather than in a more narrow sense as internal and external control exerted by a person or group, then empowerment characterizes this process of conversion. Power in this broader sense is both personal and social."[50] Later in her article, Cooey discusses the ambiguity of her understanding of power in a way that helps to illuminate the point I am making about the shifting and unstable nature of power: "Ambivalence toward power, rather than avoided or denied, needs to be regarded as necessary, useful, and a source for self-reflection — in short, as a means by which to detect, analyze, and assess different modes of power."[51]

The transformative nature of women's power does not deny the worth nor the power of personal and institutional forms of control but recognizes the constant need to question, criticize, and reflect upon the uses of power. Power is always a relational reality and a means to an end: it does not exist in its own nor ought it be sought for its own sake. As a nurturing power, women's power fosters the development of the person and the community, not for its own sake, but for the sake of the good of all. As an embodied power, women's power seeks to empower all in solidarity. As a critical power, women's power seeks out abuses of power and calls them to be transformed. As a power for leadership in the church, women's power is a necessary and invaluable resource.

EMPOWERMENT FOR LEADERSHIP IN THE CHURCH

How can these aspects of women's empowerment work in relationship to and on the margins of the structures of the church?

As I have indicated above, the power of solidarity is a power that increases as it is shared. While particular places of power are closed to women in the church today — that of eucharistic president, of episcopal jurisdiction — many other forms have stretched to include women: canon lawyers, theologians, diocesan officials, parish administrators. The power of solidarity can involve both stretching and breaking hierarchical, dualistic, and undifferentiated forms of leadership in these and in other places where women exercise power, as well as challenging forms of leadership in places closed to women. The power of solidarity means that office is a function, not a role. Emphasizing the relational nature of leadership involves attention to language: how leadership is described, how leaders speak to include and empower. It also means stressing the diversity of ministries in the church, providing avenues for the expression of these ministries and the support necessary to keep them going.

The solidarity of women also needs to be developed by women ourselves and to be given the kind of support by the institutional church that has historically been extended to men. This involves including more than "token women" in the few positions available to women, but should include the kind of support given recently by Rembert Weakland, archbishop of Milwaukee, in consulting women of his see on their views on the abortion issue. A leadership that incorporates the power of solidarity is not afraid of its power and is willing to share this leadership. Recognizing the solidarity of groups and fostering small groups within larger structures is an important task for any structure. Developing a spirit of partnership and of co-operation is the first and most crucial step in empowering leadership in the church.

The power of marginality is another critical element in empowerment. It means that women, by standing on the margins of the structures of power, are able to be critical of abuses of power. Even for those women in positions of prominence, marginality remains; leadership is always unstable, subject to the dynamics of power relationships. This is a temptation as well as an opportunity. The temptation is that in gaining access to power where women have traditionally not possessed it, women run the risk of using power in unilateral ways. Unilateral power is unstable and also insecure; it can be lost and so is held all the more tenaciously. The privilege of marginality is that one never completely possesses power, but is empowered.

The power of marginality is what permits the honest use of power in oneself and in others. The constant self-critical dimension is a capacity that needs to be developed not only by the underside of power, but also by those who are in traditional positions of power. Building opportunities for the widest possible consultation on issues that concern all members of the church is a process that will include and listen to the marginal. This is necessary so that the use of power can become and remain an honest use of power.

Marginality also means recognition of alternative forms of power. The kinds of communities Rosemary Ruether envisions in *Women–Church* exist "on the margins:" not inside, yet not wholly outside. These communities provide the necessary places for sustenance of those on the margins, a respite from the heavy doses of all-male symbolism that assail women and men in the "official" liturgies of the church. These marginal communities do not exist to replace the church but to expand it.

The power of embodiment for leadership means recognizing our fragile and vulnerable condition as human beings. It also means that embodiment is a shared human condition, not one possessed only by women. This recognition involves restoring a badly-needed balance to our understanding of the person: as both physical and mental, not as a disembodied intellect. While rationality is surely one of the greatest human capacities, it requires the balance of the "heart."[52] Being full human beings also involves an appreciation of human sexuality. While structures beyond the powers of individuals continue to deprive the church of the ministry of married priests and of women, leadership requires positive attention to human embodiment in our educational institutions, in our liturgical celebrations, in pastoral situations. Courageous leadership can be exercised by those who are aware of and appreciative of their own embodiment and that of others.

On a broader level, the embodiment of the diversity of ministries and leaders in the church is also an act of empowerment. Paul's description of the diversity of ministries and gifts to the church in Corinth remains a compelling model in the present: "There are varieties of gifts, but the same spirit. There are varieties of service, but the same Lord" (1 Cor. 12:4–5). It is crucial that a mutual recognition and affirmation of the power of all ministries be incorporated on all levels of the church.

The power of knowledge suggests related possibilities. The presence of women in some positions of leadership has indicated the willingness of some church leaders to incorporate women's knowledge. The importance of the education of all the church cannot be overstated. Empowerment of the knowledge of women requires that women be supported by the church in our education and that women's knowledge be incorporated in pastoral and educational institutions on every level. This entails pastoral guidance and educational ministry by and for women, for children, the sick, seminarians, pastors.

The "subjugated" and subversive nature of the knowledge of women means that it will not always be readily accepted nor appreciated by others. Indeed, it will often be perceived as threatening, wrong, or, more often, trivial. This ignorance of the power of women's knowledge is a temptation on the part of women and of others to dismiss this knowledge. Therefore the power of solidarity is necessary to keep this knowledge alive and growing. Women's knowledge will continue, if not in the center then on the margins of the church as a reminder of the fragility of all forms of knowledge.

All of these aspects of the empowerment of women are transformative: of our understandings of power over to shared conceptions of power; of the need for cooperation; of the willingness to shed old images and expectations.

The feminist contribution to reconceiving power and leadership in the church is found in these aspects that promote transformation: solidarity, marginality, embodiment, knowledge. These are inspired by the tradition itself, in the "dangerous memories" of the life and death of Jesus and in the communities that have kept these memories alive.[53] These memories have taken various forms over the centuries: prophets, mystics, reformers. They are kept alive today in the work of those who are struggling to empower the powerless.

To return to the image that opened this essay, we might envision our current situation this way: while the mighty still occupy their thrones, the lowly have moved on to other places, put the chairs in a circle, and begun to construct the new church. Whether or not the mighty will follow this movement is yet to be known.

12

THE CHURCH AND HISPANICS IN THE UNITED STATES: FROM EMPOWERMENT TO SOLIDARITY

Roberto S. Goizueta

In their pastoral letter on the U.S. economy, the Catholic bishops of the United States boldly declared that, as individuals, as a nation, and as a church, "we are called to make a fundamental 'option for the poor.'"[1] The notion of a preferential option for the poor has a long history in the church, though the term itself has gained prominence only since Vatican II, and especially in the wake of the Latin American bishops' meetings at Medellín and Puebla. In their conference at Medellín, Colombia, in 1968, the Latin American bishops committed the church in Latin America to becoming a "Church of the poor."[2] In their subsequent meeting at Puebla, Mexico, in 1979, the bishops proclaimed: "We affirm the need for conversion on the part of the whole Church to a preferential option for the poor."[3]

In this essay, I will examine the notion of a preferential option for the poor and its implications for a theology of empowerment. I will propose that, if we understand that notion not only as an ethical imperative or commandment but as, in fact, a precondition for authentic Christian faith, we will be led beyond a theology of empowerment to a theology of solidarity with the poor. Out of the commitment to solidarity will emerge new understandings of faith and discipleship. Out of that commitment will emerge, in short, a process of conversion.

Standing at the threshold of Christianity's third millennium, North American Christians are faced with new calls to solidarity and conversion. As we approach the year 2000, one of those calls issues from the growing Hispanic communities in the United States. This call is addressed with special urgency to the Catholic Church in the United States, which, if current projections are correct, will be a predominantly Hispanic church by the early part of the next century.[4] As a call to conversion, the Hispanic presence in the church is, in the words of the U.S. bishops, "a moment of grace" and a "blessing from God."[5]

Challenged to respond to this moment of grace, the church in the United States is at an important crossroads in its history. Will the church — grown increasingly comfortable over the past decades as its members have become increasingly wealthy and powerful — respond to this challenge, to this graced moment, and thereby open itself to the blessing represented by the Hispanic presence? As the U.S. bishops have implied in their pastoral letter on Hispanic ministry, the Hispanic presence makes concrete the call to make a preferential option for the poor. As we enter the third millennium, therefore, the call for the church in the United States to make an option for the poor will be tested in the church's commitment to the fastest growing segment, and one of the poorest segments, of its own membership, the Hispanic, or Latino, communities of the United States.[6] It is in the context of this historical and historic challenge that I will thus address the issues of empowerment, solidarity, and the option for the poor. At the conclusion, I will adumbrate some sources of empowerment already present within Hispanic communities in the United States, particularly within the popular religiosity of those communities.

THE PREFERENTIAL OPTION FOR THE POOR

Catholic Social Teaching

Prior to the explicit discussions of a preferential option for the poor, as these are presented in the U.S. bishops' pastoral letter on the U.S. economy and the Latin American documents of Medellín and, especially, Puebla, the providential role played by the poor has been repeatedly affirmed throughout the church's history, from the Scriptures themselves to the recent papal encyclical *On Social Concern*.[7] Over the past hundred years, that role has found eloquent and forceful articulation in the series of papal documents that comprise what has come to be known as "Catholic social teaching."

Drawing not only on the Scriptures but also on the natural law tradition, Catholic social teaching has been grounded in two interrelated, foundational principles: the inherent human dignity of every person as a child of God and the responsibility of all Christians to promote the common good. Both of these principles are, in turn, interpreted in the context of the organic cosmology of natural law tradition, wherein the whole of creation is seen as a living organism. Each part of this organism plays a role essential to the orderly and harmonious functioning of the whole. Consequently, to impair any part of the organism, no matter how small or seemingly insignificant, would be to undermine the whole organism and, hence, the divine will. This cosmology is also reflected, of course, in the doctrine of the Mystical Body of Christ.[8]

As each individual person is born into this intricate organism, or network of relationships, each individual is, by nature, an inherently social entity: to be a person is to be a social being, formed and informed by one's articulation within the complex organism we call "creation" or, in the human sphere, "society." The person's social responsibility to the good of the whole, to the common good, derives, herefore, from ontology, i.e., from the person's very nature as inrinsically and constitutively social, not from some contractual duty extrinsic to the individual, which he or she may then choose to accept or reject. The common good, or the good of the whole, is thus violated whenever any part of that whole is violated, whenever anyone is denied his or her rightful dignity as a child of God.[9]

While Vatican II, and especially the document *Gaudium et Spes*, played a crucial role in the ongoing development of Catholic social teaching, the council also reflected a methodological shift, the full ramifications of which would not be felt until several years later at Medellín and Puebla. The bishops at the Second Vatican Council asked the church to look to the "signs of the times" in order to discover there the church's true meaning and mission.[10] No longer could the church afford to see itself as somehow above the fray of history, proclaiming eternal truths discovered in some rarefied spiritual realm unsullied by "secular" concerns. God is not to be found outside the vicissitudes of history, but in "the joy and hope, the grief and anguish" of God's people, especially "those who are poor or afflicted in any way."[11]

At Medellín and Puebla the Latin American bishops took up the challenge to look to the "signs of the times," where God's will for the church is revealed. Those signs, they argued, are of a people ground down by overwhelming poverty, injustice, and oppression, and of that people's courageous struggle for liberation from the shackles of slavery in order to reclaim their dignity as children of God. If the church's mission, as historical and concrete, is mediated by the signs of the times, then the church must become a church of the poor, a church intimately identified with the suffering of its people and, therefore, with their struggle for justice.[12] The preferential option for the poor then becomes, in the words of the Puebla documents, "the privileged, though not the exclusive, gauge of our following of Christ," with the consequence that the poor, or marginalized, are no longer merely an object of the church's evangelizing activity, but are themselves agents of evangelization.[13]

The significance of the poor for the church and society is also affirmed in the U.S. bishops' pastoral letter on the U.S. economy, where the bishops assert that "the obligation to provide justice for all means that the poor have the single most urgent economic claim on the conscience of the nation"; the suffering of the poor "is a measure of how far we are from being a true community of persons."[14] If the common good is the criterion, or "gauge," for determining a society's commitment to justice, the lives of its poor and marginalized are the principal criterion for determining a society's commitment to the common good. The key criterion for our solidarity with others, therefore, is our solidarity with the poor.

Liberation Theology

Grounded in the experience of the Latin American people and drawing upon the church's social teaching, especially as that was articulated in a Latin American context at Medellín and Puebla, liberation theologians have taken that teaching to its logical conclusions by making explicit what has, for the most part, remained implicit in the official documents: the preferential option for the poor is more than an ethical imperative; it is the precondition for authentic Christian faith. What is most revolutionary — and controversial — about liberation theology is not the ethical priority accorded the struggle for social justice; that priority has consistently been argued — and quite explicitly — in Catholic social teaching. What is most revolutionary is the epistemological priority accorded that struggle, a priority that nevertheless is already latent in Puebla's affirmation of the role of the poor as not only objects of evangelization but also agents of evangelization.

For liberation theologians, the preferential option for the poor derives not only from Scripture and not only from Catholic social teaching, but from ontology, from the very nature of the person and therefore all human institutions. If the signs of the times (i.e., history) are those of conflict and exploitation, to say that we are historical beings is to say that we are necessarily involved in that conflict. Even the refusal to take sides in the conflict is itself to make an option: one's silence functions as implicit consent to the ongoing conflict and exploitation. As victims of that conflict, the people of Latin America have been able to perceive it in a way very difficult for those of us who benefit from the conflict.

The victims of history are able to perceive the conflicts and discontinuities of history. The victors, on the other hand, have a vested interest in obscuring the conflicts while purveying the illusion of an essentially ordered, harmonious history, a history of "progress." The victims remind us that, though creation is indeed an organism comprised of mutually interrelated and interdependent parts, that organism remains severely broken and weakened. If, out of self-interest, we simply assume that the organism is fundamentally healthy, we undermine the harmony and unity that lies before us as an ideal to be realized rather than as an *a priori*.[15]

If history is conflictual and all persons are by definition historical beings, then a Christian, *qua* human being, is necessarily enmeshed in that conflict: to opt out of the conflict would be to opt out of our humanity, to jump out of our skins, an ontological impossibility. If neutrality is impossible — since even a "neutral" person would *ipso facto* be opting for the status quo — then the question is not whether a Christian ought to take sides (the presumption being that "taking sides" would somehow undermine the universality of the person's love for others) but rather which side ought the Christian to take.

Turning to the Scriptures to search for an answer to that question, Gustavo Gutiérrez finds there two major, overarching themes: (1) the gratuity and universality of God's love, and (2) God's preferential option for the poor.[16] At first blush, these themes appear to contradict each other — unless they are interpreted from the perspective of the poor, from the perspective of a conflictual history. From that perspective, the themes are revealed not as mutually contradictory but as, on the contrary, mutually implicit. Because human beings are by nature historical, embodied spirits (as Karl Rahner would say, "spirits in the world"), God's love for us manifests itself in history. It could not be otherwise, unless we were disembodied spirits. Consequently, if that history is conflictual, then God can no more avoid that conflict than can human beings. If human historicity precludes human neutrality, so too does the historicity of God's love preclude divine neutrality. In a situation of conflict, wherein certain groups are systematically denied their dignity as persons, a neutral God would be a God whose "neutrality" would effectively function to condone the oppression.[17]

Consequently, God's identification with the victims affirms and safeguards God's transcendence. If God were not identified with the victims, the outcasts, God's silence in the face of their suffering would make God an accomplice in their victimization. This point is illustrated with great poignancy in a scene from Elie Wiesel's autobiographical novel *Night*. As a child in a Nazi concentration camp, the author remembers standing among a number of Jews who were witnessing the hanging of another Jewish child: " 'Where is God? Where is He?' someone behind me asked.... And I heard a voice within me answer him: 'Where is He? Here He is — He is hanging here on this gallows....' "[18]

In that experience of horrific cruelty, the young Wiesel instinctively sensed that a God who is not hanging on the gallows alongside the victims is a God who is an accomplice of the hangman. If God is transcendent, if God is truly "other," then God's otherness is revealed, in history, through human otherness, especially through those persons who are most "other," those who, as victims, live on the margins of our societies. Because they suffer the consequences of our false idols, e.g., wealth, power, domination, the poor and marginalized are witnesses to the fraudulent nature of our "God" and are thus revelatory of the true God, the God who refuses to be identified with "the system," with power, privilege, and domination. As incomprehensible to and within the dominant systems, the poor mediate a God who is also incomprehensible to the dominant systems. This is the God who, in Dorothy Day's words, comforts the afflicted and afflicts the comfortable. Only the image of God hanging from the cross, crucified as a common criminal, is powerful enough to strip us of our safe and comfortable images of God, images that function to legitimate our self-indulgent lifestyles. This God, who transcends, refuses to be identified with, and is thus crucified by, the dominant power structures, is visible only to those persons whose own vantage point is outside the power structures. The preferential option for the poor provides us with the lenses with which to see God, because unless we can see God there where we would least expect to find God, among the hungry, the naked, the sick, the crucified criminals (like Jesus Christ), we will not see the true God at all. And the "God" to whom we pray will not be the God of the Scriptures but the God of power, domination, wealth, and privilege, a God who comforts the comfortable and afflicts the afflicted.[19]

To say that God opts for the poor is not, however, to idealize or romanticize the poor. The poor are themselves called upon to make a preferential option for the poor and to reject the idols of power and domination.[20] Too often the poor are themselves seduced by the dominant ideologies of power, wealth, and consumerism. The privileged position of the poor does not derive from their personal morality but from their socio-historical location outside the dominant power structures of our societies. Since, as "other" to those systems, the poor cannot be comprehended by those systems, they are the mediators of a God who, as mystery, cannot be comprehended by or reduced to those systems. Like the crucified Jesus, the poor stand as the guarantee of God's transcendence. The preferential option for the poor tells us nothing about the moral quality of the poor themselves; rather, it tells us something about God.[21]

Empowerment or Solidarity?
The preferential option for the poor is not only an exigency that proceeds from Christian faith, but is the very precondition for Christian faith. Our option for the poor empowers us to perceive God's own option for the poor. It provides us with the epistemological tools to

be able to perceive historical conflicts thereby enabling us to discover God's presence in that reality. By their very existence, the poor force us to maintain a fundamental honesty about reality. That is why we fear and despise them. That is why we hide them in ghettos, in institutions, behind walls, and on the "other side of the tracks." We cannot bear reality. And yet, as Jon Sobrino observes, "honesty about the real... is the first prerequisite of spirituality."[22] Unless we can see reality as it really is, we cannot hope to find God's presence in that reality; our God will be an illusory God just as our vision of reality is an illusion.[23]

It is not enough, however, to be honest about reality. We must then remain faithful to that reality, especially when it leads us "where we did not expect to be led," just as Jesus remained faithful to reality even on the cross, even in the face of the overwhelming reality of God's silence.[24] The preferential option for the poor is thus the condition for the possibility of authentic Christian faith (honesty about the real) and Christian discipleship (fidelity to the real). In the paradoxical way typical of the gospel, one cannot perceive the necessity of making an option for the poor unless and until one has already made that option. One cannot know God's will unless and until one does God's will.

We are called to identify ourselves with the struggles of the poor, therefore, not principally because of what we can bring to them, but because of what they can bring to us, namely, the God of Jesus Christ. Solidarity with the poor is the foundation of Christian faith and discipleship. We must listen before we can speak. For centuries the poor have been forced to listen to us; now we are called to be silent and listen to them, to become disciples of the poor, the human other, in order to be disciples of God, the Divine Other.[25]

Empowerment of the poor must follow upon and be grounded in solidarity, otherwise our desire to help the poor will likely be a response not to the needs of the poor but to our own needs, thereby perpetuating the oppression of the poor. To give more power to the powerless, or to share our power, is not necessarily to question the very definition of power and the power relationships that characterize modern Western societies. Yet it is that definition which must itself be questioned if the "empowerment" of the poor is not to result in a mere inversion of power relationships, with those who were formerly oppressed now becoming oppressors or allying themselves with their former oppressors. The notion of empowerment connotes a redistribution of power. Yet that notion presupposes the very power relationship, i.e., the benevolent, paternalistic master yielding some power to the servant, that has perpetuated the oppression of whole populations through the centuries. We still set the rules of the game, but we are now willing to let others play.

True empowerment must be based in solidarity, in an identification with the struggling poor and the marginalized. The most basic form of empowerment is that which occurs when the powerful remain silent and allow the powerless to speak and be heard. Perhaps the poor will say that what they want is not more power, not a greater stake in our political and economic games, but a different game altogether.[26]

HISPANICS IN THE UNITED STATES: A BLESSING FROM GOD

While the notions of a preferential option for the poor and empowerment are often used to describe the church's pastoral ministry to Hispanics in the United States, it is crucial that those terms be understood correctly if the church is to avoid simply replicating old patterns of exploitation. It is crucial, for instance, that, as important and influential as Catholic social teaching has been in bringing social justice to the forefront of the church's concerns, the social teaching be interpreted in the light of the experience of marginalized peoples and the theologies arising out of that experience. Within that experience, the preferential option for the poor is seen not as fundamentally an ethical issue but a theological, epistemological issue. Consequently, theologies arising out of a people's historical experience of oppression will perceive social justice not only as "doing the right thing" (ethics) but as "being honest about reality" (epistemology), in order to allow reality itself to provide the lenses for reading Scripture and tradition (theology), thereby empowering us to do "the right thing," i.e., accompany God's transformative presence in reality. Because the countenances of the poor are the mirrors of reality, we cannot be honest about reality unless we are identified with the poor, unless we are in solidarity with the poor, thereby — however imperfectly — looking at the world, and therefore God, from the perspective of the outcasts.

The history of Hispanics, or Latinos, in the United States is a history of suffering that mediates God's presence to church and society in North America. The One who is a transcendent, marginalized, outcast God is mediated through a *mestizo* people. The epistemological and theological significance of Hispanic-American *mestizaje* has been analyzed by the most prominent Hispanic-American theologian, Virgilio Elizondo.[27] As *mestizo* peoples, communities and individuals born out of a history of racial, ethnic, cultural, political, economic, and religious conflicts, all Latinos carry in their bodies the marks of marginalization, of people whose mixed heritage precludes full acceptance within the dominant societies. However, as the offspring of Native American, African, European, and most recently

Anglo-American cultures, Hispanic-American cultures symbolize the possibility of genuine unity, for these cultures are themselves a bridge: between Europe and America, between the white race and races of color, between Latin America and Anglo America.

As those seeking to empower Latinos and Latinas promote a unity grounded in the pluralistic cultural, educational, religious, political, and economic values of the dominant society, the danger of theologies of empowerment is that these will presuppose an understanding of pluralism, and hence of empowerment, that may prove alien to Hispanic-Americans and that, furthermore, may yield new forms of oppression. If empowerment is not grounded in solidarity, the interpretation and hence results of empowerment will be determined not by the poor but by the powerful, i.e., those doing the "empowering."

And just who are those doing the empowering? The answer to that question will determine the concrete nature of such empowerment and the historical form it will take. The poor reveal to all of us the truth about reality, the truth about ourselves. The answer to the above question, therefore, is revealed in the process of identification and solidarity with the struggles of the poor. In the case of Latinos and Latinas in the United States, their struggles for justice unmask the cultural presuppositions underlying Anglo notions of empowerment and pluralistic participation.

At the very heart of Hispanic-American cultures is an organic worldview. That organic worldview is inherited from the many cultures that gave birth to Latino cultures: Native American, African, and Ibero-Catholic. The organic worldview perceives creation, and humanity, as an organic unity. Whether derived from Native American animism or Roman Catholic natural law theory (as evidenced, for instance, in the tradition of Catholic social teaching), this worldview understands the human person as an inherently, intrinsically, and constitutively social entity. The person is defined by his or her social and communal ties, to family, town, church, country, etc.: to take a photograph of one's family is to take a photograph of oneself. Just as, psychologically, newborn infants at the mother's breast experience themselves as a part of the mother before experiencing themselves as separate, individual entities, so too, ontologically, a person is, by his or her very nature, given birth by and nurtured within the womb of socio-historical relationships. These are internal determinants of personal identity. Hispanic-Americans cannot escape this belief, for the reality to which it speaks is their heritage as *mestizos*.[28]

In the United States, the organic worldviews of the cultures that have heretofore formed and informed Latino cultures are now encountering another worldview that, in the process of encounter, has begun to inform Hispanic-American self-understanding. This Anglo-

American worldview is characterized by what Robert Bellah has called "ontological individualism," defined as "a belief that the individual has a primary reality whereas society is a second-order, derived or artificial construct."[29] As Paul Wachtel notes, "the individual is portrayed as *influenced* by the society in which he lives, but he is not really perceived as an organic part of it.... The 'community'... is a temporary and voluntary association of separate individuals."[30]

The conflict between an organic worldview and an individualistic worldview has important implications for those institutions and individuals who, though identified with the dominant society, seek to empower Hispanic-Americans. If the notion of empowerment is interpreted naively and exclusively within the individualistic worldview of the dominant Anglo society, one of two consequences may result: (1) Hispanics will be forced to surrender their communally-based culture in order to be accepted in the dominant society, or (2) Hispanics will be "empowered" and incorporated into North American society, but only as *marginalized* peoples, because the notion of empowerment would continue to be defined by the dominant society, hence the dominant Anglo society would continue to decide the nature and extent of Hispanic empowerment and participation. The Anglo individual could then welcome Hispanics as one additional culture to be included in the "melting pot" but, in doing so, would be blind to the ways in which his or her *a priori* historicity has already defined the process of inculturation itself. Consequently, such a melting pot could not be genuinely pluralistic, since it would insist on the historicity of the marginalized cultures while remaining inattentive to the full ramifications of the historicity of those who continue to exercise control.[31]

In the context of Anglo-American pluralism, the nature and extent of Hispanic participation would likely be severely circumscribed. Anglo-American individualism is by no means averse to the inclusion of more, and different, voices in socio-political decision-making processes. On the contrary, since it presupposes the individual's unfettered "freedom to choose" from among the widest range of alternatives possible (whether in the supermarket or the marketplace of ideas), individualism may indeed seek greater inclusiveness in order to maximize those alternatives. If an individual can, as it were, stand outside history and society in order to forge his or her identity by choosing from among a range of historical ideologies, cultures, religions, etc., then to maximize the alternatives would be to maximize individual freedom.

Yet such ignorance of the intrinsic historicity and social nature of human beings prevents those in power from recognizing how, despite their unimpeachable intentions, they continue to deny the poor their dignity by continuing to arrogate to themselves the function of "gatekeepers" in society, the ones who alone decide which voices will be heard and on what terms they will be heard. Hispanic-Americans would then no longer be forced to surrender their culture in order to participate in North American society; they would now be allowed to participate... as long as they "play by the rules." Those rules, however, must not be questioned. Hispanics can then continue to maintain their culture alive, but only within their own communities, i.e., only as long as they do not make any claims on the dominant Anglo society, which can rest content in the knowledge that it has "empowered" the poor to affirm their cultural self-identity while nevertheless persisting in the illusion that it has nothing to learn from the poor. Only if grounded in a solidarity with the poor will the very notions and interpretations of terms like "empowerment," "freedom," and "pluralism" be open to reinterpretation from the perspective of marginalized peoples. Otherwise, Anglo-Americans will continue to impose their own brand of freedom on the poor, all the while insisting that, in so doing, they are empowering the poor. One can only empower others if one is disempowered — that, after all, is the meaning of the cross. And one is disempowered by those whose broken bodies bear the marks of one's complicity in oppression. One is disempowered when one encounters the truth, when one encounters reality in all its starkness. And the poor are the truth — not, again, because of who they are, but because of who God is.[32]

To empower Hispanic-Americans, then, is to believe that Anglo society has something to learn from them. An encounter with this *mestizo* people, who have been born out of a rich, though often painful confluence of histories and cultures, calls into question the worldview of Anglo culture. It calls the dominant society beyond its cultural and ideological assumptions to new ways of seeing. It calls all of us to strive for a genuine pluralism whose very definition is forged in the struggle for justice, not imposed by the dominant social groups.

POPULAR RELIGIOSITY
AS A SOURCE OF EMPOWERMENT

The possibility of empowerment — if it is to be true empowerment — rests in the hands of the poor themselves. The weak must speak so that the powerful may listen... in order then to be able to speak not on behalf of but alongside the poor.[33] This implies that the history of oppression also contains within it the seeds of liberation; despite their social marginalization, the poor are not totally powerless, but, deep within their spirit, maintain some sense of their inherent dignity as children of God.[34]

Among Hispanics, nothing has been more important in helping

maintain that sense of dignity than the popular religiosity of Hispanic communities. If Latinos and Latinas are to be empowered, a principal source of that empowerment will be their deep religious faith as expressed, especially, in popular religion. In popular religiosity, the people's sense of dignity and, hence, the possibility of empowerment derives from the very organic cosmology that is so alien to Anglo culture. That is why popular religiosity is so readily derided (both by Anglos and by Hispanics who have identified with Anglo society), and why it is so crucial in the empowerment of Hispanics. As a principal conduit of the organic worldview inherited by Hispanics from their progenitor cultures, popular religiosity represents a major existential connection between *mestizo* Hispanic communities and their own histories. The demise of popular religiosity would thus imply not only the destruction of those histories but also the destruction of the organic, communal worldview that, as contradictory to the dominant worldview, remains a source not only of conflict — as Hispanic communities seek "acceptance" in Anglo society — but also of resistance.

This type of cultural genocide is, in fact, what often happens when "Bible-based" forms of evangelicalism enter into Hispanic communities. These present themselves as an alternative not only to "institutional" Catholicism, but also to Catholic, quasi-Catholic, and non-Catholic forms of popular religiosity, all of which are considered to be pagan. When devotions to saints and other such religious expressions are threatened, however, also threatened is the very organic worldview that, because it presupposes a creation interdependent both in space and time, forms the basis for the notion of a communion of saints united through space and time. Derived from its roots in both Catholic and indigenous cultures, this organic cosmology is then replaced by the individualistic worldview of Anglo-American religion. What is destroyed is not merely a particular form of religious expression, but an entire culture and history.

This, indeed, is the danger of certain notions of empowerment: their "empowerment" having been achieved, Hispanics can now assume their rightful place among the success stories of our society. The memories of suffering that are kept alive and re-lived in popular religion are replaced by a "biblical" religion that, though often presenting itself as an alternative to the religion of the dominant society, effectively suppresses these memories of suffering under the individualistic, realized, and thoroughly Anglo eschatology of the "born again Christian." Because the memories of suffering are a principal source of any oppressed community's empowerment and liberation, the relativization or repression of those memories seriously undermines the community's struggle for liberation. The memories of suffering are a constant reminder that the meaning of history (or the meaning of empowerment) is not — and will not be — determined by the victors, the "successful" alone. The Christian paradigm for a liberative memory of suffering is, of course, the gospel.[35]

The crucial significance of popular religiosity for the liberative empowerment of Hispanics in the United States has been argued by Orlando Espín and Sixto García: "Popular religiosity is one common element that emerges from the rich variety of the Hispanic-American world. It is probably the least 'Angloed' area of any of the Hispanic-American cultures, the least 'invaded' and thus the more deeply 'ours.' It can be seen as a font of Hispanic-American worldviews and self-concepts."[36] By popular religiosity they mean "the set of experiences, beliefs and rituals which more-or-less peripheral human groups create, assume and develop...and which to a greater or lesser degree distance themselves from what is recognized as normative by church and society, striving...to find an access to God and salvation which they feel they cannot find in what the church and society present as normative."[37]

The above definition of popular religion reveals the connection between an oppressed community's memories of suffering, as re-lived in popular religiosity, and the possibility of a liberative empowerment. The memories of suffering and popular religion maintain alive a community's self-identity as over against the dominant society. Hence, unless a theology of empowerment is grounded in a practical solidarity with the oppressed communities and their memories of suffering, the process of empowerment will be defined not by the memories of suffering but by the dominant society's nostalgic memories of conquest, which romanticize the suffering of the poor. Popular religiosity is born out of an oppressed community's self-understanding not only vis-à-vis God but also vis-à-vis the dominant society. As such, popular religion resists the dominant society's attempts to repress the poor's memories of suffering and, hence, their very identity.[38]

The liberative intent of popular religiosity is nowhere revealed with greater poignancy than in one of the most widespread and powerful of Hispanic religious devotions, the devotion to Our Lady of Guadalupe. This devotion was born out of the ashes of the conquest, "like the resurrection itself,...at the moment when everything appeared to be finished."[39] Like so many other devotions to Our Lady, Guadalupe is intimately tied to a people's memories of suffering. It is the poor, the children, the Indians, the *mestizos*, the blacks who are consistently remembered in these devotions as the bearers of revelation, the privileged recipients of the Good News.[40]

If grounded in a solidarity with the suffering of Hispanics in the United States, their empowerment will find its source in their own history. Popular religiosity is central to that history, for the popular religious devotions and practices of the Hispanic people effect a retrieval of history as a history not of conquest but of suffering. As expressions of a dispossessed people's refusal to accept the meaning imposed on history by the conquerors, the memories of suffering re-lived in popular religion are the seedbed of genuine empowerment, a liberative self-empowerment. And yet, of course, that *self*-empowerment is itself but a participation in God's own liberating work in history, God's own preferential option for the poor and identification with the poor in their suffering and in their resistance to domination. For popular religion effects not merely the retrieval of a people's history of suffering and not merely the consequent affirmation of a people's self-identity over against the dominant society; even more importantly, popular religion affirms the theological and salvific significance of that history and that identity.[41]

The preferential option for the poor, with its roots in Catholic social teaching and liberation theology, implies a suspicion of all theologies of empowerment, no matter how well-intentioned, that emerge from the dominant society. These need to be critiqued from the perspective of the victims themselves, for that perspective is, as we have seen, the perspective of the transcendent God, the God of the victims, the crucified God. Unless they are thus critiqued, they will continue to function as instruments of oppression, even if that oppression is now in the form of paternalism rather than outright genocide. For the criteria and definition of empowerment (and "democracy," "pluralism," etc.) will remain those of the cultural, political, and economic elites. Once again our society will have rejected the histories of the victims as vehicles of God's salvific truth, thereby reinforcing the ongoing *dis*-empowerment of the poor.

In their popular religiosity (e.g., the elaborate rituals surrounding Good Friday), Hispanics are identified with the human Jesus, the broken, battered, and crucified Jesus. Yet this is no masochistic self-indulgence; on the contrary, the affirmation of the crucified Jesus' humanity is, at the same time, the poor person's affirmation of his or her own humanity as one who continues to be crucified. And the beginning and precondition of any genuine empowerment is the poor person's cry, "I am a person; I am a human being." That cry effectively dethrones the oppressor, for it denies the oppressor the ability to impose his or her own meaning on the lives and histories of the poor. Among other things, it denies the oppressor the ability to define the process of empowerment. At the moment the outcast utters those revolutionary words, "I am a person," he or she literally comes into being as *someone* "that has a history, a biography, freedom," as an irreducible person who transcends all attempts at control: "Even in the extreme humiliation of a prison, in the cold of the cell and the total pain of torture, even when the body is nothing but a quivering wound, a person can still cry: 'I am another; I am a person; I have rights.' "[42]

CONCLUSION

If it is to be truly empowering and liberating, the preferential option for the poor, with its history in Catholic social teaching, must ultimately be interpreted and given meaning by the poor themselves, otherwise it will be either ignored or coopted and interpreted by the powerful in such a way that its challenging call to conversion will be effectively silenced. Yet the dominant society resists such a conversion process, for this epistemological shift implies that the poor divest the dominant society of the ability not only to define who they are but also who God is. Even more threatening is that, when the powerful are converted to the poor, the powerful surrender their power to define themselves, for they must now look at themselves through the eyes of the victims. What is most threatening about a genuine theology of empowerment, born in solidarity with the poor or out of a preferential option for the poor, is that it forces everyone to confront not only the brokenness of the victims of history but also — and as a result — our common brokenness and ultimate powerlessness, thereby enjoining all to struggle against that oppression and domination that results from the desperate need to deny human powerlessness, the need to create an illusion of omnipotence. It is only by identifying with the victims in their suffering that the powerful discover their own powerlessness — even to help the victims. The only appropriate form of "help" is that of solidarity, accompanying and joining the victims in their struggle for justice. Those who for years have perpetuated or benefited from historical injustice cannot empower those who have been victimized by that injustice; the powerful can only help remove the obstacles to the self-empowerment of the poor.[43]

As the church in the United States becomes a Hispanic church, we are thus called to retrieve Catholic social teaching, while nevertheless reading that teaching from the perspective of the poor. Then the demographic reality, the signs of the times, will give birth to a new theological reality. Hispanics are in a unique position to help forge this new reality, for their heritage spans the societies of the Americas. Hispanic-Americans stand with one foot in the Third World and one foot in the First World.[44] Hence, when Latinos and Latinas seek empowerment, they do so not to assume a greater share of the power presently exercised by Anglos, but to "usher in new life for the betterment of everyone."[45] As *mestizos*, Hispanics cannot reject outright any of the traditions to which they are heir; to do so would be to commit cultural suicide. Rather they seek to "freely and consciously assume the great traditions flowing through our veins and transcend them, not by denying [them] but by synthesizing them into something new."[46] The promise of the Hispanic-American is not merely a utopian vision but a concrete reality coursing through the veins of every Hispanic-American.

13

LOOKING TO THE LAST AND THE LEAST: A SPIRITUALITY OF EMPOWERMENT

Michael Downey

The title of this essay derives from the writings of Sallie McFague, who views the word and work of Jesus in light of his relationship to "the last and the least."[1] His message is a word of hope to those at the margins of social and religious institutions.

This essay proposes to provide an understanding of power and empowerment. By looking to the last and the least, those at the margins of the social-symbolic order, we can learn from them about the nature of power and empowerment. From the outset it must be noted that I am not attempting to chart a program for empowering the marginalized. It is rather more an issue of learning from the last and the least so that dominant understandings of power and empowerment, as well as those who live within such perspectives, might be transformed. From this goal, two questions follow: What can be learned about the nature of power and empowerment from those at the margins; and what might this contribute to an understanding of Christian spirituality?

My response to these questions employs the following strategy. First, it is necessary to examine the notions of margin and marginality. Second, an explanation of that ever-so-slippery term "spirituality" will be offered. Third, different understandings of power will be treated. Fourth, a hermeneutics of marginality will be described with the aim of bringing it to bear on the question of a spirituality of empowerment. Fifth, attention will be drawn to the significance of the kenosis of Christ and the life of Jesus as the parabolic Word of God for a spirituality of empowerment. Sixth, some elements of the process of empowerment will be described. Finally, the characteristics of a spirituality of empowerment will be suggested in light of the goal of emancipatory transformation so that all may participate in the fullness of human flourishing.

LIFE AT THE MARGINS

The terms "margins" and "marginalization" are used with increased frequency to describe those at the edge of the social-symbolic order and its ideology. Said another way, those at the margins do not fit, or are not in step with, prevalent modes of being and perceiving.

The image of margin or marginalization conveys three distinct notions. First, the margin represents the periphery, the place that does not have much importance because it is distant from the center where power is located. Second, the margin has no substance, it contains nothing, it is constituted by absence and emptiness. Third, the margin also communicates the notion of borderline or limit or edge, as a margin demarcates the edge of a written or typed page. Those at the margin are often viewed as the border between order and chaos.[2]

Referring to a person or group as marginalized is a practice of rather recent custom. To which person or group the designation applies is not always as clear as it may first seem. Those at the margins are not always the minority of a population. The majority of the Latin American population is comprised of the poor, yet the poor are marginalized by the systems of power and influence that shape their lives. Women are marginalized in the Roman Catholic Church, barred from official deliberation and decision-making that affect their lives, though they by no means constitute the minority of the ecclesial population. And lay persons, the great mass of the people of God, live at the margins of a hierarchical system comprised of celibate, male clerics.

Marginalized people may be said to be those who live at the margins or edges of a social body. The people at the "center" may be viewed as the "mainstream." The reasons for marginalization vary. Marginalization may result from poverty that relegates one to a lower economic status or class than that of the mainstream. It may have a somatic base; mentally and physically handicapped persons are often viewed as marginalized because of their difference from "normal people" with healthy and robust minds and bodies. Gender or sexual identity may also place one at the margins of a social body: women in a "man's world," and homosexuals in a world where heterosexual relationships are the norm, same-sex relationships being viewed as unnatural or abnormal. A person or group may be marginalized because of race or language.[3]

In the Roman Catholic Church, besides those noted above, those at the margins include, but are by no means limited to, single persons in parishes where the virtues of marriage and family life are extolled in sermonizing week after week, the divorced and remarried, laicized priests, and couples in interchurch marriages.

Common to all of these persons and groups is the element of difference from that which is identified as the acceptable, regular, normal,
or status quo. Such differences more often than not place persons and
groups in positions of powerlessness in the face of economic systems,
political structures, or religious institutions and their predominant
ideologies. The marginalized are those who have little or no access
to the power of the dominant ideology, or at least their access to it
is more restricted than that of those at the center. As a result, those
at the margins have little or no determination over the systems of
meaning and value, the predominant modes of perceiving and being,
which, nonetheless, profoundly affect them. They may be said to be
voiceless.

Related to the notion of the marginalized are the terms "the
alienated" and "the oppressed." The alienated are those who are
marginalized primarily for economic or political reasons. The term
"alienation" also bears emotional connotations, e.g., when women
or youth are described as alienated from the church. Oppressed peoples are marginated because of victimization arising from more active
forms of violence.

Another related term, "scapegoat," signifies the worst form of
marginalization. With origins in the Mosaic ritual of the Day of
Atonement (Lev. 16), the scapegoat was one of two goats chosen to
be sent out alive into the wilderness to die, the sins of the people
having been symbolically laid upon it, while the other was appointed
to be sacrificed. The scapegoat is the person or group who is blamed
for the failure or wrongdoing of others and cast out, expelled, or at
least ostracized from the social body. Such a person or group is often
already distinct from the main body by reason of national identity,
social status, or religious practice. In many Christian countries, Jews
have been used as scapegoats at various times in history, often with
religious sanctioning, which added to the ideological justification for
their marginalization.

It might also be useful to note that the image of Christ as scapegoat has functioned throughout Christian history, sometimes bearing
positive significance, particularly for marginalized peoples. A contemporary understanding of Christ as scapegoat in light of the experience
of marginalization deserves fuller attention, but lies beyond the scope
of this essay.

INTERLUDE: SELF-SCRUTINY

As a white, middle-class, well-educated male, it may appear that I
fit easily at the center of the social-symbolic order and its dominant
ideology. I am part of the center, the "majority" that pushes persons
and groups to the margins of church and society. But as I live at

the center, I am unable to dismiss the voices from the periphery: the cries and shouts of Christian feminist, liberation, political, and Third World theologians that address me from the margins of that center to which I have easy access by virtue of race, gender, and class. If I would stand with those on the margins, with those who speak from the margins, I must place myself outside the center of the order, to some measure, which provides possibilities for new modes of communion and solidarity with those who suffer from the effects of the social-symbolic order.

Care must be taken at this point. Some freely choose to stand with those at the margins, while others are at the margins because they have to be — there is no choice. The two should not be confused. The experience of life at the margins and the experience of those who freely choose to stand in solidarity with them is never the same, and caution must be exercised in the face of the temptation to appropriate facilely the experience of those who have no choice but to live at the margins.[4] For example, the experience of being mentally handicapped and, as a result, being cast to the margins of the mainstream, is of a radically different sort than that of "normal" persons who live in intentional communities with the mentally handicapped.[5]

To make the decision to freely stand with those at the margins results in what Rebecca Chopp calls a "center/margin viewpoint."[6] It entails a willingness to see "from beneath," from the viewpoint of the useless, the suspect, the abused, the oppressed, the despised, the powerless. In short, it is to see from the vantage of suffering.[7] From this viewpoint, I begin to understand that the dominant social-symbolic order works for no one. As a result, my own discourse about God, Christ, church, and Christian life must change. I must first listen to the suffering of those at the margins and "name" the psychic destructiveness of the center for what it is.[8] From this perspective, Christian life and practice are aimed, in part, at the emancipatory transformation of the center. The "normal" modes of perceiving and being are challenged through the powers of the weak. Emancipatory transformation is not, then, a matter of assimilating the last and the least, the wounded and the weak, into systems that themselves have caused such an awesome threat to human life and the world as we know it.

SPIRITUALITY:
THE SPIRIT AT WORK IN PERSONS

What exactly is spirituality? More specifically: What is Christian spirituality? The terms are often used with a great measure of imprecision. But more succinct and clearer definitions are emerging.

It must be recognized that Christian spirituality refers to both a lived experience and an academic discipline. In both instances, "the referent of the term 'spirituality' is Christian religious experience as such."[9] That is to say, the term refers to experience precisely as religious and as Christian. Because it is Christian, theological insights and accuracy are crucial to it. Because it is religious, it is affective as well as cognitional, communal as well as personal, focused at once on God and others. And because it is experience, it pertains to everything that constitutes the living of Christian life.[10] James Wiseman suggests that rather than focusing on "what" the Christian believes (*credenda*) or "what to do" as a consequence of belief (*agenda*), the focus of spirituality is on the *agendum* of the whole of Christian life in relation to God.[11]

Writers like Jean Leclercq and Walter Principe view Christian spirituality in a similar light. Principe defines spirituality in terms of all dimensions of a person's faith commitment "that concern his or her striving to attain the highest ideal or goal," namely, "an ever more intense union with the Father through Jesus Christ by living in the Spirit."[12]

From another vantage, I have suggested that spirituality is concerned with the Holy Spirit at work in persons: (1) within a culture; (2) in relation to a tradition; (3) in remembrance of Jesus Christ; (4) in light of contemporary events, hopes, sufferings, and promises; (5) in efforts to combine elements of action and contemplation; (6) with respect to charism and community; (7) as expressed and authenticated in praxis. The Spirit at work in all these dimensions of personal (inclusive of the social and political) life, gives rise to a great diversity of spiritualities.[13]

What these perspectives have in common is the understanding that spirituality is concerned with the *dynamic* and *concrete* character of the *relationship* of the human person to God *in actual life situations*. Moreover, the relationship is one of *development*, of growth in the life of faith, and thus covers the whole of life. Spirituality concerns religious experience as such, not just concepts or obligations.

The life situation that is our concern here is that of those who live at the margins and fissures of the center. In looking to them, our purpose is to uncover an understanding of power that arises from the work of the Spirit in the experience of marginalization, which differs considerably from views of power that prevail at the center.

UNDERSTANDINGS OF POWER

One way to speak of power is in terms of the ability to act. Power effects change; it brings something about. Most understandings of power suggest that some have it, while others do not. Those who have power can use it for good or for ill. Powerful people can abuse others through exercises of power that dominate, control, manipulate, and violate. The powerless often submit to such exercises of power, by choice or circumstance, and thus are controlled, manipulated, and violated. Often such exercises of power are said to be for a greater or higher good, such as God's will or the divine plan. Abuses of power of the most subtle sort are visited upon children "for their own good" by their parents.[14]

This "some have it, some don't" understanding of power rests on an asymmetrical dualism rooted in a restricted and restrictive view of an all-powerful God.[15] In this view, God is all-powerful, external to the world as the power that controls it. Human beings are ultimately powerless, subject to domination by the divine sovereign, or to divine benevolence. Such a view of God as the divine sovereign who is "in charge" and who exercises power vis-à-vis human beings "for their own good," can serve to justify exercises of power that dominate, control, and manipulate those without power and can be counterproductive.

Feminist studies and the "linguistic turn" as it has affected much of religious and theological studies bring new perspectives to bear on prevalent notions of power.[16] From these perspectives, power is understood in terms of "naming," giving voice, speaking. Power speaks, it "names" one's experience as one's own, it gives voice to one's silent suffering and the suffering of a people at the hands of those "in charge." To have power is to have a say. For Rebecca Chopp, "power is the ability to take one's place in whatever discourse is essential to action, and the right to have one's part matter."[17] Power is "talking back," a form of resistance to the practices and principles of control, domination, and oppression.

Whether it is viewed as the ability to speak or to act and change, self-determination is at issue. To have power, to speak or act, is to be the subject of one's own history. If this is the case, then dualistic and asymmetrical views of power that accentuate a separation between divine and human power, must give way to other views that recognize the unity and interdependence of divine and human power.[18] This necessitates a fuller appreciation of the nature of God's relationship with the world in and through the work of the Spirit that is the very life, presence, and power of God in, through, and to the world. Such an appreciation allows for understanding power as a unified and interdependent reality, thus making possible the recognition and exercise of power through processes of relationality built on mutuality, reciprocity, and collaboration.

This relational view of power stands in direct opposition to the view of power that rests on asymmetrical dualism, which gives rise to the position that "some have it, some don't." The latter view treats power as something given by unilateral bestowal by those who have it to those who do not. In the relational view, power is unified and interdependent because it originates in the unity and interdependence of divine and human power that is the Spirit. This necessitates recognizing that power rests at the heart of all creation, even and especially in the most vulnerable of creation, and allowing it to stand forth.

The keynote of the unilateral approach to power is *order*. In the attempt to preserve order, especially when it is judged to be divinely ordained, control, manipulation, domination, and forms of violence both subtle and overt continue to be justified and tolerated, even in God's name. The hallmarks of the relational view of power are fidelity, nurture, attraction, self-sacrifice, passion, responsibility, care, affection, respect, and mutuality.[19]

Here it must be noted that in fact most exercises of power do operate in the manner of "some have it, some don't." That is to say that some do hold power and others are in fact powerless. Structures do control and dominate. So what good is the effort to describe different modes or views of power more in keeping with a relational perspective? For any real change to take place, a linguistic and epistemological reorientation is required. This demands not only a description of what actually is and must be. It also requires a description that suggests what may or might be. The intention of this essay is not to offer a specific program for proper exercises of power and empowerment. It is to suggest views of what may or might be, what is possible for each and for all in our common desire for human flourishing.

A HERMENEUTICS OF MARGINALITY[20]

In light of our concern to spell out the contours of a spirituality of empowerment, it is useful to ask at this point: Which of these approaches to power is more in keeping with the lordship of Christ, properly understood, and the power of the Holy Spirit? The answer depends upon how one views Christ's lordship or how one remembers the word and the work of Jesus as expressing God's intention for the world both now and to come.

In every age the Christian community has attempted to find appropriate ways of giving praise and thanks to God in prayer, in light of changing circumstances and different exigencies. The prayer life of individuals and communities depends in no small measure on the way they remember Christ. Put another way: Persons and groups make decisions about which elements in the life of Jesus, God's Word, are central to the task of being and becoming Christian in a particular time, place, culture, and tradition. This has been done in every age.

Put more simply still: Hearers of the Word hear the Word in certain ways.

The term "hermeneutics of marginality" describes a way of looking, understanding, judging, deciding, and acting from the margins, in solidarity with those who live and speak from the periphery: from the fissures, the cracks, the edges of the center. Adopting such a hermeneutical stance, deciding that one will perceive and be in the world from the margins, is to risk being at odds with what is judged to be "normal," "established," "reliable," and "traditional." Looking to Jesus and hearing his words from a hermeneutics of marginality implies a twofold acknowledgement: First, it sees Jesus' ministry as focused on the margins and on the radical reordering of present reality and, second, it recognizes and "names" the experience of God at the margins. More succinctly: To view the word and the work, the meaning and message of Jesus in this way is to attend to the presence and action of God manifest in the margins and in those who manifest God's Spirit there.

What is the view of Jesus that emerges when one looks and hears from the margins? From the perspective of the margins, one might say that it is the Kenotic Christ, whose lordship and dominion are disclosed precisely in his self-emptying (Phil. 2:6–11), in his refusal to lay claim to exercises of authority and power grounded in unilateral, asymmetrical dualism — the power of "the world." In his refusal of this type of power, in fact in his powerlessness, the power and lordship of Jesus are disclosed. Jesus' refusal of external, "worldly" power and his acceptance of the human condition enabled him to enter the life of others at their most vulnerable point. But this is power of a sort very different from the power of "the world." It is the power of an infant at Bethlehem and a crucified minister and teacher of mercy on Golgotha. And this power differs completely from that which brings about change by control, domination, or manipulation; it is power manifest in care, compassion, self-sacrifice, reciprocity, and mutuality.

A hermeneutics of marginality looks to the Kenotic Christ precisely within the context of a proclamation of good news for those at the edges, the fissures of the social and religious bodies. A fuller appreciation of the Kenotic Christ thus requires attention to the power of the Word.

THE PARABOLIC POWER OF THE WORD

Listening to the Word at the margins requires attention to the proclamation and manifestation of God's action and presence in Christ Jesus in a distinctive manner. Just as every point of view is *a* view of a point, so the place where one stands determines what one hears. When standing at the margins, we hear the Word in ways that orient us to a new sense of time through remembrance of what God has done, is now doing, and will do in and through Christ. Proclaiming and hearing the Word from the edge is an act of memory and of hope — remembrance, in the fullest sense of the term (from the Greek, *anamnesis*), and trust in the divine promise yet to be realized.

Here it may be useful to emphasize that it is the Spirit who enables us to remember the words and work of Jesus. Remembering is made possible by the activity of the Holy Spirit who, in recalling Jesus to mind, makes us understand and actualize his presence (John 14:26). Thus, in speaking of the power of the Word in both proclamation and hearing and in speaking of different ways of remembering Christ and his message that results from this, we are describing the work of the Spirit in persons — a spirituality mediated in and through the Word.

A fuller appreciation of Jesus as God's Word from a hermeneutics of marginality demands an understanding of the way the Word works. Paul Ricoeur has written extensively on the nature and function of religious language. His insights on parable are particularly instructive for the purposes of this essay. Ricoeur suggests that parables work on a pattern of orientation, disorientation, and reorientation.[21] The parable begins in the ordinary world with its familiar and unquestioned assumptions and modes of perception. But in the course of the story a radically different view is introduced that shocks and disorients the hearer(s). Through the interplay of the two contrasting perspectives, a tension is created that gives rise to a redescription of the world and a reorientation of the hearer's mode of perceiving and being in the world.

This insight can be extended in such a way that we may speak of the parabolic power of the Word. That is to say, the way in which the parable works is also the way the Word, more generally speaking, works. In a similar vein, Walter Brueggemann suggests that the Word is both a radical critique of conventional standards, and a source of energy for the building of a new world more in keeping with God's promise.[22]

The parabolic power of the Word, whose rhythms fill the ears and the hearts of those gathered at the edges to be "washed" in its ebb and flow, wages a radical critique on conventional standards and the unquestioned, yet tightly held, assumptions about God, self, and others. But it also energizes the hearers of the Word to live and to work for a radically new future, the contours of which are discerned in the proclamation of the Crucified and Risen One, who through his *kenosis* lived and died in solidarity with those who suffer at the edges.

In the proclamation and hearing, the Word shocks and disorients the hearers. The present situation, the now in which voices are lifted to God in praise and thanksgiving, is called into question and radically critiqued by a Word that tells of the mighty being cast from their thrones, of the poor holding pride of place (as in the Magnificat, Luke 1:46–55), and of the child who shall be the prophet of the Most High (as in the Benedictus, Luke 1:68–79). Indeed the Word overturns our conventional standards, our ordinary ways of perceiving and judging. Hearing this Word summons to a redescription of reality: the poor are at the top of the ladder; the rich and proud of heart are not to be the center of attention; children speak of God and have something to say — believe them!

Thus, the Word demands a reorientation in the direction of the future, the time of God's promise, the hour when the power of love will cast out all fear, when love will prevail over all evil. Listening to the Word at the margins entails giving the parabolic quality of the Word in its entirety a chance in our hearing. This implies that all the words, psalms, hymns, canticles, readings, and benedictions that are proclaimed and heard from the margins give expression to parable's pattern: orientation, disorientation, reorientation.

For example, the parable of the prodigal son begins with an orientation that appeals to ordinary, commonplace sensibilities. Then disorientation enters when it shocks and shatters those sensibilities, calling into question all standards of fairness and justice. Finally a reorientation invites the hearers to live from the perspective of unrestricted forgiveness and mercy. The effect of this and other parables of Jesus is to "destabilize" tightly held views and expectations of the God-world relation, so that human beings can live by a new vision that is glimpsed in the word and work of Jesus.[23]

This new vision is also seen, in part, in the meal stories of the New Testament. Jesus eats with sinners as well as with "the saved." This shatters expectations and perceptions of righteousness and holiness. It also challenges perceptions of the "unworthy." Those on the "outside" are on the "inside" through Jesus' eating at table with them. Thus, those who would live by the meaning and message of Jesus are invited to reorient their ways of relating along the lines of "inclusivity," with particular attention to those at the margins of society and religious institutions — "the last and the least." "Not the holiness of the elect, but the wholeness of *all* is the central vision of Jesus."[24]

The position that the parabolic power of the Word needs to be given its chance in our hearing is rooted in the conviction that the life, ministry, death, and resurrection of Jesus is the parabolic Word of God. That is to say that the pattern of Christ's self-emptying in the *kenosis* and in the *pasch*, which is the point of reference in all Christian life and spirituality, is itself an expression of the pattern of orientation, disorientation, reorientation.

The parabolic power of the Word as orientation, disorientation, reorientation, or description, deconstruction, redescription is nowhere more pronounced than in the life, dying, and rising of Christ. The destabilizing effect of the parables that is expressed in the life of Jesus himself through the inclusion of all at the table, especially the last and the least, is consummated in the cross. The cross is the necessary path in bringing about the new mode of perceiving and being expressed in the parables and the table stories. This is a way of radical identification with all others, which entails a commitment to solidarity with the suffering and with victims of all ages. It also requires nonhierarchical, nondualistic modes of relationship with all others, particularly the wounded and the weak, the voiceless, those at the margins, the last and the least.

The parabolic power of the Word destabilizes, shocks, and shatters our standard ways of thinking about things and invites us to live by a vision in which the proud-hearted are scattered in their conceit and the poor are exalted. In light of this redescription of reality and of life within it, Christian life is rooted in the *kenosis*, the self-emptying of Christ, described in the Philippians hymn (2:6–11). Union with God requires a commitment to downward mobility in order to live in mutual love with the wounded and the weak, in imitation of Christ's self-emptying, rather than the upward mobility, the "upscale" vision of, let us say the "yuppies," the new ascendancy whose hallmark is conspicuous consumption.[25]

The Word of God is a bold proclamation of the discontinuity and contrast between present, conventional standards and ways of being and the future to which God calls and commands. On the one hand, the Word wages a strident critique, reminding the hearers that the power of evil and sin still has sway in the world. On the other, it offers the hope and consolation that this power will come to an end. Thus, there is cause for repentance as well as celebration, sorrow as well as joy, lamentation as well as praise and thanksgiving. From the vantage of the margins, we see that authentic Christian living in our day entails recognizing suffering and naming the negative factors in ecclesial and social life together with the positive ones for which we rightly give thanks to God. And this implies that we do so particularly, though not exclusively, in prayer in all its expressions: "private" and public, individual and liturgical.[26]

The parabolic power of the Word as it is proclaimed and heard at the margins reorients the hearers to the realization that the way of the cross is necessary in bringing about the new world, the new mode of being envisioned in the parables and in the stories of Jesus sitting at table with the "unworthy." This is a way of radical identification with all others, particularly the last and the least. The cross symbolizes the willingness to relinquish controlling and triumphalist tactics in favor of solidarity with victims, the wounded and the weak, the last and the least. Thus, a model of Christian life in the Spirit transformed by this hearing of the Word in and for our time would recognize that authentic Christian praxis lies in the acceptance of the invitation to solidarity with the Crucified Christ in and through the practice of solidarity with those who suffer.

POWER AND EMPOWERMENT
FROM THE MARGINS

In light of this way of viewing Jesus focused on the singular importance of his *kenosis* and this way of proclaiming and hearing the Word as a work of the Spirit, what can be learned about power and empowerment in Christian life?

Whether it be viewed in terms of the ability to speak or to act and change, the power of the Spirit mediated in the Word is unified and interdependent. Divine and human power are not in competition. While they are distinct, they are not separate realities. Similarly, the power exercised by human beings need not necessarily be viewed in terms of "the haves and have nots." A Christian exercise of power thus becomes a matter of relinquishing approaches to power rooted in asymmetrical dualism, which result in competition, control, domination, and manipulation for the preservation of what is judged to be proper order. This "normal," "accepted," "approved," "traditional" way of perceiving and being in the world, from the perspective of the margins, does not work. And from the "center/margin" perspective that I have adopted throughout this essay, an uncritical acceptance of the social-symbolic order and its ideology contributes to the psychic destructiveness of the center. Thus, the parabolic power of the Word and the *kenosis* of Christ that lies at its core confronts that power which preserves and protects the center. From the center, refusing to lay claim to power is to be in a position of powerlessness; from the periphery it is to share in the power of the Spirit of Christ who in his teaching and very presence wages the ultimate criticism of the dominant ideology, the prevalent order. Brueggemann writes:

> He [Jesus] has, in fact, dismantled the dominant culture and nullified its claims. The way of his ultimate criticism is his solidarity with marginal people and the accompanying vulnerability required by that solidarity. The only solidarity worth affirming is solidarity characterized by the same helplessness they know and experience.[27]

From the perspective at the margins, power possesses a whole new purpose. The end, the objective, in any proper exercise of power from a hermeneutics of marginality is to provide for the possibility of others becoming ever more fully the subjects of their own history, rather than the subjects of the powerful, rich, and robust. It is to speak with one's own voice and to tell one's own story, not to speak in the voice of another or adopt the modes of discourse in which one's own voice is, at best, only a faint echo. Put another way, power is for emancipatory transformation, the process by which persons come to do the truth in love freely, not for the preservation of tradition and order. Such power enables persons to become their own subjects, to speak their own voice. In this lies authentic empowerment.

From this perspective, power is understood to be expressed in manifold ways. It is enriched rather than diminished by difference. Those "in charge" are not viewed as the sole custodians of power, but rather as servants of its manifold presence. Other views of power merely tolerate difference in light of an exacting need for control. But a relational view of power rooted in a hermeneutics of marginality does not merely tolerate difference. It demands, enables, and encourages difference. Persons and communities are enriched, not diminished, by differences. Because it is in the confrontation with those who are different from themselves that those at the center can discover their own powerlessness, their own "marginalization" and alienation from their deepest selves. Authentic solidarity with those who suffer, with others who are gaining voice at the margins, is possible only to the measure that those at the center accept their own powerlessness and marginalization, which is disclosed as they are confronted by the powers of the weak.

Within the context of this relational view of power that is exercised for the purpose of emancipatory transformation, the question that needs to be addressed is: What is the nature of empowerment and how does it take place? How does empowerment happen if power is not simply handed on unilaterally by those who have it to those who do not?

Walter Brueggemann's treatment of the nature of prophecy as radical critique of the priestly, royal, dominant consciousness from the perspective of the marginal ones is pertinent here. It suggests clues for understanding how empowerment works within a hermeneutics of marginality.[28]

First, there is the task of uncovering symbols that convey the experience of life at the edges. This is not a matter of inventing symbols. It is rather a question of digging deeply into the consciousness of those at the margins to find therein particular histories that have provided the basis for contradicting the dominant ideology or prevalent order that has made them invisible, voiceless, powerless. Such symbols, retrieved in memory and in hope, can offer possibilities for life and future to those who have been pushed and shoved to the margins.

The retrieval of symbols and stories of life at the margins is a way of pushing and shoving back.

For example, there is the symbol of the weak and frail Abel, victim of the violence of his strong and robust brother Cain. It is from the blood of the weaker, slain brother that salvation comes. Similarly, it is from Jacob, the younger brother, again much more frail and fair (but far more clever and inventive!) than the sinewy Esau, that the promise of salvation continues. There is God's promissory address to the darkness of chaos, to barren Sarah, to oppressed slaves of the Egyptians. "The promise of God is first about an alternative future," and it is offered to those who have no future or possibility in the reigning order of the center.[29]

Second, there is the task of bringing to public expression the horrors and the hopes of those at the margins. This may be the hardest task of all. For if those at the margins are powerless and voiceless, how is speech possible? To this question there is no easy answer. But we see examples in those survivors of the Holocaust who are willing to bring to public expression the horrors that they and millions of the voiceless dead suffered at the hands of the Nazis.[30]

Just as the recovery of the symbols of the marginalized entails digging deeply into the consciousness of those at the margins to find therein symbols of contradiction, so too speaking of the horror and the hope of the margins requires a recognition that there are and have always been modes of discourse within which those at the margins have "talked back" to the center from which they have been excluded. Learning to bring the horrors of the margins to public expression requires speaking about that of which many are not conscious, cannot believe, or flatly deny. The hope expressed from the margins is often an absurdity too embarrassing to speak about, because it opposes what those at the center proclaim as facts. Christian hope at the margins is "the refusal to accept the reading of reality which is the majority opinion; and one does that only at great political and existential risk."[31]

Third, empowerment requires listening to the language of grief and lamentation so that one can learn to speak it to others. From the perspective of the margins, the old order is passing away; those at the center must grieve its loss. Exercises of power grounded in asymmetrical dualism have resulted in violence and in the suffering of innocent millions. But the voices of these millions, both living and dead, speak about hope and newness that redefines the present situation. It is the voice of rejected Joseph assuring his brothers that things do work out for good and the voice of Mary of Nazareth proclaiming the greatness of the God who fills the hungry with good things, casts down the proud and mighty, lifts up the poor and lowly, and reserves for them pride of place. Indeed, the whole history of Israel begins in God's attentiveness to the cries of the marginal ones. Christian faith rests in the Crucified and Risen One who lived and died in solidarity with those at the margins. And his Spirit is nowhere more vibrant than in the voices of those who cry out in pain and possibility from the edges to the center.

A SPIRITUALITY OF EMPOWERMENT

To speak of spirituality is to speak of the Spirit at work in persons. This Spirit is the life and power of God in, through, and to the world. A Christian spirituality emerges as a result of the Spirit manifest and mediated in the word and work, meaning and message of Jesus. And different Christian spiritualities, different ways of living in and by the Spirit, arise as a result of the way the Spirit works within different cultures, specific traditions, various ways of remembering Christ, and so on.[32]

This essay has attempted to develop a spirituality of empowerment from the vantage of a hermeneutics of marginality. What are the contours of this spirituality of empowerment?

First, this spirituality is rooted in a view of power that is unified and interdependent, grounded not in the asymmetrical dualism that derives from a faulty notion of the separation of divine and human power. Rather, such a spirituality is grounded in a relational view of power that is exercised authentically to the degree that it is aimed at emancipatory transformation, so that human persons, especially the last and the least, the wounded and the weak, might become subjects of their own history in order to do the truth in love freely.

Second, the *kenosis* of Christ is central to this spirituality. Within the context of this way of remembering Christ through the work of the Spirit, prevalent exercises of power rooted in competition, domination, manipulation, and control are to be critiqued and relinquished in order to cultivate expressions of power built on reciprocity, mutuality, and care.

Third, this spirituality is characterized by attentiveness to the work of the Spirit in the parabolic pattern of the Word that orients, disorients, and reorients to ways of perceiving and being more in keeping with the lordship of the Kenotic Christ. As a result:

(a) Christian life destabilizes conventional expectations and standards of the center and upsets "normal" divisions and dualisms. Those at the edges, on the outside, invisible at the margins, are those who receive God's self-disclosure.

(b) Christian life is inclusive and requires the recognition of the strengths already existing in the wounded and the weak, the outsider.[33]

(c) Christian life requires antihierarchical and antitriumphalist ways of human relationship, expressed in the self-emptying of Christ, the king who became a servant and who suffers alongside the wounded and the weak, the outsider, the last and the least.[34]

Fourth, this spirituality rests in the confidence that the life, breath, and power of God in and through the Spirit resides at the heart of all creation, even and especially the wounded and the weak, the most vulnerable. Its most pressing mandate is to let life continue, rather than to harness, control, and master it. Its most compelling exercise is in letting life be instead of forcing itself in the name of good order.

Fifth, those who would live by this spirituality recognize that the challenge of empowerment does not lie in handing over power from those who have it to those who do not. Empowerment involves much more than the passing on of power. It entails seeking forgotten symbols that convey the life of the Spirit at the margins, learning to hear with open ears and speak with full voice about the horrors and hopes of those at the margins and, finally, offering a new description of ways of perceiving and being in the world more in keeping with God's intention for the world both now and to come.

CONCLUSION

Perhaps the greatest risk in discourse about power and empowerment is the failure to get beyond understandings of power grounded in the "some have it, some don't" approach. Such understandings lead to strategies, often quite well-intentioned and benign (though more often than not patronizing), of turning over, giving up, or passing on to others this slippery reality we call power.

The view of power and empowerment from a hermeneutics of marginality is of a very different kind. Most importantly, authentic exercises of this power are aimed at the emancipatory transformation of persons and the radical critique and transformation of power as it is exercised at the center. Thus, it is not a matter of giving those at the margins a share in the power of those at the center of church and society. It is a matter of recognizing new ways of perceiving and being more in keeping with the word and the work of the Crucified and Risen One whose power was disclosed in his refusal to lay claim to the power of lords, kings, priests, and patriarchs.

To share in this power is to listen to those who speak in a different voice. It is to turn one's ears and eyes from the center to the edge of church and society. It is to live from and for fidelity, nurture, attraction, self-sacrifice, passion, responsibility, care, affection, respect, and mutuality. It is to accept the mandate: Let life continue, but not as it has been with the center defining life and the quality of human life. And it is to set aside the inordinate desire for order and to recognize, enable, and encourage otherness, specificity, particularity, solidarity, and transformation.[35]

The spirituality of empowerment is one of surrender to the Spirit, the breath of God anointing to speech and bringing to voice, blessing difference, specificity, solidarity, transformation, and anticipation.

Notes

1 · The Politics of Meeting: Women and Power in the New Testament by Tina Pippin (pages 13–24)

1. Jay Murphy, "Interview with Fredric Jameson," *Left Curve*, no. 12 (1988): 9.
2. Jim Merod, *The Political Responsibility of the Critic* (Ithaca, N.Y.: Cornell University Press, 1987), 191.
3. Rosemary Radford Ruether, *Sexism and God-Talk* (Boston: Beacon Press, 1983), 32.
4. For example, see the discussion in Carter Heyward, "Suffering, Redemption, and Christ," *Christianity and Crisis* 49 (December 11, 1989): 381–86.
5. Chap. 5 in *Sexism and God-Talk*.
6. Elizabeth A. Meese, *Crossing the Double-Cross: The Practice of Feminist Criticism* (Chapel Hill: University of North Carolina Press, 1986), 141–42.
7. Jonathan Culler, *On Deconstruction: Theory and Criticism after Structuralism* (Ithaca: Cornell University Press, 1982), 44.
8. Patrocinio P. Schweickart, "Reading Ourselves: Toward a Feminist Theory of Reading," in *Gender and Reading: Essays on Readers, Texts, and Contexts*, ed. Elizabeth A. Flynn and Patrocinio P. Schweickart (Baltimore: Johns Hopkins University Press, 1986), 49.
9. Max Weber, *Economy and Power*, ed. Günther Roth and Claus Wittich, vol. 1, sec. 16 (New York: Benminster Press, 1968), 53, quoted in Martin Hengel, *Christ and Power*, trans. Everett R. Kalin (Philadelphia: Fortress Press, 1977), 2.
10. Hengel, ibid., 81.
11. Jürgen Habermas, "Hannah Arendt's Communications Concept of Power," *Social Research* 44 (Spring 1977): 6–7
12. Ibid., 18.
13. Janice Capel Anderson, "Mary's Difference: Gender and Patriarchy in the Birth Narratives," *Journal of Religion* 67 (1987): 185.
14. Ibid., 186.
15. Barbara Johnson, *A World of Difference* (Baltimore: Johns Hopkins University Press, 1987), 143.
16. Ibid., 3.
17. Ibid., 7.
18. Toril Moi, *Sexual/Textual Politics: Feminist Literary Theory* (New York: Methuen, 1985).

19. In particular, Fernando Belo, *A Materialist Reading of the Gospel of Mark*, trans. Matthew J. O'Connell (Maryknoll, N.Y.: Orbis Books, 1981), and Ched Myers, *Binding the Strong Man: A Political Reading of Mark's Story of Jesus* (Maryknoll, N.Y.: Orbis Books, 1988).

20. Belo, ibid., 32.

21. Pierre Macherey, *A Theory of Literary Production* (New York: Routledge & Kegan Paul, 1985).

22. Susan Wells, *The Dialectics of Representation* (Baltimore: Johns Hopkins University Press, 1985), 165.

23. Rosalind Coward and John Ellis, *Language and Materialism* (Boston: Routledge & Kegan Paul, 1977), 88.

24. Hans Conzelmann, *The Theology of St. Luke*, trans. Geoffrey Buswell (New York: Harper & Row, 1961), 172, note 1.

25. Jane Schaberg, *The Illegitimacy of Jesus* (New York: Harper & Row, 1987), 96.

26. Ibid., 99–103.

27. Robert Tannehill, "The Magnificat as Poem," *Journal of Biblical Literature* 93 (1974): 275.

28. Kristeva is explained by Moi, *Sexual/Textual Politics*, 167.

29. C. Hugo Zorrilla, "The Magnificat: Song of Justice," in *Conflict and Context: Hermeneutics in the Americas*, ed. Mark Lau Branson and C. Rene Padilla (Grand Rapids: William B. Eerdmans, 1986), 237.

30. David Peter Seccombe, *Possessions and the Poor in Luke-Acts* (Linz: Studien zum Neuen Testament und seiner Umwelt, 1982), 94.

31. Ibid., 95.

32. Zorrilla, "The Magnificat," 237.

33. Northrop Frye, *The Great Code: The Bible and Literature* (New York: Harcourt Brace Jovanovich, 1982), 183.

34. Zorrilla, "The Magnificat," 235.

35. Ernesto Cardenal, *The Gospel in Solentiname*, trans. Donald D. Walsh (Maryknoll, N.Y.: Orbis Books, 1976), 25.

36. Ibid., 31.

37. Rita Brock, *Journeys by Heart: A Christology of Erotic Power* (New York: Crossroad, 1988), 71.

38. Ibid., 74.

39. Ibid., 76.

40. Beverly Harrison, *Making the Connections*, ed. Carol S. Robb (Boston: Beacon Press, 1985), 14.

41. Elisabeth Schüssler Fiorenza, *In Memory of Her* (Crossroad, 1983), 350.

2 · Power and Authority in Early Christian Centuries
by David N. Power (pages 25–38)

1. See J. G. Dunn, *Jesus and the Spirit: A Study of the Religious and Charismatic Experience of Jesus and the First Christians as Reflected in the New Testament* (Philadelphia: Westminster Press, 1975), 76–82.

2. Ibid., 81.

3. See J. H. Schutz, *Paul and the Anatomy of Apostolic Authority* (New York: Cambridge University Press, 1984).

4. Dunn, *Jesus and the Spirit*, 110–14.

5. Out of the massive literature on this subject, a useful synthesis is found in R. E. Brown, *The Churches the Apostles Left Behind* (New York: Paulist Press, 1984).

6. For early church developments, see H. Von Campenhausen, *Ecclesiastical Authority and Spiritual Power in the Church of the First Three Centuries* (Stanford: Stanford University Press, 1969). There is a useful chapter, entitled "The Emergence of Orthodoxy," in W. H. C. Frend, *The Rise of Christianity* (Philadelphia: Fortress Press, 1984), 229–57.

7. On the formation of the canon, see H. Von Campenhausen, *The Formation of the Christian Bible* (Philadelphia: Fortress Press, 1972).

8. On the rule of faith, see J. N. D. Kelly, *Early Christian Creeds* (New York and London: Longmans, Green, 1950).

9. This point was made in Faith and Order Paper 103, *Spirit of God, Spirit of Christ: Ecumenical Reflections on the Filioque Controversy* (London: SPCK; Geneva: World Council of Churches, 1981), 7.

10. See Geoffrey Wainwright, *Doxology: The Praise of God in Worship, Doctrine, and Life* (New York: Oxford University Press, 1980), 251–83.

11. There is a helpful collection of texts from early Christian sources in R. B. Eno, *Teaching Authority in the Early Church*, Message of the Fathers of the Church 14 (Wilmington, Del.: Michael Glazier, 1984). For Ignatius, see 32–35.

12. See ibid., 42–50.

13. For example, *The Apostolic Tradition of Hippolytus* on confessors and healers. See G. J. Cuming, *Hippolytus: A Text for Students* (Bramcote, Nottingham: Grove Books, 1987), 14, 15.

14. This contrast is shown, for example, in Edward Schillebeeckx, *The Church with a Human Face: A New and Expanded Theology of Ministry* (New York: Crossroad, 1985).

15. For questions that this phenomenon puts to the church today, see A. Faivre, "Les premiers chrétiens interpellent le Synode des Évêques," *Revue des Sciences Religieuses* 63 (1989): 17–46.

16. On ordination in the early church, see W. Vos and G. Wainwright, eds., *Ordination Rites: Papers Read at the 1979 Congress of Societas Liturgica* (Rotterdam: Liturgical Ecumenical Center Trust, 1980).

17. See Eno, *Teaching Authority*, 84–96; J. D. Laurance, *Priest as Type of Christ: The Leader of the Eucharist in Salvation History according to Cyprian of Carthage* (New York: Peter Lang, 1984).

18. See Eno, ibid., 126–40.

19. Y. Congar, *Power and Poverty in the Church* (Baltimore: Helicon, 1965), 56. The essay "Historical Development of Authority," 40–80, is helpful for an understanding of this period as a whole.

20. Eno, *Teaching Authority*, 131.

21. Ibid., 132.

22. On his approach to councils, see ibid., 138.

23. See Y. Congar, *L'Ecclésiologie du Haut Moyen-Âge* (Paris: Ed. du Cerf, 1968), 141–51.

24. Isidore of Seville, *De Ecclesiasticis Officiis* V, 5 (*PL* 83, 781–82).

25. J. Fontaine, ed., *Sulpice Sévère: Vie de Saint Martin de Tours*, Sources Chrétiennes 133–34 (Paris: Ed. du Cerf, 1967–69).

26. See G. H. Luttenberger, "The Priest as Member of a Ministerial College: The Development of the Church's Ministerial Structure from 96 to c. 300 A.D.," *Revue de Théologie Ancienne et Médiévale* 43 (1976): 5–63.

27. See G. J. Cuming, *Hippolytus: A Text for Students*.

28. David N. Power, "The Holy Spirit: Scripture, Tradition and Interpretation," in G. Wainwright, ed., *Keeping the Faith: Essays to Mark the Centenary of Lux Mundi* (Philadelphia: Fortress Press, 1988), 152–78.

29. Vatican II, *Constitution on the Church*, no. 13.

3 · Rebirth of the Word: Empowerment in the Middle Ages by J. A. Wayne Hellmann (pages 39–48)

1. See Franco Andrea Dal Pino, *I Frati Servi di S. Maria delle origini dall' aprovazione* (Louvain: Storiografia. Fonti. Storia., 1972), 468–72.

2. See Marsha L. Dutton, "Intimacy and Imitation: The Humanity of Christ in Cistercian Spirituality," in *Erudition at God's Service*, Studies in Medieval Cistercian History 9, ed. John Sommerfeldt (Kalamazoo, Mich.: Cistercian Publications, 1987), 34–38.

3. As quoted in ibid., 33 (SC 2:3; SBOp 1:9; CF 4:10).

4. As quoted in ibid., 57 (SC 2:2; SBOp 1:9; CF 4:9).

5. Marsha Dutton, "The Cistercian Source: Aelred, Bonaventure, and Ignatius," in *Goad and Nail*, Studies in Medieval Cistercian History 10 (Kalamazoo, Mich.: Cistercian Publications, 1985), 170.

6. See Caroline Walker Bynum, *Docere Verbo et Exemplo: An Aspect of Twelfth-Century Spirituality* (Missoula, Mont.: Scholars Press, 1979), 21.

7. English translation by Bynum, ibid., 42: Latin text in *PL* 176: 897–98.

8. See Grover Zinn, "Historia Fundamentum Est: The Role of History in the Contemplative Life according to Hugh of Saint Victor," ed. G. A. Shriver, *Contemporary Reflections on the Medieval Christian Tradition: Essays in Honor of Ray C. Petrie* (Durham, N.C.: Duke University Press, 1974).

9. Richard of St. Victor, *The Twelve Patriarchs*, 78; ed. Grover Zinn, *Richard of St. Victor* (New York: Paulist Press, 1973), 136 (*PL* 196:56).

10. Alan of Lille, *The Art of Preaching*, trans. Gillian Evans (Kalamazoo, Mich.: Cistercian Publications, 1981), 16.

11. Ibid., 21.

12. M. D. Chenu, *Nature, Man, and Society in the Twelfth Century*, trans. Jerome Taylor and Lester K. Little (Chicago: University of Chicago Press, 1968), 253.

13. Francis of Assisi, "First Letter to the Custodians," *Francis and Clare: The Complete Works*, trans. R. Armstrong and I. Brady (New York: Paulist Press, 1982), 53.

14. Francis of Assisi, "A Letter to the Clergy," ibid., 50.

15. Francis of Assisi, "Letter to the Entire Order," ibid., 60.

16. Francis of Assisi, "First Version of the Letter to the Faithful," ibid., 63.

17. Francis of Assisi, "Second Version of the Letter to the Faithful," ibid., 67.

18. Ibid., 109.

19. Ibid., 137.

20. Bonaventure, "Tree of Life," trans. E. Cousins, *Bonaventure* (New York: Paulist Press, 1978), 119.

21. As quoted by Marsha Dutton, "Cistercian Source," 165 (Cant. 1:21).

22. See Marsha Dutton, "Cistercian Source."

23. Ibid., 165.

24. See Francis of Assisi, "The Salutation of the Virtues," *Francis and Clare: The Complete Works*, 152.

25. See Francis of Assisi, "Later Rule," ibid., 137.

26. Humbert of Romans, "On the Formation of Preachers," in *Early Dominicans*, ed. Simon Tugwell (New York: Paulist Press, 1982), 184.

27. Ibid., 187.

28. Meister Eckhart, "German Sermon IV," in *Meister Eckhart, Teacher and Preacher*, ed. Bernard McGinn (New York: Paulist Press, 1986), 251.

29. Ibid., 344.

30. M. D. Chenu, *Nature, Man, and Society in the Twelfth Century*, 219.

31. Ibid., 236.

4 · Religious Life as a Space of Empowerment by Mary Milligan (pages 49–59)

1. *Dogmatic Constitution on the Church (Lumen Gentium)*, no. 43.

2. Ibid.

3. *Decree on the Appropriate Renewal of the Religious Life (Perfectae Caritatis)*, no. 1.

4. Ibid., no. 2.

5. Ibid., no. 8.

6. Ibid.

7. Johannes Baptist Metz, *Poverty of Spirit* (Glen Rock, N.J.: Newman Press, 1968).

8. Odilo Engels, "Religious Orders," in *Sacramentum Mundi*, ed. Karl Rahner et al. (New York: Herder and Herder, 1970), 298.

9. Ibid., 298.

10. Peter Brown, "The Notion of Virginity in the Early Church," in *Christian Spirituality: Origins to the Twelfth Century*, ed. Bernard McGinn, John Meyendorff, and Jean Leclercq (New York: Crossroad, 1987), 428.

11. Ibid., 429.

12. Ibid., 436.

13. The Charitable Sisters of the Holy Infant Jesus, popularly called the Ladies of Saint-Maur, founded by Nicolas Barré in 1682, are a case in point.

14. This was the well-known situation of the Daughters of Charity of St. Vincent de Paul. Other congregations professed one or two all-inclusive vows rather than the three that required enclosure.

15. The desire to avoid enclosure seems to have been one of the reasons that Jean-Pierre Médaille, founder of the Sisters of St. Joseph in the seventeenth century, established each small group of sisters as autonomous.

16. M. L'abbé Balme-Frézol, *De l'instruction des femmes* (Paris, 1866), as cited in A. M. Meynard *Réponses canoniques et pratiques sur le gouvernement et les principaux devoirs des religieuses à voeux simples* (Clermont-Ferrand, 1891), 279–80.

17. The origins of this project date back to 1980; funding from the Lilly Endowment made possible its first colloquium held at Cushwa Center, Notre Dame, in 1987. A national conference was held in St. Paul, Minnesota, in June 1989.

5 · Pope John Paul II's Vision of Collaboration and Empowerment by Leonard Doohan (pages 60–76)

1. Mieczyslaw Malinski, *Pope John Paul II: The Life of Karol Wojtyla* (New York: Seabury Press, 1979), 198.

2. Ibid., 188–89.

3. See ibid., 202.

4. Antoni Gronowicz, *God's Broker: The Life of Pope John Paul II* (New York: Richardson and Snyder, 1984), 396.

5. Pope John Paul II, "First Address as the Bishop of Rome to the World," *L'Osservatore Romano* 43 (1978): 3–4. These speeches can be found in *John Paul II and the Laity*, Leonard Doohan, ed. (Cambridge, Mass.: Human Development Books, 1984).

6. "Address to the International Council of Catholic Men" *L'Osservatore Romano* 45 (1978): 4. Throughout this essay, the references are to the English weekly edition of *L'Osservatore Romano*.

7. "Need of Apostolate of the Laity for Community of Christ's Church," *L'Osservatore Romano* 26 (1980): 16.

8. "Address to the Catholic Students at Guadalajara, Mexico," *L'Osservatore Romano* 7 (1979): 8.

9. "Man's Answer to God's Call to Service," *L'Osservatore Romano* 4 (1979): 3.

10. "Address in Guadalupe to Students of the Mexican Catholic Universities," *L'Osservatore Romano* 8 (1979): 5.

11. "Address in the Mexican Diplomatic Corps," *L'Osservatore Romano* 7 (1979): 3.

12. "A Message of Hope to the Asian People," *Origins* 10 (1981): 612.

13. "Address to Youth, Wzgorze Lecha, Gniezno, Poland," *Origins* 9 (1979): 58.

14. "Address to the Boys and Girls in Catholic Action," *L'Osservatore Romano* 5 (1981): 14.

15. "Be Mediators Not Politicians," *Origins* 10 (1980): 11.

16. "Sustain Your Courage in the Face of Difficulties of the Times," *L'Osservatore Romano* 46 (1981): 10.

17. "Adequate Response to the Needs of Society Today," *L'Osservatore Romano* 24 (1980): 5.

18. "Catechesis Continues Activity of Jesus, the Teacher," *L'Osservatore Romano* 22 (1980): 9.

19. *Redeemer of Man* (*Redemptor Hominis*), *Origins* 8 (1979): 639.

20. "Catechesis Continues Activity of Jesus," 9.

21. "Address to Lay Church Workers," *Origins* 10 (1980): 394.

22. "Address to Italian Catholic Union of Secondary Teachers," *L'Osservatore Romano* 15 (1981): 8.

23. "Address to the National Union of Charitable and Welfare Institutions," *L'Osservatore Romano* 17 (1979): 11.

24. For a selection of speeches dealing with this section, see *John Paul II and the Laity*, chap. 1: "Definitions of the Lay Person."

25. "The Experience and Meaning of Your Freedom," *L'Osservatore Romano* 17 (1981): 2. For additional references to this section, see *John Paul II and the Laity*, chap. 2: "The Condition of the Laity."

26. "Adequate Response," 5.

27. "Communion and Liberation," *L'Osservatore Romano* 15 (1979): 6.

28. For this section, see *John Paul II and the Laity*, chap. 3: "The Relationship between Laity and Hierarchy."

29. See ibid., chap. 5: "Ministry of Laity."

30. See ibid., chap. 6: "Family Life."

31. "The Vocation and Function of the Laity Is to Renew Society of Which They Are a Part," *L'Osservatore Romano* 20 (1987): 10–11.

32. "The Secret of the Maturation of the Laity Lies in the Threefold Bond with the Ministry of Christ," *L'Osservatore Romano* 10 (1987): 10.

33. *Lord and Lifegiver* (*Dominum et Vivificantem*), encyclical letter, May 30, 1986, (no. 60), Washington, D.C.: USCC, 121.

34. "Participation of the Laity in the Church's Life Is a Responsibility Which Demands Dedication and Consistency," *L'Osservatore Romano* 26 (1987): 8.

35. Ibid., 8.

36. "Who Are the Laity?" *L'Osservatore Romano* 9 (1987): 2.

37. "Address to Youth in Austria," *Origins* 13 (1983): 272.

38. "Christian Maturity the Essential Basis of the Apostolate of the Laity," *L'Osservatore Romano* 32 (1987): 2.

39. "Knowledge, Participation and Commitment Are Essential to Effective Apostolate," *L'Osservatore Romano* 44 (1986): 6.

40. "Establish Models of Christian Life in Conformity with the Faith," *L'Osservatore Romano* 4 (1986): 11.

41. "The Pope's Address to Laity in San Francisco," *Origins* 17 (1987): 323.

42. "Knowledge, Participation," 6.

43. "Who Are the Laity?" 2.

44. "In the Mission of Salvation the Clergy and Laity Complement One Another," *L'Osservatore Romano* 41 (1987): 22.

45. Ibid.

46. Ibid., 22, 24.

47. "Unity in the Church's Mission with Diversity in Apostolates or Ministries," *L'Osservatore Romano* 8 (1982): 6.

48. "Participation of the Laity in the Church's Life," 8.

49. "The Goal of Unity and Communion Is to Bear Witness in a Credible Manner," *L'Osservatore Romano* 50 (1986): 20.

50. Ibid.

51. "Apostolic Exhortation on the Family" (*Familiaris Consortio*), *Origins* 11 (1981): 445 (no. 21).

52. "In the Service of the Kingdom Following the Lead of the Spirit in Communion of Faith, Thought and Discipline with the Pastors," *L'Osservatore Romano* 51 (1986): 11.

53. "Prayer Is the Soul of the Parish Community," *L'Osservatore Romano* 8 (1985): 9.

54. "Holy Father Makes Appeal for Help in Ethiopia," *L'Osservatore Romano* 1 (1985): 5.

55. "Apostolic Letter on the Christian Meaning of Human Suffering" (*Salvidici Doloris*), *Origins* 37 (1984): 622.

56. "Apostolic Exhortation on the Family," 444 (no. 19).

57. "Address to Members of Labor Organizations," *L'Osservatore Romano* 5 (1987): 11.

58. "A New Solidarity Based on Work Is Necessary," *L'Osservatore Romano* 26 (1982): 10; see also 12 and 20.

59. Ibid., 10.

60. See "The Peacemaking Weapons on the Strong," *Origins* 15 (1986): 542.

61. See ibid., 539.

62. "Beyond Violence and Hate: Church and Society," *Origins* 44 (1987): 782–83.

63. "The Inculturation of the Gospel Is at the Heart of the Mission of the Church in the World," *L'Osservatore Romano* 4 (1986): 3.

64. "Growth in Unity and Mutual Collaboration," *L'Osservatore Romano* 11 (1987): 12.

65. Ibid.

66. See "Communion, Participation, Evangelization," *Origins* 10 (1980): 135.

67. See "Address to the Plenary Session of Cardinals," *Origins* 9 (1979): 357–58.

68. "Address to the U.S. Bishops," *Origins* 9 (1979): 290.

69. See "Christian Life in Africa," *Origins* 10 (1980): 27.

70. "The Contribution of the Laity Is Rooted in Their Characteristic Identity," *L'Osservatore Romano* 36 (1987): 2.

71. "I Come at the Service of Unity in Love," *L'Osservatore Romano* 22 (1982): 2.

72. "The Pope in Ireland," *Origins* 9 (1979): 270.

73. "Who Is the Priest?" *Origins* 10 (1980): 143.

74. *Redeemer of Man, Origins* 8 (1979): 639.

75. "Communion and Liberation," 6.

76. All the references in this section are from the Apostolic Exhortation on the Laity, *Christifideles Laici*; the page references are to the edition in *Origins* 18 (1989): 561–95.

77. Gronowicz, *God's Broker*, 438.

7 · Empowering Lay Leadership in the Church by Robert F. Morneau (pages 89–102)

1. Pope Paul VI, *Evangelii Nuntiandi, On Evangelization in the Modern World* (Washington, D.C.: United States Catholic Conference, 1976), 49–50 (no. 68).

2. Pope John Paul II, *Christifideles Laici, Apostolic Exhortation on the Vocation and Mission of the Lay Faithful in the Church and in the World, Origins* (National Catholic News Service, 1989), 571 (no. 23).

3. Edward C. Sellner, "Lay Leadership in the 1990s," *America* 161, no. 6 (September 16, 1989): 135.

4. Pope John Paul II, *Christifideles Laici*, 565 (no. 7).

5. *Dogmatic Constitution on the Church* (*Lumen Gentium*), in *The Documents of Vatican II*, Walter M. Abbott, S.J., ed. (New York: Herder and Herder, 1966), 57 (no. 30).

6. Pope John Paul II, *Christifideles Laici*, 572 (no. 23).

7. Ibid., 577 (no. 34).

8. John Henry Cardinal Newman, "Prospects of the Anglican Church," in *Essays and Sketches* (New York: Longmans, Green and Company, 1975), 1:362.

9. Martin Buber, *Pointing the Way*, trans. Maurice S. Friedman (New York: Schocken Books, 1974), 158.

10. Jon Sobrino, *Christology at the Crossroads*, trans. John Drury (Maryknoll, N.Y.: Orbis Books, 1978), 55.

11. Pope John Paul II, *Christifideles Laici*, 563 (no. 2).

12. John Courtney Murray, S.J., *The Problem of God: Yesterday and Today* (New Haven: Yale University Press, 1964), 79.

13. *Decree on the Apostolate of the Laity* (*Apostolicam Actuositatem*), *The Documents of Vatican II*, 517 (no. 29).

14. Pope John Paul II, *Christifideles Laici*, 589 (no. 57).

15. Ibid., 575 (no. 30).

16. Evelyn and James Whitehead, *Christian Life Patterns* (New York: Doubleday, 1979), 21.

17. Jon Sobrino, *Christology at the Crossroads*, 281.

18. Henri Nouwen, *Reaching Out* (New York: Doubleday, 1975), 61.

19. Goethe, *Faust*, trans. with an introduction by Walter Kaufmann (New York: Doubleday, 1961), 115.

20. Romano Guardini, *The Lord* (Chicago: Henry Regnery, 1954), 16–17.

21. William Reiser, *An Unlikely Catechism: Some Challenges for the Creedless Catholic* (New York: Paulist Press, 1985), 159.

22. Jim Wallis, *The Call to Conversion* (San Francisco: Harper & Row Publishers, 1981), 126.

23. *Dogmatic Constitution on the Church* (*Lumen Gentium*), 67 (no. 40).

24. John Paul II, *Christifideles Laici*, 589 (no. 58).

25. *Selected Poetry of Jessica Powers*, ed. Regina Seigfried and Robert Morneau (Kansas City: Sheed & Ward, 1989), 38.

8 · Priests and Laity: Mutual Empowerment
by Roger M. Mahony (pages 103–117)

1. See, for example, *Dogmatic Constitution on the Church* (*Lumen Gentium*), nos. 10–11.

2. See *Constitution on the Sacred Liturgy* (*Sacrosanctum Concilium*), no. 14. An important consequence of the community's share in the priesthood of Jesus is the constitution's restriction on private Masses, with only an ordained priest present; no. 27.

3. See *Decree on the Apostolate of the Laity* (*Apostolicam Actuositatem*), no. 3.

4. For example, *Pastoral Constitution on the Church in the Modern World* (*Gaudium et Spes*), no. 10.

5. For example, *Decree on the Church's Missionary Activity* (*Ad Gentes*), nos. 11, 13.

6. See, for example, *Pastoral Constitution on the Church in the Modern World*, no. 44; *Decree on the Church's Missionary Activity*, no. 22.

7. See *Decree on the Church's Missionary Activity*, no. 12; *Pastoral Constitution on the Church in the Modern World*, chap. 4.

8. Fortunately there is growing interest in these questions of Christian mission in society. We find it in discussions of lay spirituality, family life, and theology of work, as well as in retreats and other reflections sponsored by the National Center for the Laity.

9. Essential contributions to such a spirituality include Pope John Paul II's encyclical letter *On Human Work* (*Laborem Exercens*) and his apostolic exhortation following the last synod of bishops, *The Vocation and the Mission of the Lay Faithful in the Church and in the World* (*Christifideles Laici*), especially chap. 3. See also *Work and Faith in Society: A Handbook for Dioceses and Parishes*, prepared by the Secretariat of the Bishops' Committee on the Laity (Washington, D.C.: USCC Office of Publishing and Promotion Services, 1986).

10. In part, I have addressed this concern in my pastoral letter to the priests of Los Angeles; see *Priestly Ministers* (Boston: St. Paul Editions, 1986).

11. Michael Himes, "Making Priesthood Work," *Church* 5, no. 3 (December 1989): 5–11.

12. Pope John Paul II acknowledges how all share in the secular dimension of life, though in different ways; see *The Vocation and the Mission of the Lay Faithful*, no. 15.

13. This is reiterated specifically in relation to ordained priests in the Second Vatican Council's *Decree on the Ministry and Life of Priests* (*Presbyterorum Ordinis*), no. 9. See also my pastoral letter, *Priestly Ministers*, 7.

14. I recognize that, in the past, we used the term "the faithful" to refer to the laity, perhaps with the connotation that they were docile toward the

clergy. The use of "Christ's faithful" in the council and in the code is to refer to all the baptized, a use which is affirmed indirectly when the Holy Father uses the expression, "the lay faithful," in *The Vocation and the Mission of the Lay Faithful.*

15. "Clergy-Laity Relationships," *Origins* 17, no. 19 (October 22, 1987): 351.

16. As I pointed out in my pastoral letter *Priestly Ministers*, 9, more than "functions," it is the priest's symbolic role that distinguishes him from the rest of the baptized.

17. See *The Vocation and Mission of the Lay Faithful*, no. 23.

18. I should acknowledge that Avery Dulles, S.J. rejects this view which he had found expressed by Karl Rahner, S.J., namely that those who are fully ministers of the Church are thereby no longer quite lay, and further expressed his opposition to the establishment of any new "orders" for ministers who are now lay; see "Can the Word 'Laity' be Defined?" *Origins* 18, no. 29 (December 29, 1988): 470–75.

19. *The Vocation and the Mission of the Lay Faithful*, no. 23.

20. "Clergy-Laity Relationship," 351.

21. See *The Vocation and the Mission of the Lay Faithful*, no. 22.

22. The two most important contemporary pastoral letters of the U.S. bishops are *The Challenge of Peace: God's Promise and Our Response* (adopted May 3, 1983) and *Economic Justice for All: Catholic Social Teaching and the U.S. Economy* (adopted November 13, 1986).

23. *Decree on the Ministry and Life of Priests*, no. 9.

24. This mission is addressed in many recent documents, such as Pope John Paul II encyclicals *On Human Work* (*Laborem Exercens*) and *Sollicitudo Rei Socialis*, and the postsynod exhortation, *The Vocation and the Mission of the Lay Faithful*, as well as in the pastoral letters of the National Conference of Catholic Bishops on war and peace and on the economy.

25. The Committee on Priestly Life and Ministry of the National Conference of Catholic Bishops has addressed the needs of priests recently in their paper on the work of a pastor, *A Shepherd's Care*, and in the document *Reflections on the Morale of Priests.*

9 · From Paternalism to Empowerment
by James R. Jennings (pages 118–129)

1. Pius XI, *Quadragesimo Anno*, no. 39, in William J. Gibbons, S.J., ed., *Seven Great Encyclicals* (New York: Paulist Press, 1963), 135. See also Pope John XXIII, *Mater et Magistra*, no. 26, in Joseph Gremillion, ed., *The Gospel of Peace and Justice* (Maryknoll, N.Y.: Orbis Books, 1976), 149.

2. *Quadragesimo Anno*, nos. 14, 30, 39, 59. For its reception in Europe, see Lillian Parker Wallace, *Leo XIII and the Rise of Socialism* (Durham, N.C.: Duke University Press, 1966), 388–94.

3. Neil Bretten, *Catholic Activism and the Industrial Workers* (Gainesville: University of Florida Press, 1976), 10–12.

4. Leo XIII, *Rerum Novarum*, no. 35, in Gibbons, *Seven Great Encyclicals*, 22.

5. Ibid., no. 36. Wallace considers Leo's endorsement of "worker only" associations as the encyclical's most revolutionary principle, 272.

6. Ibid., no. 2.

7. Richard L. Camp, *The Papal Ideology of Social Reform* (Leiden, Netherlands: Brill, 1969), 12.

8. Donal Dorr, *Option for the Poor* (Maryknoll, N.Y.: Orbis Books, 1983), 19–20.

9. Gregory Baum, *Theology and Society* (Mahwah, N.J.: Paulist Press, 1987), 32; Camp, *The Papal Ideology of Social Reform*, 25–31.

10. Eric O. Hanson, *The Catholic Church in World Politics* (Princeton, N.J.: Princeton University Press, 1987), 119. The era is called "neo-Christianity" in Paul Steidl-Meier, *Social Justice Ministry* (New York: Le Jacq Publishing, 1984), 149–53.

11. *Rerum Novarum*, no. 29.

12. Dorr, *Option for the Poor*, 29–51.

13. Cited in an unpublished dissertation of Bernard F. Evans, "The Campaign for Human Development: An Analysis of the Theological Basis for the Campaign" (Washington, D.C.: Catholic University of America, 1985), 70.

14. *Rerum Novarum*, nos. 16, 24, 29, 32.

15. Ibid., no. 14.

16. Ibid., no. 20.

17. Gremillion, *The Gospel of Peace and Justice*, 2. For a summary review of the era, see Dorr, *Option for the Poor*, 57–86; Camp, *The Papal Ideology of Social Reform*, 13–21; 32–40; 57–68; 87–100.

18. A typical set of stipulations on the selection of bishops appears in the 1933 concordat with Austria. Before publicly announcing the name of a new bishop, the Vatican agreed to send the nominee's name to the Austrian government, "in order to learn whether it has reasons of a general political character to oppose such a nomination." If none was communicated within fifteen days, the Vatican would make the appointment public. Hanson, *The Catholic Church in World Politics*, notes that among the provisions of the 1985 concordat with Italy, Catholicism is no longer deemed the state religion and bishops do not have to take an oath of allegiance to the Italian state, as was required in the concordat with Mussolini in 1929 (137).

19. *The Decree on the Bishops' Pastoral Office in the Church* (*Christus Dominus*), no. 20, in Walter M. Abbott, S.J., ed. *The Documents of Vatican II* (New York: America Press, 1966), 411.

20. "Guidelines for the Study and Teaching of the Church's Social Doctrine in the Formation of Priests," *Origins* 19, no. 11 (August 3, 1989): 175–78.

21. John XXIII, *Pacem in Terris*, nos. 40–45, in Gremillion, *The Gospel of Peace and Justice*.

22. Dorr, *Option for the Poor*, 158.

23. "Medellín Documents," "Peace," no. 18, in Gremillion, *The Gospel of Peace and Justice*.

24. Paul VI, *Octogesima Adveniens*, no. 46, in Gremillion, ibid.

25. Dorr, *Option for the Poor*, 209–10.

26. Ibid., 219.

27. Ibid., 207–51.

28. John Paul II, *Sollicitudo Rei Socialis*, no. 39, *Origins* 17, no. 38 (March 3, 1988): 654.

29. For a detailed review of CHD's first fifteen years, see James Jennings, ed., *Daring to Seek Justice* (Washington, D.C.: USCC, 1986).

30. Ibid., 69.

31. Ibid., 73.

32. Ibid., 55–56.

33. George Weigel, *Catholics and the Revival of American Democracy* (New York: Paulist Press, 1989), 151.

34. William T. Poole and Thomas W. Pauken, *The Campaign for Human Development: Christian Charity or Political Activism?* (Washington, D.C.: Capitol Research Center, 1988), v.

35. U.S. Bishops, "Economic Justice for All," *Origins* 16, no. 24 (November 27, 1986).

36. Ibid., 431, 447, 447.

10 · Liturgy and Empowerment:
The Restoration of the Liturgical Assembly
by Bob Hurd (pages 130–144)

1. Portions of the present essay appeared in my previous article "Restoring the Liturgical Assembly," *Today's Liturgy* 12, no. 1 (December 1989–February 1990): 13–16.

2. My summary of historical patterns in this section is indebted to the following studies: Robert Cabié, *The Church at Prayer*, vol. 2, *The Eucharist*, ed. A. G. Martimort, trans. Matthew J. O'Connell (Collegeville, Minn.: Liturgical Press, 1986); Bernard Cooke, *Ministry to Word and Sacraments* (Philadelphia: Fortress Press, 1976), 525–73; Michael Downey, *Clothed in Christ* (New York: Crossroad, 1987), 42–50; Josef Jungmann, *The Early Liturgy* (Notre Dame: University of Notre Dame Press, 1959); Theodor Klauser, *A Short History of the Western Liturgy*, trans. John Halliburton (Oxford: Oxford University Press, 1979); David N. Power, *Unsearchable Riches: The Symbolic Nature of Liturgy* (New York: Pueblo Publishing Co., 1984), 35–60.

3. Cited in Jungmann, *The Early Liturgy*, 17.

4. The sacrificial connotations of the Eucharist are as old as the Eucharist itself. But in the New Testament period these connotations were counterbalanced and relativized by other ideas and images. The Eucharist was not only a sacrifice but a meal of fellowship, an eschatological banquet, a celebration of thanksgiving and praise. In the succeeding period the notion of Eucharist as sacrifice begins to predominate and obscure these other meanings.

5. Cited in Hervé-Marie Legrand, "The Presidency of Eucharist according to the Ancient Tradition," *Living Bread, Saving Cup*, ed. R. Kevin Seasoltz (Collegeville, Minn.: Liturgical Press, 1982), 218.

6. Klauser, *A Short History of the Western Liturgy*, 34.

7. Robert Cabié, *The Church at Prayer*, vol. 2, *The Eucharist*, 139.

8. Ibid., 138.

9. The expression is borrowed from Michael Downey's *Clothed in Christ*, 122.

10. Legrand, *Living Bread, Saving Cup*, 219.

11. See Aquinas's treatment of the knowledge of Christ in *Summa Theologiae*, III, qq. 9, 10, and 11.

12. See Cabié, *The Church at Prayer*, vol. 2, *The Eucharist*, 190–92, and Burkhard Neunheuser, "The Relation of Priest and Faithful in the Liturgies of Pius V and Paul VI," *Roles in the Liturgical Assembly*, trans. Matthew J. O'Connell (New York: Pueblo Publishing Co., 1981), 207–19.

13. Ralph A. Keifer, *To Give Thanks and Praise: The General Instruction of the Roman Missal with Commentary for Musicians and Priests* (Washington, D.C.: Pastoral Press, 1980), 33.

14. See *Vatican Council II: The Conciliar and Post-Conciliar Documents*, ed. Austin Flannery (Northport, N.Y.: Costello Publishing Co., 1986), 17.

15. Legrand, *Living Bread, Saving Cup*, 216–17.

16. Published by G.I.A. Publications, 7404 South Mason Avenue, Chicago, IL 60638.

17. Keifer, *To Give Thanks and Praise*, 34.

18. *Vatican Council II: The Conciliar and Post-Conciliar Documents*, 1.

19. For an analysis of the prayer of the faithful with a view toward making it truly assembly-centered in practice, see Bob Hurd, "The Prayer of the Faithful: Finding the Assembly's Voice," *Liturgy: The Art of Celebration* 8, no. 2 (Spring 1990), (Washington, D.C.: Liturgical Conference).

11 · "He Has Pulled Down the Mighty from Their Thrones, and Has Exalted the Lowly": A Feminist Reflection on Empowerment by Susan A. Ross (pages 145–159)

My thanks to my colleague and friend Bill French, whose comments helped me express these ideas more clearly.

1. Anne E. Carr, *Transforming Grace: Christian Tradition and Women's Experience* (San Francisco: Harper & Row, 1988), 11.

2. Judith Andre, "Power, Oppression and Gender," *Social Theory and Practice* 11, no. 1 (Spring 1985): 116.

3. Ibid., 119.

4. Ibid., 120.

5. Jürgen Habermas, *Knowledge and Human Interests*, trans. Jeremy Shapiro (Boston: Beacon Press, 1971).

6. Michel Foucault, *Power/Knowledge: Selected Interviews and Other Writings, 1972–1977*, trans. Colin Gordon et al., ed. Colin Gordon (New York: Pantheon Books, 1980).

7. Bernard Loomer, "Two Kinds of Power," *Process Studies* 6 (Spring 1976): 5–32.

8. Elizabeth Janeway, *Powers of the Weak* (New York: Alfred Knopf, 1980).

9. See Catherine Keller, *From a Broken Web: Separation, Sexism, and Self* (Boston: Beacon Press, 1986).

10. This is the nature of the self developed by Keller, which she contrasts with both a "separate" and a "soluble" self. The separate self sees relationship as threatening, while the soluble self is so immersed in relationship that it lacks an adequate sense of self. See especially chap. 1, "The Separate and the Soluble," 7–46.

11. Sallie McFague, *Models of God: Theology for a Nuclear, Ecological Age* (Philadelphia: Fortress Press, 1985).

12. This is not meant to be an exhaustive list of critical feminist principles, but rather inclusive of issues that I see related to power and empowerment. See Rebecca S. Chopp, *The Power to Speak: Feminism, Language, God* (New York: Crossroad, 1989), who lists "specificity, difference, solidarity, embodiment, anticipation, and transformation" as terms that "play continually throughout feminist discourses of emancipatory transformation" (23).

13. This is not to say that single women, for example, are and ought to be powerless, but that a woman alone is in a less powerful economic and often psychological position than is a man alone. Also, women's solidarity is often conceived in distorted ways that demonstrate fear of women's power: e.g., "the monstrous regiment of women." The vulnerability of women alone and the ridicule of women in solidarity represent fear of women's power.

14. For extended discussions of this issue, see Nancy Chodorow, *The Reproduction of Mothering: Psychoanalysis and the Study of Gender* (Berkeley: University of California Press, 1978); Dorothy Dinnerstein, *The Mermaid and the Minotaur: Sexual Arrangements and Human Malaise* (New York: Harper & Row, 1977); and Carol Gilligan, *In a Different Voice: Psychological Theory and Women's Development* (Cambridge: Harvard University Press, 1982); and Keller, *From a Broken Web*, for the best known and most highly developed articulations of this position.

15. John A. Coleman, S.J., in his address, "Power, the Powers, and a Higher Power," *Proceedings of the Catholic Theological Society of America* 37 (1982): 1–14, quotes Max Weber's definition of power: "Power is the probability that one actor in a social relationship will be in a position to carry out his own will despite resistance, regardless of the basis on which this probability rests" (p. 3).

16. See Susan Brooks Thistlethwaite, *Sex, Race, and God: Christian Feminism in Black and White* (New York: Crossroad, 1989), especially chap. 1, "Experience in White Feminist Theory," 11–26.

17. See Sharon Welch, *Communities of Resistance and Solidarity: A Feminist Theology of Liberation* (Maryknoll, N.Y.: Orbis Books, 1985).

18. See, for example, Sallie Westwood and Parminder Bhachu, *Enterprising Women: Ethnicity, Economy and Gender Relations* (London and New York: Routledge, 1988).

19. The movement of "French feminism" has developed this conception of difference, based on the "differentiated" and "multiple" nature of women's sexuality. See Elaine Marks and Isabelle de Courtivon, eds., *New French Feminisms: An Anthology* (New York: Schocken, 1981).

20. See Chopp, *Power to Speak*, 15: "Marginal implies also the notion of borderline or limit or edge, as a margin defines the edges of a text. Here

women are cast as the border — literally, the margin, which demarcates order and chaos."

21. See Welch, *Communities of Resistance*, 26ff.

22. Marsha Hewitt, "Feminist Critical Theory," *Ecumenist* 27, no. 6 (September–October 1989): 87.

23. Sandra Schneiders, "Women and Power in the Church: A New Testament Reflection," in *Proceedings of the Catholic Theological Society of America* 37 (1982): 126.

24. Ibid., 124.

25. See the Vatican Declaration on the Admission of Women to the Ministerial Priesthood, in Arlene Swidler and Leonard Swidler, eds., *Women Priests: A Catholic Commentary on the Vatican Declaration* (New York: Paulist Press, 1977). While the first draft of the U.S. bishops' pastoral letter, "Partners in the Mystery of Redemption," condemns the "sin of sexism," women's "unique" role is still highlighted.

26. See Hewitt, "Feminist Critical Theory," 86.

27. See Letty Russell, "People and the Powers," *Princeton Seminary Bulletin* (n.s.) 8, no. 1 (1987): 13–14. Russell relies on Janeway, *Powers of the Weak*.

28. See Ruether, *Women-Church: Theory and Practice of Feminist Liturgical Communities* (San Francisco: Harper & Row, 1985).

29. See Sherry Ortner, "Is Female to Male as Nature Is to Culture?" in Michele Z. Rosaldo and Louise Lamphere, eds., *Woman, Culture, and Society* (Stanford: Stanford University Press, 1974). See also Susan A. Ross, "'Then Honor God in Your Body' (1 Cor. 6:20): Feminist and Sacramental Theology on the Body" *Horizons* 16, no. 1 (Spring 1989): 7–27, for a survey of Roman Catholic attitudes toward women and the body.

30. See Alison Jaggar, *Feminist Politics and Human Nature* (Totowa, N.J.: Rowman and Allenheid, 1983), for a helpful discussion of liberal, romantic, and Marxist-socialist feminism.

31. See especially Carol Christ, *The Laughter of Aphrodite: Reflections on a Journey to the Goddess* (San Francisco: Harper & Row, 1987).

32. See Matthew Fox, *Original Blessing: A Primer in Creation Spirituality* (Santa Fe: Bear and Co., 1983).

33. Indeed, this is the point that Sherry Ortner makes in her groundbreaking article, "Is Female to Male as Nature Is to Culture?"

34. See Peter Brown, *The Body and Society: Men, Women, and Sexual Renunciation in Early Christianity* (New York: Columbia University Press, 1988), and Carolyn Walker Bynum, *Holy Feast and Holy Fast: The Religious Significance of Food to Medieval Women* (Berkeley: University of California Press, 1987).

35. "Partners in the Mystery of Redemption," no. 34.

36. See Susan Brooks Thistlethwaite, "Every Two Minutes: Battered Women and Biblical Interpretation," in Letty Russell, ed., *Feminist Interpretation of the Bible* (Philadelphia: Westminster, 1985); Mary D. Pellauer, "Moral Callousness and Moral Sensitivity," in Andolsen, Gudorf, and Pel-

lauer, eds., *Women's Consciousness, Women's Conscience* (Minneapolis: Winston Press, 1985).

37. See William C. French, "Nature and the Web of Responsibility: Reflections on a Mother's Death," *Second Opinion* 10 (March 1989): 80–102.

38. See Christine Gudorf, "Sexuality and the Family: Part 1: Sexual Ignorance in the Age of Information," *Second Opinion* 10 (March 1989): 10–37.

39. See Mary Field Belenky et al., *Women's Ways of Knowing: The Development of Self, Voice, and Mind* (Boston: Beacon Press, 1986).

40. See Rosemary Radford Ruether, ed., *Womanguides: Readings Toward a Feminist Theology* (Boston: Beacon, 1985).

41. This is one of the major points of liberation theology, with which feminist theology shares many concerns. See Welch, *Communities of Resistance.*

42. See Alison M. Jaggar, "Love and Knowledge: Emotion in Feminist Epistemology," in *Gender/Body/Knowledge: Feminist Reconstructions of Being and Knowing,* ed. Alison M. Jaggar and Susan Bordo (New Brunswick, N.J.: Rutgers University Press, 1989).

43. Beverly Wildung Harrison, "The Power of Anger in the Work of Love: Christian Ethics for Women and Other Strangers," in Carol S. Robb, ed., *Making the Connections: Essays in Feminist Social Ethics* (Boston: Beacon Press, 1985).

44. Jaggar, "Love and Knowledge," 161.

45. Harrison, "The Power of Anger in the Work of Love," 13.

46. See Sandra Harding, "The Instability of the Analytical Categories of Feminist Theory," *Signs* 13, no. 3 (1988).

47. See Johannes Baptist Metz, "Messianic or Bourgeois Religion?" in *The Emergent Church: The Future of Christianity in a Post-Bourgeois World,* trans. Peter Mann (New York: Crossroad, 1981).

48. See Thistlethwaite, *Sex, Race, and God,* for an examination of this issue.

49. See James Cone, *My Soul Looks Back* (Nashville: Abingdon Press, 1982), on a black male theologian's reflection on sexism in black liberation theology.

50. Paula Cooey, "The Power of Transformation and the Transformation of Power," *Journal of Feminist Studies in Religion* 1, no. 1 (Spring 1985): 30.

51. Ibid., 36.

52. Despite the warning of the Vatican official who feared that women on marriage tribunals would be misled by their "tender hearts" and would fail to make the kinds of "tough" decisions required by this office; on "heart" as a feminist theological term, see Rita Nakashima Brock, *Journeys by Heart: A Christology of Erotic Power* (New York: Crossroad, 1988).

53. The term is used by Johannes B. Metz in *Faith in History and Society: Toward a Practical Fundamental Theology* (New York: Seabury Press, 1980), and also developed by Welch, *Communities of Resistance,* chap. 3: "Dangerous Memory and Alternate Knowledges," 32–54.

12 · The Church and Hispanics in the United States: From Empowerment to Solidarity by Roberto S. Goizueta (pages 160–175)

1. National Conference of Catholic Bishops, *Economic Justice for All: Pastoral Letter on Catholic Social Teaching and the U.S. Economy* (Washington, D.C.: NCCB, 1986), 45.

2. CELAM (Conference of Latin American Bishops), *Documentos finales de la II conferencia del Episcopado latinoamericano* (Bogotá: Ediciones Paulinas, 1969), 172–80.

3. John Eagleson and Philip Scharper, eds., *Puebla and Beyond: Documentation and Commentary* (Maryknoll, N.Y.: Orbis Books, 1979), 264.

4. Allan Figueroa Deck, *The Second Wave: Hispanic Ministry and the Evangelization of Cultures* (New York: Paulist, 1989), 12.

5. National Conference of Catholic Bishops, *The Hispanic Presence: Challenge and Commitment* (Washington, D.C.: NCCB, 1984), 3.

6. See ibid., 6–7; Deck, *The Second Wave*, 9–25. Hispanics in the United States continue to debate the relative appropriateness of the terms "Hispanic" and "Latino/a." To reflect the current lack of consensus over the use of those terms, I will use them interchangeably.

7. John Paul II, *On Social Concern* (Washington, D.C.: USCC, 1987).

8. See Donal Dorr, *Option for the Poor* (Maryknoll, N.Y.: Orbis Books, 1983), especially 252–75.

9. Ibid.

10. Austin Flannery, ed., *Vatican II: The Conciliar and Post-Conciliar Documents* (Collegeville, Minn.: Liturgical Press, 1975), no. 4, 905.

11. Ibid., no. 1, 903–4.

12. USCC, Division for Latin America, *Second General Conference of Latin American Bishops, The Church in the Present Day Transformation of Latin America in the Light of the Council, II (Conclusions).* (Washington, D.C.: USCC, 1973), 34–41, 97, 191.

13. Eagleson and Scharper, eds., *Puebla and Beyond: Documentation and Commentary*, no. 396, 178; no. 1145, 265.

14. USCC, *Economic Justice for All*, 44, 46.

15. One can illustrate this point by using a commonplace example: nothing can be more destructive for an individual suffering from terminal cancer than, out of fear, to deny the diagnosis while laboring under the assumption that he or she is healthy. An aspirin will not do. In such a situation, a presumption of health guarantees self-destruction. Only an honest acknowledgment of the sickness and a commitment to treatment will promote the health of the patient.

16. Gustavo Gutiérrez, *On Job* (Maryknoll, N.Y.: Orbis Books, 1987), xi–xix.

17. Archbishop Desmond Tutu suggests that "if you are neutral in a situation of injustice, you have chosen the side of the oppressor. If an elephant has his foot on the tail of the mouse, and you say you are neutral, the mouse will not appreciate your neutrality" (quoted in Robert McAfee Brown, *Unexpected News* [Philadelphia: Westminster, 1984], 19).

18. Elie Wiesel, *Night* (New York: Avon, 1958), 76.

19. See Roberto S. Goizueta, "Liberation Theology: Retrospect and Prospect," *Philosophy and Theology* 3, no. 1 (Fall 1988): 32.

20. Jon Sobrino, *Spirituality of Liberation* (Maryknoll, N.Y.: Orbis Books, 1988), 112.

21. Eagleson and Scharper, eds., *Puebla and Beyond: Documentation and Commentary*, 265; Gutiérrez, *On Job*, 39–49.

22. Sobrino, *Spirituality of Liberation*, 17.

23. Ibid.

24. Ibid., 17–19.

25. Enrique Dussel, *Philosophy of Liberation* (Maryknoll, N.Y.: Orbis Books, 1985), 16–66.

26. Ibid.

27. Virgilio Elizondo, *Galilean Journey: The Mexican-American Promise* (Maryknoll, N.Y.: Orbis Books, 1983). I use the term *mestizo* here in its broadest sense, as referring to people of mixed race and culture. This would then include people of mixed black and white heritage, or *mulattos*, who predominate in certain areas of the Americas.

28. See Deck, *The Second Wave*, 99–132.

29. Robert Bellah et al., *Habits of the Heart* (Berkeley: University of California Press, 1985), 334.

30. Paul Wachtel, *The Poverty of Affluence* (New York: Free Press, 1983), 118.

31. See Roberto S. Goizueta, "Liberating Creation Spirituality," *Listening* 24, no. 2 (Spring 1989): 105–12.

32. Gutiérrez, *On Job*, 39–49. A variant of this second form of oppressive pluralism is the pluralism that, in its "openness" to different cultural and religious experiences, presumes a universality that essentially suppresses particularity, or otherness. The "openness" of this kind of pluralism masks an underlying refusal to respect and accept the other as other, as making claims on me, but from his or her distinct history. I then continue to define the other in terms of my own history — which is naively universalized — and he or she continues to be marginalized (see Goizueta, "Liberating Creation Spirituality," 104–8).

33. See Dussel, *Philosophy of Liberation*, 39–41.

34. Ibid.

35. Johann Baptist Metz, *Faith in History and Society* (New York: Seabury, 1980), 113–14, 88–118.

36. Orlando Espín and Sixto García, "Hispanic-American Theology," in *Proceedings of the Catholic Theological Society of America* 42 (1987): 114.

37. Ibid., 115.

38. Ibid.

39. Virgilio Elizondo, *The Future Is Mestizo* (Bloomington, Ind.: Meyer-Stone, 1988), 60.

40. See ibid., 57–66; Elizondo, *Galilean Journey*, 122–25; and José Juan Arrom, *Certidumbre de América* (Madrid: Editorial Gredos, 1971), 184–214.

41. Espín and García, "Hispanic-American Theology," 114–15.

42. Dussel, *Philosophy of Liberation*, 41.
43. See Goizueta, "Liberating Creation Spirituality," 85–93.
44. Elizondo, *The Future Is Mestizo*, 84.
45. Ibid.
46. Ibid.

13 · Looking to the Last and the Least: A Spirituality of Empowerment by Michael Downey (pages 176–192)

1. Sallie McFague, *Models of God: Theology for an Ecological, Nuclear Age* (Philadelphia: Fortress Press, 1987). See especially 45ff.

2. Rebecca Chopp, *The Power to Speak: Feminism, Language, God* (New York: Crossroad, 1989), 15.

3. As an example of the importance of race and language in shaping perspectives different from those of the dominant ideology, see Michael Galvan, Marina Herrera, and Jamie Phelps on the issue of providence and responsibility from Native American, Hispanic, and African-American perspectives respectively, in "Providence and History: Some American Views," *Proceedings of the Catholic Theological Society of America* 44 (1989): 4–18.

4. Madonna Kolbenschlag, "Spirituality: Finding Our True Home," in *Women in the Church 1*, ed. Madonna Kolbenschlag (Washington, D.C.: Pastoral Press, 1987), 197–213.

5. For a treatment of life in an intentional community with mentally handicapped persons, see Michael Downey, *A Blessed Weakness: The Spirit of Jean Vanier and L'Arche* (San Francisco: Harper & Row, 1986).

6. Chopp, *The Power to Speak*, 16.

7. Gustavo Gutiérrez, *The Power of the Poor in History* (Maryknoll, N.Y.: Orbis Books, 1983), 231ff.

8. Chopp, *The Power to Speak*, 16.

9. Sandra M. Schneiders, "Theology and Spirituality: Strangers, Rivals, or Partners," *Horizons* 13 (1986): 267.

10. Ibid.

11. James A. Wiseman, "Teaching Spiritual Theology: Methodological Reflections" *Spirituality Today* 41 (1989): 145–46.

12. Walter Principe, "Toward Defining Spirituality," *Studies in Religion/ Sciences religieuses* 12, no. 2 (Spring 1983): 139. See also Jean Leclercq's introduction to *The Spirituality of Western Christendom*, ed. E. Rozanne Elder (Kalamazoo, Mich.: Cistercian Publications, 1976), xi–xxxv.

13. Michael Downey, "Liturgy's Form: Work of the Spirit" *Studies in Formative Spirituality* 9, no. 1 (1988): 17–26. See also Downey, "Recovering the Heart Tradition," *Spirituality Today* 38 (1986): 337–48.

14. For an analysis of the roots of the abuses of authority and power from a psychoanalytic perspective, see Alice Miller, *For Your Own Good: Hidden Cruelty and the Roots of Violence* (New York: Farrar, Straus, Giroux, 1983).

15. McFague, *Models of God*, 17.

16. For a treatment of the linguistic turn in theology see Michael Scanlon, "Language and Praxis: Recent Theological Trends," in the *Proceedings of the Catholic Theological Society of America* 43 (1988): 80–89.

17. Chopp, *The Power to Speak*, 2.

18. McFague, *Models of God*, 17.

19. Ibid., 21.

20. A "feminist hermeneutics of marginality" is ably described by Rebecca Chopp in *The Power to Speak*, 43–46. One of the purposes of the present essay is to extend some of her insights beyond the concerns of feminism.

21. Paul Ricoeur, "Biblical Hermeneutics," *Semeia* 4 (1975): 126.

22. Walter Brueggemann, *The Prophetic Imagination* (Philadelphia: Fortress Press, 1978); see especially chaps. 3 and 4.

23. For a fuller treatment of the destabilizing effect of the parables see Sallie McFague *Models of God*, especially 45ff.

24. Elisabeth Schüssler Fiorenza, *In Memory of Her* (New York: Crossroad, 1983), 120–21.

25. An analysis of the "yuppie strategy" is found in Barbara Ehrenreich, *Fear of Falling: The Inner Life of the Middle Class* (New York: Pantheon, 1989).

26. For a fuller appreciation of lamentation as a way of "naming the negative," see Brueggemann, *The Prophetic Imagination*, chap. 3. See also Michael Downey, "Worship between the Holocausts," *Theology Today* 43 (1986): 75–87.

27. Brueggemann, *The Prophetic Imagination*, 81.

28. Here I am indebted to the work of Walter Brueggemann, especially chaps. 3 and 4 of *The Prophetic Imagination*.

29. Ibid., 66.

30. See, for example, Elie Wiesel, *Night* (New York: Avon Books, 1960). See also Wiesel, *The Trial of God* (New York: Random House, 1979).

31. Brueggemann, *The Prophetic Imagination*, 67.

32. Michael Downey, "Liturgy's Form: Work of the Spirit."

33. For a fine example of a view of power that recognizes the strengths of the poor and of those who suffer, see the work of Gustavo Gutiérrez, especially *We Drink from Our Own Wells: The Spiritual Journey of a People* (Maryknoll, N.Y.: Orbis Books, 1984).

34. McFague, *Models of God*, 48.

35. Chopp, *The Power to Speak*, 84.

BIBLIOGRAPHY

Andre, Judith. "Power, Oppression and Gender." *Social Theory and Practice* 11 (1985): 107–22.

Apostolicam Actuositatem (Decree on the Apostolate of the Laity). In *Vatican II: The Conciliar and Post-Conciliar Documents*. Ed. Austin Flannery. Northport, N.Y.: Costello Publishing Co., 1977.

Aquinas, Thomas. *Summa Theologiae*, Ia, q. 25. Question 25, "De divina potentia," is found in the Blackfriar's edition of the *ST*, vol. 5 on God's Will and Providence (qq. 19–26).

Baptism, Eucharist and Ministry. World Council of Churches' Faith and Order Commission paper no. 111. Geneva: WCC, 1982.

Basic Christian Communities in the Church. Pro Mundi Vita 62 (1976).

Bausch, William J. *Ministry: Traditions, Tensions, Transitions*. Mystic, Conn.: Twenty-Third Publications, 1983.

Bavarel, Michel. *New Communities, New Ministries*. Maryknoll, N.Y.: Orbis, 1983.

Bennis, Warren, and Burt Nanus. *Leaders*. New York: Harper & Row, 1985.

Berkhof, Hendrik. *Christ and the Powers*. Trans. John Howard Yoder. Scottdale, Pa.: Herald Press, 1962.

Bernardin, Joseph Cardinal. *In Service of One Another: Pastoral Letter on Ministry*. Chicago: Catholic Publishing Co., 1985.

Bittlinger, Arnold. *Gifts and Ministries*. Grand Rapids, Mich.: Eerdmans, 1973.

Boff, Leonardo. *Church: Charism and Power*. New York: Crossroad, 1985.
———. *Ecclesiogenesis: The Base Communities Reinvent the Church*. Maryknoll, N.Y.: Orbis, 1986.

Brewer, James H., J. Michael Ainsworth, and George E. Wynne. *Power Management*. Englewood Cliffs, N.J.: Prentice-Hall, 1984.

Brock, Rita Nakashima. *Journeys by Heart: A Christology of Erotic Power*. New York: Crossroad, 1988.

Brown, Raymond E. *The Churches the Apostles Left Behind*. New York: Paulist Press, 1984.

Burns, James McGregor. *Leadership*. New York: Harper & Row, 1978.

Bussert, Joy M. K. *Battered Women: From a Theology of Suffering to an Ethic of Empowerment*. New York: Division for Mission in North America, Lutheran Church in America, 1986.

Caird, George. *Principalities and Powers: A Study in Pauline Theology*. Oxford: Clarendon, 1956.

Campenhausen, Hans von. *Ecclesiastical Authority and Spiritual Power in the Church of the First Three Centuries.* Stanford: Stanford University Press, 1969.

Charry, Ellen T. "Female Sexuality as an Image of Empowerment: Two Models." *Saint Luke's Journal of Theology* 30 (1987): 201–18.

Chenu, Marie-Dominique. *Nature, Man, and Society in the Twelfth Century.* Trans. Jerome Taylor and Lester K. Little. Chicago: University of Chicago Press, 1968.

Chopp, Rebecca S. *The Power to Speak: Feminism, Language, God.* New York: Crossroad, 1989.

Christian Brother's Conference. *Power and Authority.* Lockport, Ill.: Christian Brothers' National Office, 1976.

Coleman, John A. "The Future of Ministry." *America* 144 (1981): 243–49.

Coll, Regina. "Power, Powerlessness and Empowerment." *Religious Education* 81 (1986): 412–23.

Congar, Yves. *L'Ecclésiologie du Haut Moyen-Âge.* Paris: Éditions du Cerf, 1968.

———. "The Historical Development of Authority in the Church: Points for Christian Reflection." In *Problems of Authority.* Ed. John M. Todd. Baltimore: Helicon Press, 1962, pp. 119–53.

———. *Jalons pour une théologie du laïcat.* Paris: Éditions du Cerf, 1953 (English translation, *Lay People in the Church.* Rev. ed. Westminster, Md.: Newman, 1967).

———. *Ministères et communion ecclésiale.* Paris: Éditions du Cerf, 1971.

———. "My Path-findings in the Theology of Laity and Ministries." *The Jurist* 32 (1972): 169–88.

———. *Power and Poverty in the Church.* Baltimore: Helicon Press, 1965.

Congregation for Divine Worship. *Directory for Sunday Celebrations in the Absence of a Priest,* June 2, 1988. Washington: United States Catholic Conference, 1988.

Cooke, Bernard. *Ministry to Word and Sacraments: History and Theology.* Philadelphia: Fortress, 1976.

Coriden, James. "Laying the Groundwork for Further Ministries." *Origins* 4 (1974): 401–10.

———. "Ministries for the Future." *Studia Canonica* 8 (1974): 255–75.

Cowan, Michael A., ed. *Alternative Futures for Worship.* Vol. 6, *Leadership Ministry in Community.* Collegeville, Minn.: Liturgical Press, 1987.

Cuneo, J. James. "The Power of Jurisdiction: Empowerment for Church Functioning and Mission Distinct from the Power of Orders." In *The Church as Mission.* Ed. James Provost. Washington: Canon Law Society of America, 1984, pp. 183–219.

Delorme, Jean, ed. *Le ministère et les ministères selon le Nouveau Testament: Dossier exégétique et réflexion théologique.* Paris: Seuil, 1974.

Dionne, J. Robert. *The Papacy and the Church: A Study of Praxis and Reception in Ecumenical Perspective.* New York: Philosophical Library, 1987.

Doohan, Helen. *Leadership in Paul.* Wilmington, Del.: Michael Glazier, 1984.

Doohan, Leonard, ed. *John Paul II and the Laity.* Cambridge, Mass.: Human Development Books, 1984.

———. *The Lay-Centered Church: Theology and Spirituality.* San Francisco: Harper & Row, 1984.

Dorr, Donal. *Option for the Poor.* Maryknoll, N.Y.: Orbis, 1983.

Dozier, Verna J. *The Authority of the Laity.* Washington: Alban Institute, 1980.

Dulles, Avery. *A Church to Believe In.* New York: Crossroad, 1982.

Elliott, John H. *A Home for the Homeless.* Philadelphia: Fortress, 1981.

———. "Ministry and Church Order in the NT: A Traditio-Historical Analysis (1 Pt 5, 1–5 & plls)." *Catholic Biblical Quarterly* 32 (1970): 367–91.

Eno, Robert E. *Teaching Authority in the Early Church.* Wilmington, Del.: Michael Glazier, 1984.

Fagan, Harry. *Empowerment: Skills for Parish Social Action.* New York: Paulist, 1979.

Fahey, Michael, ed. *Catholic Perspectives on Baptism, Eucharist and Ministry.* Lanham, Md.: University Press of America, 1986.

Faivre, Alexandre. *The Emergence of the Laity in the Early Church* (English translation of *Les laïcs aux origines de l'Eglise* [Paris: 1984]). Trans. David Smith. New York: Paulist, 1990.

———. *Naissance d'une hiérarchie: Les premières étapes du cursus clérical.* Paris: Éditions Beauchesne, 1977.

Fedwick, Paul J. *The Church and the Charisma of Leadership in Basil of Caesarea.* Toronto: Pontifical Institute of Medieval Studies, 1979.

Fiorenza, Elisabeth Schüssler. *In Memory of Her: A Feminist Theological Reconstruction of Christian Origins.* New York: Crossroad, 1983.

Floristán, Casiano, and Christian Duquoc, eds. *Charisms in the Church.* Concilium 109. New York: Seabury, 1978.

Foucault, Michel. *Power/Knowledge: Selected Interviews and Other Writings, 1972–1977.* Trans. Colin Gordon et al. Ed. Colin Gordon. New York: Pantheon Books, 1980.

Freire, Paulo. *Pedagogy of the Oppressed.* New York: Herder and Herder, 1971.

Gaudium et Spes (Pastoral Constitution on the Church in the Modern World). In *Vatican II: Conciliar and Post-Conciliar Documents.* Ed. Austin Flannery. Northport, N.Y.: Costello Publishing Co., 1977.

Gibb, Cecil A., ed. *Leadership: Selected Readings.* Baltimore: Penguin, 1969.

Glendon, Barbara. *Corporate Responsibility: Case Studies and Empowerment Strategies.* Mystic, Conn.: Twenty-Third Publications, 1985.

Granfield, Patrick. *The Limits of the Papacy.* New York: Crossroad, 1987.

Greenleaf, Robert K. *Servant Leadership.* New York: Paulist, 1977.

Gutiérrez, Gustavo. *The Power of the Poor in History: Selected Writings.* Maryknoll, N.Y.: Orbis, 1983.

———. *We Drink from Our Own Wells: The Spiritual Journey of a People.* Maryknoll, N.Y.: Orbis, 1984.

Hahn, Cecilia A., and James R. Adams. *The Mystery of Clergy Authority.* Washington: Alban Institute, 1979.

Henderson, Frank. *Ministries of the Laity.* Ottawa: Canadian Conference of Catholic Bishops, 1978.

Hengel, Martin. *Christ and Power.* Trans. Everett R. Kalin. Philadelphia: Fortress, 1977.

Hoge, Dean. *The Future of Catholic Leadership: Response to the Priest Shortage.* Kansas City, Mo.: Sheed and Ward, 1987.

Holmberg, Bengt. *Paul and Power: The Structure of Authority in the Primitive Church as Reflected in the Pauline Epistles.* Philadelphia: Fortress Press, 1980.

Hunt, Mary E. "Sharing Feminism: Empowerment or Imperialism?" *Journal of Women and Religion* 1 (1981): 33–46.

———, and Laura Ann Quinonez. "Toward Communal Empowerment." In *Authority, Community and Conflict.* Ed. Madonna Kolbenschlag. Kansas City, Mo.: Sheed and Ward, 1986, pp. 44–50.

Janeway, Elizabeth. *Powers of the Weak.* New York: Alfred Knopf, 1980.

John Paul II. *Christifideles Laici* (Apostolic Exhortation on the Vocation and Mission of the Lay Faithful in the Church and in the World). *Origins* 18 (1989): 561–95.

Jouvenel, Bertrand de. *On Power.* Boston: Beacon, 1962.

Kerkhofs, Jan. "From Frustration to Liberation?" In *Minister? Pastor? Prophet?: Grass-roots Leadership in the Churches.* Ed. Lucas Grollenberg et al. New York: Crossroad, 1981, pp. 5–12.

Kinast, Robert L. *Caring for Society: A Theological Interpretation of Lay Ministry.* Chicago: Thomas More Press, 1985.

Lagarde, Georges de. *La naissance de l'esprit laïque au déclin du Moyen-Âge.* 2 vols. Paris: Beatrice-Nauwelaerts, 1956.

Lassey, William R., and Marshall Sashkin, eds. *Leadership and Social Change.* Rev. 3d ed. San Diego: University Association, 1983.

Lee, Bernard J., and Michael A. Cowan. *Dangerous Memories: Household Churches and Our American Story.* Kansas City: Sheed and Ward, 1986.

Legrand, Hervé-Marie. "The Presidency of the Eucharist according to the Ancient Tradition." *Worship* 53 (1979): 413–38.

Lemaire, André. "The Ministries in the New Testament: Recent Research." *Biblical Theology Bulletin* 3 (1973): 133–66.

Lips, Hilary M. *Women, Men, and the Psychology of Power.* Englewood Cliffs, N.J.: Prentice-Hall, 1981.

Loomer, Bernard. "Two Kinds of Power." *Criterion: Journal of the University of Chicago Divinity School* 15 (1976): 11–29.

Lukes, Steven. *Power: A Radical View.* New York: Macmillan, 1974.

Lumen Gentium (Dogmatic Constitution on the Church). In *Vatican II: The Conciliar and Post-Conciliar Documents.* Ed. Austin Flannery. Northport, N.Y.: Costello Publishing Co., 1977.

McKenzie, John L. *Authority in the Church.* Kansas City, Mo.: Sheed and Ward, 1966, 1986.

May, Rollo. *Power and Innocence.* New York: Norton, 1972.

May, William W., ed. *Vatican Authority and American Catholic Dissent*. New York: Crossroad, 1987.

Meeks, Wayne A. *The First Urban Christians: The Social World of the Apostle Paul*. New Haven: Yale University Press, 1983.

Mitchell, Nathan. *Mission and Ministry*. Wilmington, Del.: Michael Glazier, 1982.

Moltmann, Jürgen. *The Power of the Powerless*. New York: Crossroad, 1983.

Myers, J. Gordon, and Richard Schoenherr. "The Baptism of Power." *New Catholic World* (September/October 1980): 217–20.

New Forms of Ministries in Christian Communities. Pro Mundi Vita 50 (1974).

Newman, David R. *Worship as Praise and Empowerment*. New York: Pilgrim Press, 1988.

O'Meara, Thomas F. *Theology of Ministry*. New York: Paulist, 1983.

Oswald, Roy. *Power Analysis of a Congregation*. Washington: Alban Institute, 1982.

Potterie, Ignace de la. "L'origine et le sens primitif du mot 'laïc.'" *Nouvelle Revue Théologique* 80 (1958): 840–53.

Powell, Cyril. *The Biblical Concept of Power*. New York: Epworth, 1963.

Power, David N. *Gifts That Differ: Lay Ministries Established and Unestablished*. 2d ed. New York: Pueblo, 1985.

———. "Liturgy and Empowerment." In *Alternative Futures for Worship*. Ed. Michael Cowan. Vol. 6, *Christian Leadership*. Collegeville, Minn.: Liturgical Press, 1987.

Power as an Issue in Theology. Proceedings of the Catholic Theological Society of America 37 (1982).

Presbyterorum Ordinis (Decree on the Ministry and Life of Priests). In *Vatican II: The Conciliar and Post-Conciliar Documents*. Ed. Austin Flannery. Northport, N.Y.: Costello Publishing Co, 1977.

Provost, James H., ed. *Official Ministry in a New Age*. Washington: Canon Law Society of America, 1981.

Rahner, Karl. "Notes on the Lay Apostolate." *Theological Investigations* 2. Baltimore: Helicon Press, 1963, pp. 319–52.

———. *The Shape of the Church to Come*. New York: Seabury, 1974.

———. "The Theology of Power." *Theological Investigations* 4. New York: Seabury, 1974, pp. 391–401.

Russell, Letty. *The Future of Partnership*. Philadelphia: Westminster, 1979.

———. *Growth in Partnership*. Philadelphia: Westminster, 1981.

———. *Household of Freedom: Authority in Feminist Theology*. Philadelphia: Westminster Press, 1987.

Sacred Congregation for the Discipline of the Sacraments. "Instruction Empowering Lay Persons to Preside at Marriage in Brazil." *Doctrine and Life* 25 (1975): 670–72.

Schillebeeckx, Edward. *Church: The Human Story of God*. New York: Crossroad, 1990.

———. *The Church with a Human Face: A New and Expanded Theology of Ministry*. New York: Crossroad, 1985.

———. *Jesus: An Experiment in Christology.* New York: Crossroad, 1979.
———. *Ministry: Leadership in the Community of Jesus Christ.* New York: Crossroad, 1981.
———, and Johannes Metz. *The Right of the Community to a Priest.* Concilium 133. New York: Seabury, 1980.
Schmitt, Donna M., and Donna C. Weaver, eds. *Leadership for Community Empowerment: A Source Book.* Midland, Mich.: Pendell Publishing Co., 1979.
Schneiders, Sandra M. "Evangelical Equality, I." *Spirituality Today* 38 (1986): 293–302; "Evangelical Equality, II." *Spirituality Today* 39 (1987): 56–67.
Sellner, Edward C. "Lay Leadership in the 1990s." *America* 161 (1989): 133–38
Sherry, Robert. "Shortage? What Vocation Shortage?" *The Priest* 41 (1985): 29–31.
Simon, Yves. *Nature and Functions of Authority.* Milwaukee: Marquette University Press, 1940.
Smith, Carolyn F., and Julia Rappaport, eds. *Studies in Empowerment: Steps toward Understanding and Action.* New York: Haworth Press, 1984.
Sölle, Dorothee. *The Strength of the Weak.* Philadelphia: Westminster, 1984.
Sullivan, Francis. *Magisterium: Teaching Authority in the Church.* New York: Paulist, 1983.
Tanner, Kathryn E. *God and Creation in Christian Theology: Tyranny or Empowerment?* New York: Blackwell, 1988.
Tillard, J. M. R. *The Bishop of Rome.* Wilmington, Del.: Michael Glazier, 1983.
Tillich, Paul. *Love, Power and Justice.* New York: Oxford University Press, 1954.
Vatican Council II: The Conciliar and Post-Conciliar Documents. Ed. Austin Flannery. Northport, N.Y.: Costello Publishing Co., 1977.
Whitehead, Evelyn Eaton, and James D. Whitehead. *Community of Faith: Models and Strategies for Developing Christian Communities.* New York: Seabury, 1982.
Whitehead, James D., and Evelyn Eaton. *The Emerging Laity.* Garden City, N.Y.: Doubleday, 1986.
Wink, Walter. *Naming the Powers: The Language of Power in the New Testament.* Philadelphia: Fortress Press, 1984.

Notes on Contributors

Bernard Cooke is Professor of Systematic Theology at Holy Cross College, Worcester, Massachusetts. Past President of the Catholic Theological Society of America (1982–83), he is also a recipient of the CTSA's John Courtney Murray Award. Noteworthy among his publications are *Ministry to Word and Sacraments, Sacraments and Sacramentality*, and, most recently, *The Distancing God.* He also edited and contributed to *Christian Marriage*, volume 5 of *Alternative Futures for Worship.*

Leonard Doohan is Professor of Religious Studies at Gonzaga University, Spokane, Washington. He lectures and gives workshops throughout the U.S. and Canada, as well as in Europe, Australia, New Zealand, and the Far East. Author of many articles and thirteen books, including *The Lay-Centered Church, The Laity's Mission in the Local Church*, and *John Paul II and the Laity*, his latest publication is a handbook for career lay ministers, *Grass Roots Pastors.*

Michael Downey is Associate Professor of Theology at Loyola Marymount University, Los Angeles. He has served on the editorial board of several journals and is editor of *The New Dictionary of Catholic Spirituality* (forthcoming, The Liturgical Press). His publications include *A Blessed Weakness: The Spirit of Jean Vanier and L'Arche* and *Clothed in Christ: The Sacraments and Christian Living* (Crossroad).

Roberto S. Goizueta received his Ph.D. in 1984 from Marquette University. He has taught at Loyola University, New Orleans, and the Mexican American Cultural Center, San Antonio. Presently, he is Executive Vice President of the Aquinas Center of Theology at Emory University. He also serves as President of the Academy of Catholic Hispanic Theologians of the United States and is the author of *Liberation, Method, and Dialogue: Enrique Dussel and North American Theological Discourse.*

J. A. Wayne Hellmann, O.F.M. Conv., is Associate Professor in the Department of Theological Studies at St. Louis University. He currently serves as Minister Provincial for the Conventual Franciscans of the Province of Our Lady of Consolation in mid-America. Notable among his writings is "The Spirituality of the Franciscans," in *World Spirituality: An Encyclopedic History of the Religious Quest, Christian Spirituality II, High Middle Ages and Reformation*, vol. 17, ed. Jill Raitt (New York: Crossroad, 1987).

Bob Hurd is a teacher, composer, and liturgist. He is Assistant Professor of Philosophy and Systematic Theology at St. Patrick's Seminary, Menlo Park, and is Associate Director of Liturgy and Music, Saint Leander's Church, San Leandro, California. His writings have appeared in *Worship, Today's Liturgy, The Thomist, Liturgy, Philosophy Today*, and *Philosophy and Theology*. His liturgical music is published by Oregon Catholic Press.

James R. Jennings, Associate Director of the U.S. bishops' Campaign for Human Development, has written frequently on the link between faith and justice. His most recent work is *Journeys with Jesus*.

Roger M. Mahony is Archbishop of Los Angeles. He serves the National Conference of Catholic Bishops in a variety of capacities. A participant in the 1987 Synod on the Laity, his writings include *Priestly Ministers* (Boston: Saint Paul Editions, 1986) and "The Magisterium and Theological Dissent" in *Vatican Authority and American Catholic Dissent* (New York: Crossroad, 1987).

Mary Milligan, R.S.H.M., is Professor of Theology at Loyola Marymount University in Los Angeles. She has served as General Superior of the Religious of the Sacred Heart of Mary and on the Executive Committee of the International Union of Superiors General. She holds her doctoral degree in spirituality from the Gregorian University in Rome.

Robert F. Morneau, Auxiliary Bishop of Green Bay, is presently Director of Diocesan Commissions in the Diocese of Green Bay, Wisconsin. He is the author of nine books, and his articles have appeared in *America, Chicago Studies, Pastoral Life, Emmanuel, Review for Religious*, and *Bible Today*. He does extensive retreat work in the U.S. and is currently in residence at St. Margaret Mary Parish in Neenah, Wisconsin.

Tina Pippin is Assistant Professor of Bible and Religion at Agnes Scott College in Decatur, Georgia, and is Founding Editor of *Paradigms: A Graduate Student Journal in Religious Studies*. She is a permanent deacon in the Episcopal Church.

David N. Power, O.M.I., is Professor of Systematic Theology and Liturgy at the Catholic University of America, Washington, D.C. He has been on the editorial board of the international theological review *Concilium* since 1969. Noteworthy among his publications are

Gifts That Differ: Lay Ministries Established and Unestablished, 2d ed. (New York: Pueblo, 1985), and *Unsearchable Riches: The Symbolic Nature of Liturgy* (New York: Pueblo, 1984). He also contributed to vol. 6, *Leadership Ministry in Community*, of *Alternative Futures for Worship* (Collegeville, Minn.: Liturgical Press, 1987).

Susan A. Ross teaches in the Theology Department of Loyola University of Chicago. Her articles and reviews have been published in *Worship, Religious Studies Review, Horizons*, and the *Journal of Religion*. She has contributed to *The Praxis of Experience: An Introduction to the Thought of Edward Schillebeeckx* (San Francisco: Harper & Row, 1989) as well as to *Suffering and Healing in Our Day* (Villanova, Pa.: Villanova University, 1990), and is currently completing a book on women, the body, and sacramental theology.